lonely planet

Best Road Trips IRELAND

FIONN DAVENPORT, ISABEL ALBISTON, BELINDA DIXON, CATHERINE LE NEVEZ, NEIL WILSON

CONTENTS

BELFAST & THE NORTH OF IRELAND p221
SCOTLAND
North Channel
NORTHERN IRELAND
GALWAY & THE WEST OF IRELAND p171
DUBLIN & EASTERN IRELAND p63
CORK & SOUTHWEST IRELAND p123
ATLANTIC OCEAN
Irish Sea
St George's Channel
IRELAND
Ballyliffin
Carndonagh
Dunfanaghy
Portstewart
Ballycastle
Falcarragh
Buncrana
Coleraine
Dunlewey
Limavady
Burtonport
Letterkenny
Derry
ANTRIM
Dungloe
DONEGAL
DERRY
Ballymena
Kells
Larne
Glenties
TYRONE
Carrickfergus
Glencolumbcille
Donegal
Antrim
Omagh
Lough Neagh
BELFAST
Bangor
Newtownards
Bruckless
Donaghmore
Lurgan
Bundoran
Craigavon
Lower Lough Erne
DOWN
Sligo Bay
Enniskillen
Armagh
Downpatrick
Ballycastle
Sligo
FERMANAGH
Monaghan
ARMAGH
Newry
Newcastle
Clones
Bangor Erris
Ballina
SLIGO
LEITRIM
MONAGHAN
Greencastle
MAYO
Boyle
Carrick-on-Shannon
Cavan
Carrickmacross
Dundalk
Newport
CAVAN
Castlebar
LOUTH
ROSCOMMON
Westport
Knock
Strokestown
LONGFORD
Kells
Slane
Drogheda
Leenane
Navan
Roscommon
Claddaghduff
Lough Ree
Mullingar
Trim
MEATH
Lough Corrib
Clifden
GALWAY
Athlone
WESTMEATH
Malahide
Maynooth
Roundstone
Oughterard
Kilbeggan
Ballinasloe
DUBLIN
Galway
Athenry
OFFALY
KILDARE
Dalkey
North Sound
Burren Village
Loughrea
Tullamore
Kildare
Newbridge
Gort
Portumna
Birr
Mountmellick
WICKLOW
Doolin
Kilfenora
Roscrea
LAOIS
Wicklow
Corofin
CLARE
Nenagh
Abbeyleix
Miltown Malbay
Ennis
Durrow
Carlow
TIPPERARY
CARLOW
Kilkee
Kilrush
Fergus Bay
Bunratty
Kilkenny
Limerick
Ferns
Adare
Kells
Dungarvan
Ballybunion
Tarbert
Cashel
Enniscorthy
Tipperary
Fethard
Listowel
LIMERICK
Clonmel
KILKENNY
New Ross
Wexford
Cahir
Rosslare Strand
Tralee
Waterford
Rosslare Harbour
WEXFORD
Annascaul
Castlemaine
Mallow
Lismore
WATERFORD
Dingle
Tramore
Kilmore Quay
Killarney
Dungarvan
Kells
Killarney National Park
KERRY
CORK
Youghal
Ardmore
Cork
Portmagee
Sneem
Kenmare
Cobh
Caherdaniel
Glengarriff
Bantry
Clonakilty
Schull
0 50 km
0 25 miles

WELCOME TO IRELAND

In Ireland, the journey is not so much long as it is deep. Distances – even between the furthest points – are relatively short: you can drive from coast to coast in under three hours, and even from tip to toe in no more than six. Yet, this small island crams a whole lot in: within the space of a few kilometres, you can travel back in time 4000 years, stumble on a sleepy village straight out of a postcard and pull the curtain back on the spectacular scenery that most likely brought you here in the first place. And pretty much everywhere you go, there's the people – a complex jumble of wit, warmth and approachability.

Narrow roads cutting through the wildest of landscapes. Gourmet city tours sandwiched between spa treatments. And, yes, traffic jams consisting of sheep: it's all here for discovery along Ireland's roads.

Beach, St John's Point (p235), Donegal
NICOLAS D'HOEDT/LONELY PLANET

MY PERFECT ROAD TRIP

FIONN DAVENPORT

DELIGHTS OF DONEGAL, p234

The first time I visited Donegal, I was 15, and in the four decades since, I've come to love it like a second home. No matter how often I see Errigal or gaze into the Poisoned Glen, it still stirs something deep inside. From the towering cliffs of Sliabh Liag to the remote wildness of Inishowen, Donegal is my happy place – vast, elemental and endlessly capable of resetting my spirit, whatever the weather.

NICOLAS D'HOEDT/LONELY PLANET

Poisoned Glen (p37), Donegal

BEST LONG DRIVES

1. **The North in a Nutshell** From turbulent history to vertiginous views, a drive that straddles an invisible border.
2. **Ring of Kerry** The most famous drive of them all, 179km of blockbuster scenery that never seems to quit.
3. **Ireland's Highlights** A week-long dive into the big-ticket attractions and scenic highlights of Ireland.
4. **Tip to Toe** A drive covering two coasts and Ireland's relatively undiscovered centre, a hub of history and culture.
5. **Wild Atlantic Way** Some 2500km of spectacular scenery and wild drama along the full stretch of the west.

BEST URBAN DRIVES

1. **A Long Weekend Around Dublin** See the capital inside and out on this three-day trip around Ireland's largest city.

2. **East to West** From cosmopolitan capital to colourful Galway, explore two sides of Ireland's urban experience.

3. **Kilkenny's Treasures** Ireland's most intact medieval city awaits on this drive that explores castles, abbeys and craft.

4. **Musical Landscapes** From busy, bustling Galway to the music towns of Clare, all to a traditional soundtrack.

5. **From Bangor to Derry** Northern Ireland's first and second cities bookend this drive across a surprisingly diverse province.

ISABEL ALBISTON

THE ANTRIM COAST, p252

The trip along the Antrim coast takes in some spectacular scenery. Driving through the undulating Antrim Glens is a wonderful way to experience their wild beauty. Soon, the sea is glimpsed from high above, before the road descends from Glenariff to the coast and the charming village of Cushendun. Home to seals and nesting seabirds, Rathlin Island is one of my favourite places, and I'll never tire of glimpsing the mythical hexagonal rocks of the Giant's Causeway.

BALLYGALLY VIEW IMAGES/SHUTTERSTOCK

Cushendun (p253), Antrim

BEST FAMILY DRIVES

1. **Family Fun** Theme parks, adventure centres and interactive sites all within an hour's drive of Dublin.

2. **The Boyne Valley** A drive that takes you atop regal hilltops and down into Neolithic passage tombs.

3. **Mountains & Moors** The wild ruggedness of Connemara is the perfect landscape for a family adventure.

4. **County Clare** An adventure through forts on remote islands and the bizarre landscape of The Burren.

5. **Northwest on Adrenaline** Surfing, hiking, tales of pirates and Ireland's tallest cliffs – take a deep breath and dive in.

BEST SCENIC DRIVES

When it comes to spectacular scenery, Ireland has it covered. The whole of the west coast, from Cork to Donegal, is where you'll find the biggest showstoppers (and probably why you're here in the first place), but there are lots of scenic hits in other parts of the country, notably in and around the Wicklow Mountains and along the Antrim *(Aontroim)* coast in Northern Ireland.

① WICKLOW MOUNTAINS

On this drive, glacial valleys and mountain passes showcase the scenic splendours of the east coast. p92

② RING OF KERRY

Postcard views greet you around every corner on one of Ireland's best-known drives. p126

③ THE WILD ATLANTIC WAY

Some 2500km of virtually non-stop blockbuster scenery stretching the length of the west coast. p22

④ MOUNTAINS & MOORS

Enjoy Connemara's brooding beauty, matched only by the splendid isolation and ruggedness of the peninsula. p190

⑤ DELIGHTS OF DONEGAL

Explore the majestic scenery and barely tamed landscape of Ireland's remote northwestern corner. p234

Left: Glendalough (p86), Wicklow; Right: Gap of Dunloe (p131), Kerry

LEFT TO RIGHT: WIRESTOCK CREATORS/SHUTTERSTOCK, CLEARSKIES/SHUTTERSTOCK

NARROW ESCAPE

While the minor roads may look impossibly narrow, unless indicated they're usually wide enough for two cars to pass each other; very narrow roads usually have designated 'passing places'.

GO WITH THE FLOW

Tour buses drive the Ring of Kerry on a counterclockwise route, so keep an eye on those blind bends!

LISFANNON BEACH

Just outside Fahan on the Inishowen Peninsula is Lisfannon Beach, one of the prettiest in the northwest.

ON THE BLACKWATER

You can take a 90-minute Blackwater cruise *(blackwatercruises.com)* from Youghal as far as Ballynatray House in County Cork.

BEST HIDDEN TREASURES

Ireland isn't just about the myriad five-star attractions. Beyond the chart toppers (where the bustling crowds just won't get out of your way for that perfect pic) are a host of sights and towns that have escaped mass attention, which is precisely why you should visit them. Here, away from all of the hype, is Ireland at its loveliest and most authentic.

① CARLOW BACK ROADS

A marvellous county largely untouched by mass tourism, meaning its delights are all yours to uncover. p96

② BLACKWATER VALLEY DRIVE

Revel in this quiet 64km route that's packed with history, culture and some pretty stunning views. p112

③ SHANNON RIVER ROUTE

This drive along Ireland's mightiest river has plenty of wonderful and little-visited spots to explore. p162

④ LOUGHS OF THE WEST

The backwaters of this County Galway drive have untarnished delights that include epic castles and islands. p196

⑤ INISHOWEN PENINSULA

This stunning peninsula is tough to get to, but your effort will be richly rewarded. p238

Left: River Blackwater (p112), Waterford; Above: Lisfannon Beach, Inishowen Peninsula (p238), Donegal

LEFT TO RIGHT: FARUTXO/SHUTTERSTOCK, JKSZ.PHOTOGRAPHY/SHUTTERSTOCK

OUR PICKS

BEST FOOD & DRINK

Ireland's best food leans heaviest on its high-quality local produce. And there's plenty of it, too: from freshly caught seafood to organic meat and homemade breads to some of the best dairy produce you'll find anywhere in the world. These days, you can eat well almost anywhere, but parts of the country really stand out, including some spots on these drives.

① A LONG WEEKEND AROUND DUBLIN

The capital has the country's highest concentration of restaurants, and some of the best. p66

② WEXFORD & WATERFORD

Some parts of Waterford's west are a gourmet heaven, largely centred on Dungarvan. p106

③ SOUTHWESTERN PANTRY

County Cork has long been a flag bearer for Ireland's foodie revolution, bringing the best of Irish to the table. p150

④ WEST CORK VILLAGES

Virtually every village in West Cork offers exceptional dining, where the standards just keep getting better. p154

⑤ THE WILD ATLANTIC WAY

From Sligo to Kerry, the Wild Atlantic Way has some exceptional dining options. p22

Left: Dublin Bay prawns; Right: Seafood chowder with soda bread, Cork (p150)

BOOK AHEAD

Be sure to book the popular and award-winning restaurants well in advance, especially during summer.

EATING TIME

The Irish typically eat their evening meal early, usually between 6pm and 7pm; many restaurants stop service after 9pm.

Knowth, Brú na Bóinne (p79), Meath

MNSTUDIO/SHUTTERSTOCK

BEST ANCIENT MONUMENTS

Ireland is old — as in, older-than-the-pyramids old. Wherever you drive to, you're likely to find a Neolithic passage grave, the ruins of a 1500-year-old monastery or a collection of stones marked in mysterious runes so old the archaeologists talk of eras rather than centuries. Some, like the UNESCO World Heritage monuments of Brú na Bóinne, are very well-known; others appear wholly undisturbed in remote fields, seemingly untouched for millennia.

① THE BOYNE VALLEY

This drive covers Ireland's most famous prehistoric monument and the markers of its most infamous battle. p78

WINTER SOLSTICE

To be in the draw for the winter solstice event at Brú na Bóinne in County Meath, email *brunaboinne@opw.ie*

DRIVING SLEA HEAD

You should drive Dingle's Slea Head clockwise so as to avoid meeting tour buses head-on.

② ANCIENT IRELAND

Exactly what you'd expect: a sojourn through the big stars of Ireland's ancient past. p82

③ DINGLE PENINSULA

A drive through a peninsula covered with prehistoric monuments, some literally scattered in fields. p134

④ THE HOLY GLEN

Explore County Tipperary's rich collection of monastic ruins, with many more than a thousand years old. p166

⑤ SLIGO SURROUNDS

A wealth of prehistoric sites, all within relatively easy reach of each other. p208

BEST ADRENALINE RUSHES

CLIMBING SLIABH LIAG

The 10km looped path to the top of the cliffs of Sliabh Liag (Slieve League) in County Donegal goes from the upper car park.

Ireland has myriad ways for you to work up a sweat, from chasing chickens around a farmyard to paragliding off the edge of a mountain. There are also plenty of family-friendly activities, whether it's indulging in a bit of mountain biking on well-marked trails to ziplining across a forest canopy. And don't forget the water-based sports, too, which run the gamut from stand-up paddleboarding (SUP) and kayaking to surfing.

1 WICKLOW MOUNTAINS

Stretch your legs on the fabulous walking and biking trails spread throughout this eastern county. p92

2 FAMILY FUN

From working farms to adventure centres – there's fun for the whole family on this route. p116

3 DINGLE PENINSULA

Take to the water for some scuba diving and surfing in the beautiful southwest. p134

4 DELIGHTS OF DONEGAL

Explore one of the world's premier surf spots on this scenic drive. p234

5 NORTHWEST ON ADRENALINE

Get breathless in the sea and climb up a mountain on this northwest roller-coaster. p242

Cliffs of Sliabh Liag (p245), Donegal

NICOLAS D'HOEDT/LONELY PLANET

WHEN TO GO

Four distinct seasons, but no extremes of weather mean Ireland is a year-round driving destination.

I LIVE HERE

SMALL TOWNS, BIG HEARTS

Noeleen Tyrrell is a yoga teacher living in Leitrim. @noeleentyrrell_yoga

When I first moved to County Leitrim, a friend from the US sent me a letter, not knowing my address. But they knew the car I was driving, so the envelope read 'Noeleen Tyrrell, The Red Mini, Dromahair'. And it arrived! From that moment, I was smitten. I'm still here almost 30 years later, and not a lot has changed. The wildness of the countryside, hedges unkempt and spilling with wild roses and columbine, a lake or mountain around every turn – this is Leitrim. People are warm and there's a sense of belonging in the relatively small population.

The best time to travel in Ireland? April to June are statistically the driest months with the most hours of sunshine, but September into early October can also be gorgeous, with long 'Indian summer' days. The coaches that clog the scenic routes have largely gone and the kids are back in school, leaving Ireland's most beautiful places that bit quieter and easier to navigate.

Irish winters are usually mild, with temperatures rarely dipping below freezing, although early morning frosts in January and February can make for treacherous conditions. Summers see most of the island's visitors, especially in the tourist hot spots of Dublin, Kerry and the southern and western coasts.

ACCOMMODATION

Accommodation is at its most expensive (and busiest) during the summer and peak holiday times, which is pretty much whenever schools are closed. Rates drop off considerably out of season, but many smaller hotels and guesthouses close up for the winter, especially in quieter areas.

A GOLDILOCKS CLIMATE

The effect of the Gulf Stream means that Ireland never gets too hot or too cold. Heavy snow is rare, while any temperature over 25°C will prompt a conversation about the 'incredible' heat. The warmest temperature ever recorded was 33°C at Kilkenny Castle. In 1887.

LOCAL DELIGHTS

One of the best food festivals in the country, **Taste of West Cork** (p151) in September features cookery demos, food-tastings, competitions and a terrific farmers market.

Events, screenings, gigs and a brilliantly boisterous parade

WEATHER WATCH

JANUARY
Avg. daytime max: **5.5°C**
Days of rainfall: **16**

FEBRUARY
Avg. daytime max: **6°C**
Days of rainfall: **13**

MARCH
Avg. daytime max: **7°C**
Days of rainfall: **13**

APRIL
Avg. daytime max: **8°C**
Days of rainfall: **12**

MAY
Avg. daytime max: **10.6°C**
Days of rainfall: **11**

JUNE
Avg. daytime max: **13.7°C**
Days of rainfall: **11**

CEZARY ZAREBSKI PHOTOGRAPHY/GETTY IMAGES

St Patrick's Day parade

that rolls through the city centre mark the 10-day **Dublin Pride** celebrations in June.

For one night a year, historic homes, museums, galleries, studios and private gardens all over Ireland open their doors for September's **Culture Night**, with talks, performances and organised visits.

A **Leprechaun Hunt**, you say? The mountains around Carlingford, County Louth, have been designated a protected habitat for the little people... by the EU. This unique one-day festival is more of a celebration than an actual hunt, and the surroundings are gorgeous. It takes place in late March/early April.

RAINFALL IN IRELAND

Average annual rainfall is approximately 1230mm, but the west and high ground get more than double the average of the east coast. The wettest point is Leenane in County Galway, which averages 2874mm a year; the driest is Dublin, which gets around 683mm a year.

MAJOR FESTIVALS

St Patrick's Day
Ireland comes to a halt on 17 March for St Patrick's Day, which has stretched out in recent years to become a multiday festival. Dublin is home to the biggest celebrations, but every town in the country hosts a parade. **March**

Electric Picnic
Stradbally Hall in County Laois is Ireland's answer to Glastonbury, but on a smaller scale. Upwards of 30,000 revellers show up with tents and wellies to participate in this three-day festival featuring some of the biggest names in music, past and present. **August/September**

Willie Clancy Summer School
Ireland's premier celebration of traditional music is the nine-day Willie Clancy Summer School in Miltown Malbay, County Clare. It's the impromptu evening sessions that really make the festival hop. **July**

Galway International Arts Festival
The Galway International Arts Festival is a two-week fiesta of theatre, comedy, music and art. **July**

JULY	AUGUST	SEPTEMBER	OCTOBER	NOVEMBER	DECEMBER
Avg. daytime max: **15.2°C**	Avg. daytime max: **15.5°C**	Avg. daytime max: **13.5°C**	Avg. daytime max: **11°C**	Avg. daytime max: **8.5°C**	Avg. daytime max: **6.6°C**
Days of rainfall: **13**	Days of rainfall: **14**	Days of rainfall: **13**	Days of rainfall: **15**	Days of rainfall: **16**	Days of rainfall: **17**

GET PREPARED FOR IRELAND

Useful things to load in your bag, your ears and your brain.

WATCH

- **An Cailín Ciúin (The Quiet Girl)** *(Colm Bairéad; 2022)* Beautiful coming-of-age drama adapted from a short story by Claire Keegan.

- **The Banshees of Inisherin** *(Martin McDonagh; 2022)* Oscar-nominated yarn about two friends on an island off the west coast who fall out, with devastating consequences.

- **Belfast** *(Kenneth Branagh; 2021)* Semi-autobiographical film chronicling the life of a young boy in working-class Belfast in the late 1960s.

- **Derry Girls** *(Lisa McGee; 2018–2022)* Hilarious teen sitcom set in Derry during the final years of the Troubles.

- **Normal People** *(Lenny Abrahamson and Hettie MacDonald; 2020)* Sally Rooney's hugely successful novel turned into a 12-part romantic psychological drama starring Paul Mescal and Daisy Edgar-Jones.

CLOTHING

Smart casual Ireland is an informal kind of place, and you won't need anything more than vaguely neat dress for even fancy dinners and the concert hall.

Lightweight layers, including T-shirts and long-sleeve shirts Very useful in a 'four seasons in one day' climate like Ireland's.

Warm sweater or fleece See above; temperatures fluctuate all the time.

Weatherproof walking shoes or hiking boots with socks You'll need something for those panoramic hikes once you've parked the car.

Jeans or long trousers Good for everyday use and in the summer months, when the west has lots of midges – small flies that come out around dusk and like to bite.

Winter coat A bracing wind can make even the mildest of temperatures feel like it's freezing cold.

Scarf, hat and gloves It can get pretty cold in winter and when the sun goes down.

Light waterproof jacket In summer, an essential item for that impromptu rain shower you hadn't anticipated.

Waterproof trousers Did we mention that it rains?

Sunglasses Good for sunny days, and especially useful when driving on sunny days in winter, when the low winter sun can be blinding.

Sun hat or cap It doesn't feel very warm, but that sun is deceptively strong.

FROM LEFT TO RIGHT: Q15/SHUTTERSTOCK, FOREST BADGER/SHUTTERSTOCK, LANDSCAPEMANIA/SHUTTERSTOCK, NICOLAS D'HOEDT/LONELY PLANET

Hiker near Cong (p197), on the border of Mayo and Galway

WORDS

Hello Dia dhuit *(dee-ah qwitch)*
Goodbye Slán leat *(slawn latt)*
How are you? Conas atá tú? *(kunass ataw too)*
Please Le do thoil *(leh duh hull)*
Turn left/right Cas ar clé/dheis *(kass er klay/yesh)*
Keep going straight ahead Gabh díreach ar aghaidh *(do djeeragh air ay)*
Entrance Bealach isteach / Slí isteach *(bal-akh iss-chah / shlee iss-chah)*
Exit Bealach / Slí amach *(bal-akh / shlee amah)*
How do I get to...? Conas a rachaidh mé go...? *(kunass ah rockig may go)*
I'm lost Tá mé ar strae *(taw may er stray)*

GET PREPARED

LISTEN

Euro-Country
(CMAT; 2025) The third LP from the queen of Irish pop has cemented CMAT's status as music royalty, with catchy tunes about serious things.

Dogrel
(Fontaines DC; 2019) Debut album of this Dublin alt rock band shows them at their riff-driven best.

Becoming a Jackal
(Villagers; 2010) Villagers is singer-songwriter Conor O'Brien, whose intricate, story-driven brilliance shines on this album.

READ

Angela's Ashes
(Frank McCourt; 1996) This bleak autobiographical account of the author's poverty-stricken Limerick childhood won the Pulitzer Prize.

Milkman
(Anna Burns; 2018) Northern Ireland's first Booker Prize winner explores the Troubles through the eyes of an anonymous 18-year-old narrator.

Juno Loves Legs
(Karl Geary; 2023) Geary's second novel is about two teenage friends struggling in 1980s Dublin.

ROAD TRIPS

Doo Lough (p34), Mayo

BONN-BONN FOTO/SHUTTERSTOCK

CONTENTS

01

EPIC TRIP: THE WILD ATLANTIC WAY

The Wild Atlantic Way was officially launched in 2015, but the 2500km stretch from Kinsale to Donegal's Inishowen Peninsula has long been Ireland's great coastal journey. It's a route shaped by elemental landscapes that define the country's most dramatic scenery. I've spent years exploring it: chasing seafood fresh from the harbour, hiking ancient clifftops and settling into pubs alive with music. While 188 Discovery Points mark the official trail, the real magic lies in the detours – and this trip follows the main route, with a few personal turns along the way.

BY FIONN DAVENPORT

HIGHLIGHTS

1

Ballydehob, p26
In West Cork, I chase island hikes and birdlife on Cape Clear before rewarding myself in Ballydehob – Michelin stars if I fancy it, bangers and mash if I don't, pints in Levis regardless.

2

Dingle Peninsula, p28
I drive the Slea Head loop for coastal views and ancient sites, then cross the Connor Pass, a mountain road with sweeping views of one of Kerry's most dramatic landscapes.

3

Dunfanaghy/Horn Head, p37
From Dunfanaghy, I drive out to Horn Head, where quiet roads lead to sweeping Atlantic views, dramatic cliffs and one of the wildest, most beautiful corners of Donegal.

Dunquin Pier, Dingle Peninsula (p28), Kerry
IRISH DRONE PHOTOGRAPHY/SHUTTERSTOCK

EPIC TRIP

DURATION: 10–14 DAYS

DISTANCE: 2500KM / 1600 MILES

GREAT FOR: FOOD & DRINK, HISTORY, OUTDOORS, FAMILY, HIKING, PHOTOGRAPHY

BEST TIME TO GO: SEPTEMBER: SOFTER LIGHT, WARMER SEAS, FEWER CROWDS AND THE BEST SEAFOOD.

01 Kinsale

Depending on where you're starting from, the colourful yachting harbour of Kinsale marks the beginning (or the end) of the Wild Atlantic Way. For me, it's always the beginning: only 25km south

LINK YOUR TRIP

16 Ring of Kerry
Between Kenmare and Dingle, this 179km-loop is Ireland's most famous drive.

17 Dingle Peninsula
Do Dingle thoroughly for history, scenery and a fabulous town.

18 Southwest Blitz
Four-day introduction to Ireland's superb southwest.

19 Southwestern Pantry
Get to grips with West Cork's rich gourmet credentials.

20 West Cork Villages
West Cork's villages are smattered across some stunning landscapes.

21 Shannon River Route
Travel along the mighty Shannon into the heart of Ireland.

24 Musical Landscapes
Immerse yourself in the musical traditions of Clare and Galway.

27 North Mayo & Sligo
Go deep into the remote wilderness of Belmullet and Achill.

30 The North in a Nutshell
Jump into Northern Ireland from rural Donegal.

★ BEST FOR:

FAMILIES

The Great Western Greenway follows a flat, traffic-free cycle path all the way to Achill Island.

LISANDRO LUIS TRARBACH/SHUTTERSTOCK

The Great Western Greenway (p34)

of Cork city, **Kinsale** is a gentle introduction to the wild west and, as I'm often corrected, in western Cork rather than West Cork – a distinction people here care about.

Whatever its geographic bona fides, Kinsale is a beaut. The best way to get a sense of it is along the **Scilly Walk**, a 6km round trip that hugs the shoreline and takes me to **Charles Fort** *(heritageireland.ie)*, the 17th-century star-shaped fort overlooking the harbour and the surrounding countryside. It's the kind of place that instantly explains why this port mattered.

Lunch at the always excellent **Bulman Bar** and then back down via High Rd, aka the 'Golden Mile', full of multimillion-euro holiday homes peering out over the water. Back in town, with its bright shopfronts and easy pace, I'm ready to begin my journey. If there's a better feeling than rolling out of Kinsale with a full stomach and a full tank, I've yet to find it.

THE DRIVE: The official starting point of the Wild Atlantic is just outside Kinsale on the R600. The road skirts the coastline west for 66km through Clonakilty and to Skibbereen.

02 Skibbereen

A couple of kilometres out of town, I take a detour south along the R604 to the dramatic headland of Old Head. There's an exclusive golf course at the tip of it, but the scenic drive is more than worth it, especially with a stop at the **Old Head Signal Tower** *(oldheadofkinsale.com)*, whose museum tells the story of the *Lusitania* tragedy; a memorial marks the spot where the ship was torpedoed offshore.

From here, I rejoin the R600 (passing the pretty beach at Garretstown) and continue westward through Timoleague before meeting the N71 on the edge of Clonakilty (p160). I make a quick stop to buy the country's best black (blood) pudding at **Twomey's** on Pearse St (it's too early for Clon's other standout cultural contribution, **DeBarra's** across the street, a music venue with few rivals anywhere). And then it's back towards the coast, through glorious **Inchydoney** (a walk on the beach here in fine weather is a must), Roscarbery and the twin villages of **Union Hall** and **Glandore**, which really come alive in summer.

Just beyond Leap (pronounced 'Lepp') the N71 skirts by Castlehaven Bay before descending gently toward Skibbereen, where I'll stop for the night. Before bed, though, I'll go south to Lough Hyne for a starlight paddle with **Atlantic Sea Kayaking** *(atlanticseakayaking.com)* on a lake that can shimmer with bioluminescence.

THE DRIVE: From Skib, follow the N71 to Newbridge and then turn onto the R595 for 8km to Baltimore. The Clear Island ferry takes 50 minutes; from there you can retrace your route back to Baltimore or take the Schull ferry (one hour) and follow the R592 to the N71 and onto Ballydehob.

03 Ballydehob

I'm now fully in the heart of West Cork. From Skib, I have choices. I head south to **Baltimore** via the coastal R595, where I could take the ferry to the car-free Gaeltacht island of **Cape Clear** to see some birdlife and go for a hike. If I've managed to secure a reservation at two-Michelin-starred **Dede** *(customshousebaltimore.com)*, I'll head back to Baltimore; if not, after a walk and some birdwatching on Clear Island, I'll take the ferry from the island to **Schull**, from where I'll turn north and drive to Ballydehob.

My reward for taking two ferries in a single day also involves high-end cuisine. Ballydehob has a thriving community of boho, artsy types, and Main St is where I'll find three of my favourite places in Ireland. Michelin-starred **Restaurant Chestnut** *(restaurantchestnutwestcork.ie)* is exceptional, but even if I don't fancy such fine dining, **Budd's** *(budds.ie)* across the street has the best bangers and mash I've ever eaten. Wherever I eat, though, my evening will be spent in **Levis** (pronounced 'leevis'; *leviscornerhouse.com*), a contender for best pub in Ireland.

THE DRIVE: It's a 31km drive southwest on the R592 to the tip of Mizen Head. For Bantry, retrace the route back and take the R591 at Toormore for a total of 43km.

04 Bantry

I head back through Schull and onto the Mizen Head peninsula. Beyond Goleen the road gets narrower and the landscapes wilder. My destination is the **Signal Station** *(mizenhead.ie)* at the tip, perched high on a small island connected to the mainland by a 45m-high footbridge. For the best views, I go up the steps to the right beyond the bridge to see Dunlough Bay spread out before me.

MacCarthy's Bar, Castletownbere, Cork

FOTOGRO/SHUTTERSTOCK

The road up to Bantry takes me up the northern side of the peninsula, where, off my left side, I have fine views of the **Sheep's Head Peninsula**. (The drive around it begins just after Durrus and is spectacular, especially the views at Seefin, just beyond Kilcrohane.) But my destination is handsome Bantry, a warren of narrow streets lined with old-fashioned independent shops, traditional pubs and excellent seafood restaurants clustered around a lovely waterfront.

THE DRIVE: Take the N71 north for 8km and turn right after the bridge at the head of the bay. Proceed 1.7km to Coomhola Bridge, turning left before it and then the first right to climb up to Priest's Leap. After 7km rejoin the N71 and drive 9km to Kenmare.

05 Kenmare

Early in the morning, I leave Bantry and make my way northwest. If I had more time, I'd continue along the N71 and take a left at Glengarriff and right into the wild heart of the Beara Peninsula. I'd need two days to give this corner justice – it's a drive that keeps interrupting itself, where every lay-by is a viewing platform, especially the stretch between Allihies and Eyeries. And of course there's the famous **MacCarthy's Bar** in Castletownbere, not to mention the **cable car** *(dursey island.ie)* to Dursey Island.

Instead I'm going north along the vertiginous, single-tracked road to Priest's Leap, 15km north of Bantry. This is the original road up to Kenmare, and I have to keep my wits about me, but my reward is monumental views across the mountains to Bantry Bay.

DON'T SWEAT THE WILD ATLANTIC WAY

There was a time when warming up on Ireland's west coast meant wrapping your hands around a mug of tea and waiting for feeling to return to your fingers. Now, increasingly, it means stepping into a wood-fired sauna, listening to the crackle of burning timber while Atlantic rollers collapse against the shore just metres away.

Sea swimming may have lit the spark, but saunas have become the flame. What began as a niche ritual among sea swimmers has become one of the most popular experiences on the Wild Atlantic Way, as barrel saunas and timber huts are now cropping up with the same inevitability as coffee vans did. Several are mobile, so you might find them in different spots – check before you go.

The ritual is simple. A brisk dip in the ocean delivers an invigorating shock, quickly followed by the slow, penetrating heat of the sauna. It's not indulgence so much as reset.

Some of the finest examples sit in places you might otherwise drive straight past. At Ventry Bay on the Dingle Peninsula, **Sona Sauna** *(@sonasauna)* overlooks one of Kerry's most beautiful beaches, its wood-fired heat offering relief after a windswept walk along the strand. Nearby, **Skellig Sauna** *(skelligsauna.ie)* at Cuas Crom Beach near Cahersiveen sits on an especially atmospheric stretch of coastline on the Ring of Kerry, within the Dark Sky Reserve.

In Connemara, **Driftwood Sauna** *(driftwoodsauna.ie)* near Spiddal has sweeping views towards the Aran Islands, while on Renville Pier in Oranmore, **Sauna Fíain** *(saunafiain.com)* is a hand-built, Finnish-style structure overlooking the water.

Further north, the **Wild Atlantic Sauna** *(@wildatlanticsauna)* at Old Head Beach in County Mayo has gorgeous views across Clew Bay towards Croagh Patrick, its barrel-shaped structure just steps from the water's edge. In Sligo, **Sauna Sásta** *(saunasasta.ie)* at Dunmoran Strand and the **West Coast Sauna** *(@westcoastsaunaireland)* at Enniscrone Pier offer restorative pauses along a coastline defined by vast beaches and shifting Atlantic light.

Even in more remote corners, the experience feels deeply rooted in place. **West Cork Sauna** *(westcorksauna.ie)* operates at piers and inlets along the Beara Peninsula and beyond, while **Sauna Suaimhneas** *(saunasuaimhneas.com)*, from the Irish for 'peace', appears at beaches across County Clare, including Lahinch and Spanish Point – ideal stopping points as you follow the coast past the Cliffs of Moher.

They also offer something travellers often seek but rarely find: genuine connection with local life. Saunas draw an easy mix of regulars and passersby, farmers and surfers, retirees and road-trippers. Conversations begin naturally, whether comparing driving routes, sharing tips on hidden beaches or commenting on the weather – Ireland's universal currency. For solo travellers especially, they offer a rare chance to slip briefly into the social fabric of a place.

DRIVE SMART, NOT WIDE

Choose Size Wisely
When choosing a rental car for the Wild Atlantic Way, comfort and practicality matter more than size. A large SUV might seem appealing, but many coastal and rural roads are narrow, winding and occasionally single-track. If you're not used to tight driving conditions, a smaller car is often the better choice – easier to manoeuvre without sacrificing comfort.

Automatic vs Manual
Transmission is another important consideration. Automatic cars make driving significantly easier, especially on the constant climbs, descents and sharp bends that define much of the route. You'll pay more for an automatic, but the reduced effort (particularly on longer days) is well worth it.

Plan Realistic Distances
Daily driving distances also require realistic planning. The Wild Atlantic Way stretches for 2500km, but few travellers cover all of it. Even with ample time, driving more than 75% would mean taking every minor detour, exploring remote peninsulas and visiting offshore islands. The temptation to pack each day with distance is understandable, but the west coast rewards a slower pace.

Slow Down and Enjoy the Journey
Roads are rarely straight, often narrow and filled with distractions: sudden viewpoints, empty beaches and villages worth exploring. What looks manageable on a map can take far longer in practice. As a rule, avoid driving more than six hours a day, and four is often ideal. This allows time to stop, explore and experience the landscape properly. With sensible pacing, you can comfortably drive the route in under a week while still enjoying everything that makes it special.

THE DRIVE: It's 92km from Kenmare to Dingle, via the N71 north through Killarney National Park to Killarney, then the L2019 for about 9km and then left onto the R561, which you follow for 55km until you meet the N86.

06 Dingle

The road from Kenmare to Killarney is arguably the most spectacular stretch of the **Ring of Kerry**, a fitting finale (if you're doing it counter-clockwise as recommended) to one of the great road trips of Europe. It takes me through the glorious **Gap of Dunloe**, the mountain pass between the Purple Mountain and the Macgillicuddy Reeks, and right into the heart of Killarney National Park. I've driven the Ring many times in my life – and would happily do the whole 179km loop again – but I have another spectacular drive ahead of me.

Once I'm out of Killarney I follow the relatively unimpressive rural road north, following the signposts for Castlemaine. Then I'm back on the coast as I skirt the southern side of the Dingle Peninsula. The road slips past the wide sweep of **Inch Beach** (a 5km-long sandy film star in its own right, having featured in three movies: *Ryan's Daughter*, *Excalibur* and *Far & Away*) before climbing over the headland, the Atlantic stretching out ahead, daring you not to stop the car. I roll into Dingle town (p140) and set about exploring one of my favourite places in Ireland.

THE DRIVE: It's about 130km from Dingle to Kilrush via Ballybunion: 50km along the R560 and N86 to Tralee and 26km along the N69 to Listowel, then take the R553 to Ballybunion and R551 to Tarbert. The 4km ferry crossing between Tarbert and Killimer takes about 30 minutes and then it's only 9km to Kilrush. Shave off 22km by continuing on the N69 from Listowel to Tarbert.

07 Kilrush

I'd happily spend a few days in Dingle, eating seafood and taking a trip out to the **Blasket Islands** before finding a stool in one of the many pubs in town – preferably with live

Connor Pass, Dingle Peninsula, Kerry
MATT ELLIOTT/SHUTTERSTOCK

traditional music. But I'm not even a quarter through my journey, so I am onward bound.

I console myself with a drive around **Slea Head** – a 47km loop around the head of the peninsula that comes with stunning views and some fine ancient sites, like the **Gallurus Observatory** *(heritage ireland.ie)*. The drive brings me back to the edge of Dingle town, but no matter, because I turn northeast and make my way through the 12km **Connor Pass** (p137), a ribbon of tarmac climbing steeply between lush green mountains, opening up to vast views over the Kerry landscape. It's narrow, exposed and demands respect, so I take it slow, using the pull-ins when needed, and let the scenery do most of the work.

I drive through **Castlegregory** and resist the temptation of the beach (and all of the water-based activities on offer, from scuba diving to surfing), meeting the N86, which skirts the edge of Tralee. From there, the road threads north through **Listowel**, home of the famous literary festival. A detour west delivers me to **Ballybunion**, a seaside town that is home to the world-famous golf course, but if you prefer you can just continue north along the N69 to the mouth of the Shannon at Tarbert. I roll onto the car ferry and cross the estuary: I've now left County Kerry behind and am in County Clare. From Killimer, it's only about 15 minutes to Kilrush.

THE DRIVE: It's 110km to the Cliffs of Moher via the Loop Head Peninsula. Follow the N67 for 12km north to Kilkee then turn left onto the R487 for the peninsula. Retrace your steps back up to Kilkee and follow the N67 for 68km to Lahinch, turning left onto the coastal R478 towards Doolin.

08 Cliffs of Moher

If I've time, and if the weather allows it, I take a boat out to **Scattery Island**, 3km southwest of Kilrush. Now uninhabited save for lots of birds, it was once home to a thriving Christian community – there are the remains of no less than six medieval churches and the best-preserved round tower to explore.

Otherwise, from Kilrush, I drive northwest as far as **Kilkee**, which

Lahinch, Clare

PATRYK KOSMIDER/SHUTTERSTOCK

sits on a sweeping semicircular bay with high cliffs at the northern end and tidal rocks to the south. Between them is a huge golden beach that is thronged in summer. Undistracted, I turn southwest and make my way to the tip of the **Loop Head Peninsula**. It's only 26km, but I may as well be driving to the end of the world, as the sea gets closer on both sides of the road the nearer I get to the lighthouse at the headland. On a good day, I'm met with wonderful views south to the mountains of Kerry and north as far as Connemara in County Galway.

I make my way back up through Kilkee and rejoin the N67 as it takes me north, past Doonbeg and up to **Miltown Malbay**. I'm in traditional music country now: there are always excellent sounds in **Friel's** and **Hillery's**; just a little bit further on is beautiful **Lahinch** (p188), a surfing hot spot that is also home to one of the best golf courses in the country. From here I turn left along the R478 and enjoy a seafood lunch in Vaughan's of Liscannor; this sets me up for my next stop, the **Cliffs of Moher** *(cliffsofmoher.ie)*.

Outside of Dublin, the cliffs are Ireland's most visited attraction, and even though I've been countless times, the thrill of staring down at the crashing sea 200m below has never left me (although these days it comes with a healthy feeling of vertigo, so I make sure to stand well back). If I can time it right, sunset is unbeatable. Depending on the season, the tour buses have long gone and the crowds have thinned, leaving the cliffs bathed in soft, fading light. I walk up to O'Brien's Tower for the views, then head south along

MARK GUSEV/SHUTTERSTOCK

Sky Road (p33), Galway

THE WILD ATLANTIC WAY & ME

The Wild Atlantic Way is the Ireland of my romantic imagination. Growing up in Dublin, the west always felt wilder, somehow beyond the familiar. Childhood trips to visit cousins on Achill Island made me feel as though I'd crossed into another country, one gloriously out of step with my own.

Much has changed since then. These days, even the smallest villages have third-wave coffee, barrel saunas and reliable 5G. But the landscapes resist domestication. They remain gloriously indifferent to comfort and convenience – vast skies, empty beaches and unpredictable weather. The roads still narrow without warning and the Atlantic still shifts from serene to savage in a single afternoon. And yes, occasionally I will run into a traffic jam made up of a flock of sheep. For all the new luxuries, the west remains elemental and untamed.

Whenever I drive the Wild Atlantic Way I set out with a plan, but a sudden glimpse of white sand or a coffee dock overlooking a scenic viewpoint will always shred the schedule. It'll only take me half an hour to drive from here to there? I never accounted for stopping to watch the fishing boat unload its catch at the harbour.

Even bad weather has its own drama. Once, on the Sky Road outside Clifden, I stepped from the car in the middle of a massive storm and was *literally* blown backwards – this was not an experience I had planned for but very much loved.

the clifftop path, which is usually quieter and feels wilder by the step.

THE DRIVE: Doolin is 9km north of the cliffs on the R478.

09 Doolin

Doolin is the unofficial capital of traditional music in Ireland. After a short drive north, my evening will end in a pub, with a peat fire and the sound of some of the best live trad you will hear anywhere on earth, but first I soak my muscles in a **seaweed bath** *(wildatlanticseaweedbaths.com)* – just north of the pier are barrels filled with heated sea water and fronds of locally harvested kelp; it's the perfect way to unwind. Then it's time for the pub: I opt for **McDermott's** *(mcdermott-s-pub.com)*, which is preferred by locals, although more touristy **O'Connor's** *(gusoconnorsdoolin.com)* is still brilliant.

THE DRIVE: The N67 delivers you right into Galway city (70km); then for coastal Connemara, follow the R336 from Galway out past Salthill and continue for about 50km. At Screebe take a left onto the R340 and follow it around the coast to Clifden.

10 Clifden

The coastal route to Clifden clocks in just under 200km, but it carries me through two of Ireland's most striking landscapes and past arguably its most colourful, energetic city. Leaving Doolin, I cut straight into the heart of The Burren, that otherworldly sweep of limestone pavement, fissured and sculpted, where wildflowers somehow flourish in the cracks (known as 'grykes') and the Atlantic is never far from view.

Along the way, I pass through Lisdoonvarna, famed for its matchmaking festival but also where I can pick up some finely smoked salmon at the **Burren Smokehouse** *(burrensmokehouse.com)*, and Ballyvaughan, where I stop for cake in **An Feár Gorta**, a cafe in an 18th-century cottage. At the northern edge of The Burren is the handsome port village of Kinvarra, where my grandfather was born and raised; from here, it's only 30km north to **Galway city** around the edge of Galway Bay. I stop for lunch and a coffee, taking a stroll among the boho shops and cafes of the West End, before pushing on west, where the city gives way to open bogland and the road begins to feel wilder with every kilometre.

I stick to the coast, passing through Bearna, then Irish-speaking *An Spidéal* (Spiddal), and soon Connemara begins to take hold. Mountains rise, lakes shimmer, stone walls criss-cross the land, and the traffic reduces to almost nothing. I drive past Carraroe and its beaches, beyond the small thatched cottage once lived in by Patrick Pearse, and into Roundstone, clustered around a busy harbour.

About 2.5km west of here are my favourite beaches in Ireland, just off the main road: **Gurteen** and, on the other side of the little peninsula, **Dog's Bay**, which on a fine day are more like beaches you'd find in the Caribbean than in Ireland. By the time I roll into Clifden, the unofficial capital of Connemara, it feels like I've crossed not just a county, but into a different rhythm altogether – one shaped by weather, water and the wide Atlantic beyond.

THE DRIVE: It's 83km to Westport; take the N59 as far as Leenaun, and then turn left onto the R335, driving past Doolough and Louisburgh to Westport.

11 Westport

One of Ireland's loveliest loop roads starts and ends in Clifden: the 20km **Sky Road** goes as far as Kingston and back, taking in rugged, stunningly beautiful coastal scenery. At one point it separates into the lower and upper road – I always take the upper road for the best views.

After that it's only 83km to Westport, but this stretch of my journey is full of distractions. After 17km I reach Letterfrack, where beautiful **Kylemore Abbey** *(kylemoreabbey.com)* is worth a couple of hours of my time. I visit the 19th-century house and gardens, stopping for a snack in the excellent restaurant. A few kilometres further on I am once more on the water, skirting alongside Killary Harbour, Ireland's only fjord. If I'd time, I'd jump onto the super-comfortable catamaran operated by **Killary Fjord Boat Tours** *(killaryfjord.ie)* for a 90-minute cruise along the harbour to Barna Island and back, keeping my eyes peeled for the pods of dolphins in the water. At the head of the harbour, Leenane is a pretty village that is popular with coach tours; if it's not too busy, I'll have a toasted sandwich in **Gaynor's Bar**, right by the water.

Beyond Leenane, the N59 continues right up to Westport, but if I took that I'd be missing one of Ireland's most scenic drives. I turn left onto the R335 and make my way northward through the

Traditional music session, Westport, Mayo
NICOLAS D'HOEDT/LONELY PLANET

desolate **Doolough Valley**, the steep sides of the surrounding mountains sliding into the steely grey waters of **Doo Lough**. Along the road is a memorial commemorating the Doolough Tragedy of 1849, when hundreds of starving victims of the Famine walked south along this road from Louisburgh to Delphi Lodge hoping for some help; none was forthcoming, and in the bitter cold, many died on the way home. By the time I hit the coast, I'm only 19km from Westport.

Westport (p182) is one of my favourite towns in Ireland, and I could easily spend a few days here, taking in its collection of cool cafes and music-filled pubs. Westport is also the starting point of the **Great Western Greenway**, a cycle track that goes 42km out to Achill; alternatively, it's only a 10-minute drive to the foothills of **Croagh Patrick** (764m), Ireland's holiest mountain and a very popular climb – the views from the summit of Clew Bay and its collection of islands are superb.

THE DRIVE: The fastest way to Sligo is to take the N5 as far as Charlestown and then turn north onto the N17 (103km); the coastal N59 is longer (166km) but much more scenic.

12 Sligo

I'm in no rush to get to Sligo: I go north along the N59 and skirt around the coast before cutting into the heart of the Belmullet Peninsula, which is largely taken up by **Wild Nephin National Park**, comprising some of Europe's greatest areas of blanket bog. The

Wild Nephin National Park, Sligo

BONN BONN FOTO/SHUTTERSTOCK

MARK GUSEV/SHUTTERSTOCK

Charge point, Galway

GOING ELECTRIC ON THE WILD ATLANTIC WAY

At 2500km through some remote landscapes, driving the Wild Atlantic Way in an electric vehicle might sound daunting, but it's entirely achievable. Driven in a straight line, the route requires fewer than three full charges, and even covering every last kilometre, you'll find plenty of opportunities to plug in along the way.

As of 2026, Ireland has around 1900 public chargers across 800 locations nationwide, including many along the west coast. These are listed and regularly updated on the Electricity Supply Board's charge point map *(esb.ie)*. Download the ESB app to view the network in real time – it lets you locate chargers, check availability and pay easily while travelling. The Irish Electric Vehicle Association *(irishevassociation.ie)* also maintains a useful list of providers, including private operators such as EasyGo and ePower, further expanding your options.

For maximum convenience, the best place to charge is often at your accommodation overnight. Many hotels, guesthouses and self-catering properties along the route now offer on-site charge points, allowing you to wake up fully powered and ready to continue. Booking platforms such as Tripadvisor offer EV-charging filters, though it's always wise to confirm before arrival.

Higher-end hotels are especially well equipped. Properties such as Ashford Castle in County Mayo, Ballynahinch Castle in Connemara, and Adare Manor and Dromoland Castle in County Limerick all offer guest charging. With a little planning, driving the Wild Atlantic Way in an EV is not just possible, but effortless.

best way to visit the park is by car; the entrance is signposted between Mulranny and Bangor Erris.

From the excellent **visitor centre** (the scones alone in the restaurant are worth the trip) there's a short trail that reveals some of the loveliest views of Achill Island, the surrounding mountains and the sea. Satisfied, I rejoin the N59 and continue northeast, skirting the coast until I reach Sligo town.

THE DRIVE: It's 190km from Sligo to Dunfanaghy via the coastal N15 and N56. An alternative is the inland route via the N15 and N13 through Letterkenny, which is shorter at 149km, and what it lacks in coastal scenery it more than makes up for in dramatic landscapes.

13 Dunfanaghy

From Sligo town, I head north on the N15; about 8km out of town, I pass the church in **Drumcliffe**, where WB Yeats' grave features his famous (self-penned) epitaph – 'Cast a cold eye on life, on death. Horseman, pass by!' – all in the dramatic shadow of Benbulben. I meet the coast a little further on at Grange, and soon I'm over the border in Donegal at **Bundoran**, one of Ireland's best-known seaside resorts. Another 45km on and I'm in Donegal town, where I take a coastal detour onto the N56.

The coastal R263 takes me through Inver, Killybegs and Muckross, passing the **Secret Waterfall** at Largy before cutting through the hills to Teelin and **Sliabh Liag**. Taller, wilder and even more dramatic than the Cliffs of Moher, this is one of Ireland's most scenic spots, and I hike up beyond the viewpoint to see them in all their glory.

I retrace my steps and rejoin the R263, pushing on through the Donegal mountains, detouring to the Gaeltacht village of Malin Beg and the horseshoe beach Silver Strand. From there it's back across rolling green hills to rejoin the N56, but not before pulling in at the **Glengesh Viewing Point** between Glencolumbcille and Ardara, a mountain pass that rivals the Connor Pass in Kerry for scenic drama.

The road beyond feels properly wild and pretty soon I'm in the Donegal Gaeltacht, the Irish-speaking corner of the county. Before I get to Gweedore I can see the pinkish-grey quartzite peak of **Mt Errigal** (751m) off to my left, the highest point in Donegal. If I have time, I take a detour to the **Poisoned Glen** at Dunlewey, where the ruin of an old church sits by dark water with Errigal reflected beyond. From here, I'm less than 25km from Dunfanaghy.

THE DRIVE: It's 107km from Dunfanaghy to Malin Head via the more scenic route: turn off the N56 at Kilmacrenan and proceed on the R249 to Rathmullan; the ferry across Lough Swilly takes 30 minutes. In Buncrana, follow the R238 coastal route and then the R242 to Malin Head.

14 Malin Head

I'm nearly at the end of my journey. Before leaving Dunfanaghy, though, I take a quick spin up **Horn Head**, the headland jutting out to sea beyond the stretch of Killyhoey Beach. On a clear day, I can see the Scottish mainland from the summit.

The fastest way to my destination at Malin Head is actually longer – following the N56 through Letterkenny and then along the N13 – but I want to follow the last bit of the Wild Atlantic Way so I turn left at Kilmacrenan and follow the R247 along the lower reaches of the Inishowen Peninsula.

I drive through Ramelton and Rathmullan and then take the ferry across Lough Swilly to Buncrana, 5km away. Here I turn northward along the coastal R238 that takes me through the beautiful **Mamore Gap** and on to Clonmany, Ballyliffin and around the bay until I reach Malin Head at the northern end of the peninsula. On a still day it feels serene; in wind, elemental. Exactly what I want from the Wild Atlantic Way.

Cliffs of Sliabh Liag, Donegal

NICOLAS D'HOEDT/LONELY PLANET

02

EPIC TRIP

★ BEST

TWO DAYS

The Connemara Peninsula and the Ring of Kerry.

IRELAND'S HIGHLIGHTS

DURATION: 7 DAYS

DISTANCE: 959KM / 596 MILES

GREAT FOR: FOOD & DRINK, HISTORY, OUTDOORS

BEST TIME TO GO: APRIL TO SEPTEMBER FOR THE LONG DAYS AND BEST WEATHER.

Trinity College, Dublin

Every time-worn truth about Ireland will be found on this trip: the breathtaking scenery of stone-walled fields and wave-dashed cliffs; the picture-postcard villages and bustling towns; the ancient ruins that have stood since before history was written. The trip begins in Ireland's storied, fascinating capital and transports you to the wild west of Galway and Connemara before taking you south to the even wilder folds of County Kerry.

LINK YOUR TRIP

19 Southwestern Pantry
From Kenmare, it's a 42km drive south to Durrus and the start of the mouth-watering Southwestern Pantry trip.

20 West Cork Villages
You can explore the gorgeous villages of West Cork from Kinsale.

01 Dublin

World-class museums, superb restaurants and the best collection of entertainment in the country – there are plenty of good reasons why the capital is the ideal place to start your trip. Get some sightseeing in on a walking tour before 'exploring' at least one of the city's storied – if not historic – pubs.

Your top stop should be the grounds of **Trinity College** *(tcd.ie)*, home to the gloriously illuminated **Book of Kells**. It's kept in the stunning 65m Long Room of the **Old Library**.

THE DRIVE: It's a 208km trip to Galway city across the country along the M6 motorway, which has little in terms of visual highlights beyond green fields, which get greener and a little more wild the further west you go. Twenty-two kilometres south of Athlone (about

halfway) is a worthwhile detour to Clonmacnoise.

02 Galway City

The best way to appreciate Galway is to amble around Eyre Sq and down Shop St towards the **Spanish Arch** and the River Corrib, stopping off for a little liquid sustenance in one of the city's classic old pubs.

Top of our list is **Tig Chóilí** *(tigchoiligalway.com)*, a fire-engine-red pub that draws them in with its two live *céilidh* (traditional music and dancing sessions) each day. A close second is **Tigh Neachtain** *(tighneachtain.com)*, known simply as Neachtain's (nock-tans) or Naughtons – stop and join the locals for a pint.

THE DRIVE: The most direct route to Roundstone is to cut through Connemara along the N59, turning left on Clifden Rd – a total of 76km. Alternatively, the 103km coastal route, via the R336 and R340, winds its way around small bays, coves and lovely seaside hamlets.

03 Roundstone

Huddled on a boat-filled harbour, Roundstone *(Cloch na Rón)* is one of Connemara's gems. Colourful terrace houses and inviting pubs overlook the dark recess of Bertraghboy Bay, which is home to lobster trawlers and traditional *currachs* (rowing boats) with tarred canvas bottoms stretched over wicker frames.

Just south of the village, in the remains of an old Franciscan monastery, is Malachy Kearns' **Roundstone Musical Instruments** *(bodhran.com)*. Kearns is Ireland's only full-time maker of traditional bodhráns (hand-held goatskin drums). Watch him work and buy a tin whistle, harp or booklet filled with Irish ballads; there's also a small free folk museum and a cafe.

THE DRIVE: The 22km inland route from Roundstone to Clifden is a little longer, but the road is better (especially the N59) and the brown, barren beauty of Connemara is yours to behold. The 18km coastal route along the R341 brings you through more speckled

♥ DON'T MISS

ENNIS' BEST TRAD SESSION PUBS

Cíaran's Bar
Slip into this small place by day and you can be just another geezer pondering a pint. At night there's usually trad music. Bet you wish you had a copy of the Guinness mural out front!

Brogan's
(facebook.com/brogansennis) On the corner of Cooke's Lane, Brogan's sees a fine bunch of musicians rattling even the stone floors from about 9pm Monday to Thursday, plus more nights in summer.

Cruise's Pub
(queenshotelennis.com) There are trad-music sessions most nights from 9.30pm.

Poet's Corner Bar
(oldgroundhotelennis.com/poets-corner-bar.html) This old pub often has massive trad sessions on Fridays.

landscape; to the south, you'll have glimpses of the ocean.

04 Clifden

Connemara's 'capital', Clifden *(An Clochán)* is an appealing Victorian-era country town with an amoeba-shaped oval of streets offering evocative strolls. It presides over the head of the narrow bay where the River Owenglin tumbles into the sea. The surrounding countryside beckons you to walk through woods and above the shoreline.

THE DRIVE: It's 154km to the Cliffs of Moher; you'll have to backtrack through Galway city (take the N59) before turning south along the N67. This will take you through the unique striated landscape of The Burren, a moody, rocky and at times fearsome space accented with ancient burial chambers and medieval ruins.

DETOUR
The Sky Road
Start: 04 Clifden

From the N59 heading north out of Clifden, signs point towards the Sky Road, a 12km route tracing a spectacular loop out to the township of Kingston and back to Clifden, taking in some rugged, stunningly beautiful coastal scenery en route. It's a cinch to drive, but you can also easily walk or cycle it.

05 Cliffs of Moher

Star of a million tourist brochures, the Cliffs of Moher (*Aillte an Mothair*, or *Ailltreacha Mothair*) are one of the most popular sights in Ireland.

The entirely vertical cliffs rise to a height of 214m, their edge falling away abruptly into the constantly churning sea. A series of heads, the dark limestone seems to march in a rigid formation that amazes, no matter how many times you look.

Such appeal comes at a price: crowds. This is check-off tourism big time and busloads come and go constantly in summer. A vast **visitor centre** *(cliffsofmoher.ie)* handles the hordes.

Like so many overpopular natural wonders, there's relief and joy if you're willing to walk for 10 minutes. Past the end of the 'Moher Wall', a 5km trail leads south along the cliffs to Hag's Head – few venture this far.

THE DRIVE: The 39km drive to Ennis goes inland at Lahinch (p188; famous for its world-class golf links); it's then 24km to your destination, through flat south Clare. Dotted with stone walls and fields, it's the classic Irish landscape.

06 Ennis

As the capital of a renowned music county, Ennis *(Inis)* is filled with pubs featuring trad music. In fact, this is the best reason to stay here. Where's best changes often; stroll the streets pub-hopping to find what's on any given night.

If you want to buy an authentic (and well-made) Irish instrument, pop into **Custy's Music Shop** *(custysmusic.com)*, which sells fiddles and other musical items as well as giving general info about the local scene.

THE DRIVE: It's 186km to Dingle if you go via Limerick city, but only 142km if you go via the N68 to Killimer for the ferry across the Shannon estuary to Tarbert. The views get fabulous when you're beyond Tralee on the N86, especially if you take the 456m Connor Pass, Ireland's highest.

07 Dingle Town

In summer, Dingle's (p140) hilly streets can be clogged with visitors, and there's no way around it; in other seasons, its authentic

Master bodhrán maker Malachy Kearns (p39)
ROBERT ORMEROD/LONELY PLANET

Malachy
Kearns

charms are yours to savour. Many pubs double as shops, so you can enjoy Guinness and a singalong among screws and nails, wellies and horseshoes.

THE DRIVE: It's only 17km to Slea Head along the R559. The views – of the mountains to the north and the wild ocean to the south and west – are a big chunk of the reason you came to Ireland in the first place.

08 Slea Head

Overlooking the mouth of Dingle Bay, Mt Eagle and the Blasket Islands, Slea Head has fine beaches, good walks and superbly preserved structures from Dingle's ancient past, including **beehive huts**, forts, inscribed stones and church sites. **Dunmore Head** is the westernmost point on the Irish mainland and the site of the wreckage in 1588 of two Spanish Armada ships.

> **PHOTO OPPORTUNITY**
>
> The Lakes of Killarney from Ladies' View on the Ring of Kerry.

The Iron Age **Dunbeg Fort** is a dramatic example of a promontory fortification, perched atop a sheer sea cliff about 7km southwest of Ventry on the road to Slea Head. The fort has four outer walls of stone. Inside are the remains of a house and a beehive hut, as well as an underground passage.

THE DRIVE: The 88km to Killarney will take you through Annascaul (home to a pub once owned by Antarctic explorer Tom Crean) and Inch (whose beach is seen in *Ryan's Daughter*). At Castlemaine, turn south towards Miltown then take the R563 to Killarney.

09 Killarney

Beyond its proximity to lakes, waterfalls, woodland and moors dwarfed by 1000m-plus peaks, Killarney has many charms of its own as well as being the gateway to the Ring of Kerry, perhaps the outstanding highlight of many a visit to Ireland.

Besides the breathtaking views of the mountains and glacial lakes, highlights of the 102-sq-km **Killarney National Park** include Ireland's only wild herd of native

Ladies' View on the Ring of Kerry

PETE SEAWARD/LONELY PLANET

red deer, the country's largest area of ancient oak woods and 19th-century Muckross House.

THE DRIVE: It's 27km along the narrow and winding N71 to Kenmare, much of it through magnificent scenery, especially at Ladies' View (much loved by Queen Victoria's ladies-in-waiting) and, 5km further on, Moll's Gap, a popular stop for photos and food.

10 Kenmare

Picturesque Kenmare carries its romantic reputation more stylishly than does Killarney, and there is an elegance about its handsome central square and attractive buildings. It still gets very busy in summer, all the same. The town stands where the delightfully named Finnihy, Roughty and Sheen Rivers empty into Kenmare River. Kenmare makes a pleasant alternative to Killarney as a base for visiting the Ring of Kerry and the Beara Peninsula.

THE DRIVE: The 47km to Caherdaniel along the southern stretch of the Ring of Kerry duck in and out of view of Kenmare River, with the marvellous Beara Peninsula to the south. Just before you reach Caherdaniel, a 4km detour north takes you to the rarely visited Staigue Fort, which dates from the 3rd or 4th century.

11 Caherdaniel

The big attraction here is **Derrynane National Historic Park** *(derrynanehouse.ie)*, the family home of Daniel O'Connell, the campaigner for Catholic emancipation. His ancestors bought the house and surrounding parkland, having grown rich on smuggling with France and Spain. It's largely furnished with O'Connell memorabilia, including the restored triumphal chariot in which he lapped Dublin after his release from prison in 1844.

THE DRIVE: Follow the N70 for about 18km and then turn left onto the Skellig Ring (roads R567 and R566), cutting through some of the wildest and most beautiful scenery on the peninsula, with the ragged outline of Skellig Michael never far from view. The whole drive is 35km long.

12 Portmagee & Valentia Island

Portmagee's single street is a rainbow of colourful houses, and is much photographed. On summer mornings, the small pier comes to life with boats embarking on the choppy crossing to the Skellig Islands.

A bridge links Portmagee to 11km-long **Valentia Island** *(Oileán Dairbhre)*, an altogether homier isle than the brooding Skelligs to the southwest. Like the Skellig Ring it leads to, Valentia is an essential, coach-free detour from the Ring of Kerry. Some lonely ruins are worth exploring.

Valentia was chosen as the site for the first transatlantic telegraph cable. When the connection was made in 1858, it put Cahersiveen in direct contact with New York. The link worked for 27 days before failing, but went back into action years later.

The island makes an ideal driving loop. From April to October, there's a frequent, quick ferry trip at one end, as well as the bridge to Portmagee on the mainland at the other end.

THE DRIVE: The 55km between Portmagee and Killorglin keep the mountains to your right (south) and the sea – when you're near it – to your left (north). Twenty-four kilometres along is the unusual Glenbeigh Strand, a tendril of sand protruding into Dingle Bay with views of Inch Point and the Dingle Peninsula.

DETOUR

Skellig Michael

Start: 12 Portmagee & Valentia Island

The jagged, 217m-high rock of **Skellig Michael** (Archangel Michael's Rock, like St Michael's Mount in Cornwall and Mont St-Michel in Normandy; *heritage ireland.ie*) is the larger of the two Skellig Islands and a UNESCO World Heritage site.

Early Christian monks survived here from the 6th until the 12th or 13th-century; their determined quest for ultimate solitude led them to this remote, windblown edge of Europe.

Skellig Michael featured as Luke Skywalker's secret retreat in the *Star Wars* movies *The Force Awakens* (2015) and *The Last Jedi* (2017), attracting a whole new audience to the island's dramatic beauty.

It's a tough place to get to, and requires care to visit, but is worth every effort. The 12km sea crossing can be rough, and there are no toilets or shelter, so bring something to eat and drink, and wear stout shoes and weatherproof clothing. Due to the steep (and often slippery) terrain and sudden wind gusts, it's unsuitable for young children or people with limited mobility.

Note that the island's fragility requires limits on the number of daily visitors. The 15 boats

Skellig Michael (p43), Kerry
STEFAN MISSING/SHUTTERSTOCK

are licensed to carry no more than 12 passengers each, for a maximum of 180 people at any one time. It's wise to book ahead in July and August, bearing in mind that if the weather's bad the boats may not sail (about two days out of seven). Trips usually run from Easter until September, depending, again, on the weather.

Boats *(about €100 per person)* leave Portmagee, Ballinskelligs and Derrynane at around 10am, returning at 3pm. Boat owners generally restrict you to two hours on the island, which is the bare minimum to see the monastery, look at the birds and have a picnic. The crossing takes about 1½ hours from Portmagee, 35 minutes to one hour from Ballinskelligs and 1¾ hours from Derrynane.

13 Killorglin

Killorglin *(Cill Orglan)* is a quiet enough town, but that all changes in mid-August, when it erupts in celebration for **Puck Fair**, Ireland's best-known extant pagan festival.

First recorded in 1603, with hazy origins, this lively (read: boozy) festival is based around the custom of installing a billy goat (a poc, or puck), the symbol of mountainous Kerry, on a pedestal in the town, its horns festooned with ribbons. Other entertainment ranges from a horse fair and bonny baby competition to street theatre, concerts and fireworks; the pubs stay open until 3am.

Author Blake Morrison documents his mother's childhood here in *Things My Mother Never Told Me*.

♥ WHY I LOVE THIS TRIP

FIONN DAVENPORT, WRITER

The loop from Dublin west to Galway and then south through Kerry into Cork explores all of Ireland's scenic heavy hitters. It's the kind of trip I'd make if I was introducing visiting friends to Ireland at its very best, a taster trip that would entice them to come back and explore the country in greater depth.

03

EPIC TRIP

THE LONG WAY ROUND

DURATION: 14 DAYS

DISTANCE: 1300KM / 807 MILES

GREAT FOR: FOOD & DRINK, HISTORY, OUTDOORS

BEST TIME TO GO: YOU'LL HAVE THE BEST WEATHER IN JUNE AND AUGUST, BUT SEPTEMBER IS IDEAL.

There's a strong case to be made that the very best Ireland has to offer is closest to its jagged, dramatic coastlines: the splendid scenery, the best mountain ranges (geographically, Ireland is akin to a bowl, with raised edges) and most of its major towns and cities – Dublin, Belfast, Galway, Sligo and Cork. The western edge – between Donegal and Cork – corresponds to the Wild Atlantic Way driving route (p22).

LINK YOUR TRIP

04 Tip to Toe
Kilmore Quay is 134km east of Ardmore, where you can pick up the toe part of this trip and do it in reverse.

14 Blackwater Valley Drive
From Ardmore, it's only 5km to Youghal, where you can explore the gorgeous valley of the Blackwater River.

01 Dublin

From its music, art and literature to the legendary nightlife that has inspired those same musicians, artists and writers, Dublin has always known how to have fun and does it with deadly seriousness.

Should you tire of the city's more highbrow offerings, the **Guinness Storehouse** *(guinness-storehouse.com)* is the most popular place to visit in town; a beer-lover's Disneyland and multimedia bells-and-whistles homage to the country's most famous export and the city's most enduring symbol. The old grain storehouse is a suitable cathedral in which to worship the black gold; shaped like a giant pint of Guinness, it rises seven impressive storeys high around a central atrium.

THE DRIVE: It's 165km of motorway to Belfast – M1 in the Republic, A1 in Northern Ireland

ESSEVU/SHUTTERSTOCK

★ BEST

TWO DAYS

Stops 7 to 9 allow you to experience the very best of the wild west, including a day trip to the Aran Islands.

Inishmore (*Inis Mór*, p51), the Aran Islands, Galway

– but remember that the speed limit changes from kilometres to miles as you cross into the North.

02 Belfast

Belfast is in many ways a brand-new city. Once lumped with Beirut, Baghdad and Bosnia as one of the four 'Bs' for travellers to avoid, in recent years it has pulled off a remarkable transformation from bombs-and-bullets pariah to a hip-hotels-and-hedonism party town.

The old shipyards on the Lagan continue to give way to the luxury apartments of the Titanic Quarter, whose centrepiece, the stunning, star-shaped edifice housing **Titanic Belfast** *(titanicbelfast.com)*, covering the ill-fated liner's construction here, has become the city's number-one draw.

The city's history is explored in some terrific museums: SS *Nomadic* and HMS *Caroline* are fixtures in the Titanic Quarter, while **Crumlin Road Gaol** *(crumlinroadgaol.com)* is a former historic prison. They all add to a list of attractions that includes beautifully restored Victorian architecture, a glittering waterfront lined with modern art, a fantastic foodie scene and music-filled pubs.

If you're keen on learning more about the city's troubled history, take a walking tour of West Belfast.

THE DRIVE: The fastest way to the causeway is to take the A26 north, through Ballymena, before turning off at Ballymoney – a total of 100km – but the longer (by 16km), more scenic route is to take the A8 to Larne and follow the coast through handsome Cushendall and popular Ballycastle.

03 Giant's Causeway

When you first see it you'll understand why the ancients believed the causeway was not a natural feature. The vast expanse of regular, closely packed, hexagonal stone columns dipping gently beneath the waves looks for all the world like the handiwork of giants.

This spectacular rock formation – a national nature reserve and Northern Ireland's only UNESCO World Heritage site – is one of Ireland's most impressive and atmospheric landscape features, but it can get very crowded. If you can, try to visit midweek or out of season to experience it at its most evocative. Sunset in spring and autumn is the best time for photographs.

Visiting the Giant's Causeway itself is free of charge but you pay to use the car park on a combined ticket with the **Giant's Causeway Visitor Experience** *(national trust.org.uk)*. Parking-only tickets aren't available.

THE DRIVE: Follow the A29 and A37 as far as Derry/Londonderry, then cross the invisible border into the Republic and take the N13 to Letterkenny before turning northwest along the N56 to Dunfanaghy. It's a total of 136km.

DETOUR

Giant's Causeway to Ballycastle

Start: 03 Giant's Causeway

Between the Giant's Causeway and Ballycastle (p232) lies the most scenic stretch of the Causeway Coast, with sea cliffs of contrasting black basalt and white chalk, rocky islands, picturesque little harbours and broad sweeps of sandy beach. It's best enjoyed on foot, following the 16.5km of waymarked **Causeway Coast Way** *(causewaycoastway.com)* between the Carrick-a-Rede car park and the Giant's Causeway, although the main attractions can also be reached by car or bus.

About 8km east of the Giant's Causeway is the meagre ruin of 16th-century **Dunseverick Castle**, spectacularly sited on a grassy bluff. Another 1.5km on is the tiny seaside hamlet of **Portbradden**, with half a dozen harbourside houses and the tiny, blue-and-white **St Gobban's Church**, said to be the smallest in Ireland. Visible from Portbradden and accessible via the next junction off the A2 is the spectacular **White Park Bay**, with its wide, sweeping sandy beach.

The main attraction on this stretch of coast is the famous (or notorious, depending on your head for heights) **Carrick-a-Rede Rope Bridge** *(nationaltrust.org.uk/carrick-a- rede)*. The 20m-long, 1m-wide bridge of wire rope spans the chasm between the sea cliffs and the little island of Carrick-a-Rede, swaying gently 30m above the rock-strewn water.

PHOTO OPPORTUNITY

Killahoey Beach from the top of Horn Head.

04 Dunfanaghy

Huddled around the waterfront beneath the headland of Horn Head, Dunfanaghy's small, attractive town centre has a surprisingly wide range of accommodation and some of the finest dining options in the county's northwest. Glistening beaches, dramatic coastal cliffs, mountain trails and forests are all within a few kilometres.

THE DRIVE: The 145km south to Sligo town will take you back through Letterkenny (this stretch is the most scenic), after which you'll follow the N13 as far as Ballyshannon and then, as you cross into County Sligo, the N15 to Sligo town.

DETOUR

Horn Head

Start: 04 Dunfanaghy

Horn Head has some of Donegal's most spectacular coastal scenery and plenty of birdlife. Its dramatic quartzite cliffs, covered with bog and heather, rear over 180m high, and the view from their tops is heart-pounding.

The road circles the headland; the best approach by car is in a clockwise direction from the Falcarragh end of Dunfanaghy. On a fine day, you'll encounter tremendous views of Tory, Inishbofin, Inishdooey and tiny Inishbeg islands to the west; Sheep Haven Bay and the Rosguill Peninsula to the east; Malin Head to the northeast; and the coast of Scotland beyond. Take care in bad weather as the route can be perilous.

05 Sligo Town

Sligo is in no hurry to shed its cultural traditions but it doesn't sell them out either. Pedestrian streets lined with inviting shopfronts, stone bridges spanning the River Garavogue and *céilidhs* spilling from pubs contrast with genre-bending contemporary art and glass towers rising from prominent corners of the compact town.

THE DRIVE: It's 100km to Westport, as you follow the N17 (and the N5 once you leave Charlestown); the landscape is flat, the road flanked by fields, hedgerows and farmhouses. Castlebar, 15km before Westport, is a busy county town.

Horn Head, Donegal
SHAWNWIL23/SHUTTERSTOCK

♥ WHY I LOVE THIS TRIP

FIONN DAVENPORT, WRITER

Not only are you covering the spectacular landscapes of mountains and jagged coastlines of the Wild Atlantic Way, but you can explore the modern incarnation of the country's earliest settlements, taking you from prehistoric monuments to bustling cities.

LOCAL KNOWLEDGE

DOOLIN'S MUSIC PUBS

Here, Doolin's three main music pubs (others are recent interlopers) are ranked top-down in order of importance to the music scene:

- **McGann's** *(mcgannsdoolin.com)* McGann's has all the classic touches of a full-on Irish music pub; the action often spills out onto the street. The food here is the best of the trio.
- **Gus O'Connor's** *(gusoconnorsdoolin.com)* Right on the water, this sprawling favourite packs them in and has a rollicking atmosphere when the music and drinking are in full swing.
- **McDermott's** *(mcdermottspub.com)* Also known as MacDiarmada's, this simple red-and-white old pub can be the rowdy favourite of locals. When the fiddles get going, it can seem like a scene out of a John Ford movie.

06 Westport

There's a lot to be said for town planning, especially if 18th-century architect James Wyatt was the brain behind the job. Westport (*Cathair na Mairt*; p182), positioned on the River Carrowbeg and the shores of Clew Bay, is easily Mayo's most beautiful town and a major tourist destination for visitors to this part of the country.

It's a Georgian classic, its octagonal square and tidy streets lined with trees and handsome buildings, most of which date from the late 18th-century.

THE DRIVE: Follow the N5 then the N84 as far as the outskirts of Galway city – a trip of about 100km. Take the N18 south into County Clare. At Kilcolgan, turn onto the N67. Ballyvaughan provides a good base to explore the heart of The Burren.

07 The Burren

The karst landscape of The Burren is not the green Ireland of postcards. But there are wildflowers in spring, giving the 560-sq-km Burren brilliant, if ephemeral, colour amid its austere beauty. Soil may be scarce, but the small amount that gathers in the cracks and faults is well drained and nutrient-rich. This, together with the mild Atlantic climate, supports an extraordinary mix of Mediterranean, Arctic and alpine plants. Of Ireland's native wildflowers, 75% are found here, including 24 species of orchid, the creamy-white burnet rose, the little starry flowers of mossy saxifrage and the magenta-coloured bloody cranesbill.

THE DRIVE: It's some 40km to Doolin, heading south first via the N67 then onto the R480, which corkscrews over the lunar, limestone landscape of The Burren's exposed hills. Next curve west onto the R476 to meander towards Doolin via more familiar Irish landscapes of green fields, and the villages of Kilfenora and Lisdoonvarna – great for pit stops and trad-music sessions.

08 Doolin

Doolin is renowned as a centre of Irish traditional music, but it's also known for its setting – 6km north of the Cliffs of Moher – and down near the ever-unsettled sea, the land is windblown, with huge rocks exposed by the long-vanished topsoil. Many musicians live in the area, and they have a symbiotic relationship with the tourists: each desires the other and each year the music scene grows a little larger. But given the heavy concentration of visitors, it's inevitable that standards don't always hold up to those in some of the less-trampled villages in Clare.

THE DRIVE: Ferries from Doolin to Inishmore take about 90 minutes to make the crossing.

09 Inishmore

A step (and boat or plane ride; p216) beyond the desolate beauty of The Burren are the Aran Islands. Most visitors are satisfied to explore only Inishmore *(Inis Mór)* and its main attraction, **Dun Aengus** *(Dún Aonghasa; heritage ireland.ie)*, the stunning stone fort perched perilously on the island's towering cliffs. Powerful swells pound the 87m-high cliff face. A complete lack of rails or other modern additions that would spoil this amazing ancient site means that you can not only go right up to the cliff's edge but also potentially fall to your doom below quite easily. When it's uncrowded, you can't help but feel the extraordinary energy that must have been harnessed to build this vast site.

The Burren
PIERRE LECLERC/SHUTTERSTOCK

AN ANCIENT FORT

For a look at a well-preserved caher (walled fort) of the late Iron Age to early Christian period, stop at **Caherconnell Fort** *(caherconnell.com)*, a privately run heritage attraction in The Burren that's more serious than sideshow.

Exhibits detail how the evolution of these defensive settlements may have reflected territorialism and competition for land among a growing, settling population. The dry-stone walling of the fort is in excellent condition.

The top-notch visitor centre also has information on many other monuments in the area. It's about 1km south of Poulnabrone Dolmen on the R480.

The arid landscape west of **Kilronan** *(Cill Rónáin)*, Inishmore's main settlement, is dominated by stone walls, boulders, scattered buildings and the odd patch of deep-green grass and potato plants.

THE DRIVE: Once you're back on terra firma at Doolin, it's 223km to Dingle via the N85 to Ennis then the M18 to Limerick city. The N69 will take you into County Kerry as far as Tralee, beyond which it's 50km on the N86 to Dingle.

10 Dingle

Unlike the Ring of Kerry, where the cliffs tend to dominate the ocean, it's the ocean that dominates the smaller Dingle Peninsula. The opal-blue waters surrounding the promontory's multihued landscape of green hills and golden sands give rise to aquatic adventures and to fishing fleets that haul in the fresh seafood that appears on the menus of some of the county's finest restaurants.

Centred on charming Dingle town, there's an alternative way of life here, lived by artisans and eccentics and found at trad sessions and folkloric festivals across Dingle's tiny settlements.

The classic loop drive around Slea Head from Dingle town is 47km, but allow a day to take it all in – longer if you have time to stay overnight in Dingle town.

THE DRIVE: Take the N86 as far as Annascaul and then the coastal R561 as far as Castlemaine. Then head southwest on the N70 to Killorglin and the Ring of Kerry. From Dingle, it's 53km.

Caherconnell Fort, Clare

PHOTO SPIRIT/SHUTTERSTOCK

11 Ring of Kerry

The Ring of Kerry is the longest and most diverse of Ireland's big circle drives, combining jaw-dropping coastal scenery with emerald pastures and villages.

The 179km circuit usually begins in Killarney and winds past pristine beaches, the island-dotted Atlantic, medieval ruins, mountains and loughs (lakes). The coastline is at its most rugged between Waterville and Caherdaniel in the southwest of the peninsula. It can get crowded in summer, but even then, the remote Skellig Ring can be uncrowded and serene – and starkly beautiful.

The Ring of Kerry can easily be done as a day trip, but if you want to stretch it out, places to stay are scattered along the route. **Killorglin** and **Kenmare** have the best dining options, with some excellent restaurants; elsewhere, basic (sometimes very basic) pub fare is the norm.

The Ring's most popular diversion is the **Gap of Dunloe**, an awe-inspiring mountain pass at the western edge of Killarney National Park. It's signposted off the N72 between Killarney and Killorglin. The incredibly popular 19th-century **Kate Kearney's Cottage** is a pub where most visitors park their cars before walking up to the gap.

12 Kenmare

If you've done the Ring in an anticlockwise fashion (or cut through the Gap of Dunloe), you'll end up in handsome Kenmare, a largely 18th-century town and the ideal alternative to Killarney as a place to stay overnight.

THE DRIVE: Picturesque villages, a fine stone circle and calming coastal scenery mark the less-taken 143km route from Kenmare to Cork city. When you get to Leap, turn right onto the R597 and go as far as Rosscarbery; or, even better, take twice as long (although it's only 24km more) and make your way along narrow roads near the water the entire way.

13 Cork City

The Republic's second city is first in every important respect, at least according to the locals, who cheerfully refer to it as the 'real capital of Ireland'. The compact city centre is surrounded by interesting waterways and is chock-full of great restaurants fed by arguably the best foodie scene in the country.

THE DRIVE: It's only 60km to Ardmore, but stop off in Midleton, 24km east of Cork along the N25, and visit the whiskey museum. Just beyond Youghal, turn right onto the R673 for Ardmore.

14 Ardmore

Due to its location off the main drag, Ardmore (p110) is a sleepy seaside village and one of the southeast's loveliest spots – the ideal destination for those looking for a little waterside R&R.

St Declan reputedly set up shop here sometime between 350 and 420 CE, which would make Ardmore the first Christian bastion in Ireland – long before St Patrick landed. The village's 12th-century **round tower**, one of the best examples of these structures in Ireland, is the town's most distinctive architectural feature, but you should also check out the ruins of **St Declan's church** and holy well, 1km east on a bluff on Ardmore's signposted 5km cliff walk.

☑ TOP TIP

THE HEALY PASS

Instead of going directly into County Cork along the N71 from Kenmare, veer west onto the R571 and drive for 16km along the northern edge of the Beara Peninsula. At Lauragh, turn onto the R574 and take the breathtaking **Healy Pass Road**, which cuts through the peninsula and brings you from County Kerry into County Cork. At Adrigole, turn left onto the R572 and rejoin the N71 at Glengarriff, 17km east.

04

EPIC TRIP

TIP TO TOE

DURATION: 10 DAYS

DISTANCE: 950KM / 590 MILES

GREAT FOR: FOOD & DRINK, HISTORY, OUTDOORS

BEST TIME TO GO: SPRING AND AUTUMN TO AVOID SUMMER CROWDS.

This 10-day trip takes in so much. You can bob on a boat beneath 600m-high cliffs, clamber over castle ruins and marvel at massive seabird colonies. Scenery-rich routes link sites telling tales of rebellion, the Troubles, famine and faith. Memorable days connect experiences rich in Irish culture, from lyrical poetry to pubs alive with traditional music. On this trip you can really discover Ireland, tip to toe, head to heart.

LINK YOUR TRIP

13 Wexford & Waterford
Scenic shorelines, birdlife and fishing villages. Start where this trips stops: Kilmore Quay.

25 Mountains & Moors
Drive deep into romantic Connemara. Pick it up from, and return to, Galway city on this trip's route.

01 Derry

Derry comes as a pleasant surprise to many visitors: a vibrant, riverside city, encircled by impressive, 17th-century fortifications. Like Belfast, it has a past of bitter sectarian divisions, but here too a remarkable healing is underway. Get a true taste of both the enormity of the problems and the progress by walking around the city, strolling atop the city walls, passing Unionist strongholds and absorbing the powerful murals of the Republican Bogside district. Be sure to visit the **Tower Museum** *(towermuseumcollections.com)*, where audiovisual exhibits bring the city's rich and complex past to life. Some time in 2027, the museum is set to close and its exhibits will move to the new **DNA Museum** *(dnamuseum.com)*.

THE DRIVE: As the A2/N13 heads west out of Derry over the River Foyle towards Letterkenny, road signs switch from mph to km/h: you've just entered

★ BEST

THREE DAYS

Stops 11 to 15 for party-town Galway, elegant Birr and the iconic Rock of Cashel.

WIRESTOCK CREATORS/SHUTTERSTOCK

Rock of Cashel (p59), Tipperary

the Irish Republic. At Bridgend follow signs left up to Grianán of Aileách (12km).

02 Grianán of Aileách

This fort encircles Grianán Hill like a halo. Ducking in through its cave-like entrance and clambering up its tiered battlements reveals eye-popping views of Lough Swilly, with Inch Island plumb in the centre; Counties Donegal, Derry and Tyrone stretch out all around.

It's thought the site was in use in pre-Celtic times as a temple to the god Dagda, becoming the seat of the O'Neills between the 5th and 12th centuries. It was demolished by Murtogh O'Brien, king of Munster, and most of these remains are a 19th-century reconstruction.

THE DRIVE: The N13 cruises west to traffic-choked Letterkenny (with some handy accommodation options). There, climb north gradually on the N56 towards Dunfanaghy, with the distant Glendowan Mountains sliding into view. Once up in the high hills, take the R255 left to Glenveagh National Park (50km) and Glenveagh Castle.

03 Glenveagh National Park

Lakes shimmer like dew in mountainous **Glenveagh National Park** *(Páirc Náisiúnta Ghleann Bheatha; glenveaghnationalpark.ie)*, where knuckles of rock alternate with green-gold bogs and oak and birch forest. In delightfully showy **Glenveagh Castle** *(glenveagh nationalpark.ie)*, rooms combine stuffed stags with flamboyant furnishings, with highlights being the tartan-and-antler-covered music room and the blue single ladies' room (formerly Greta Garbo's).

The exotic gardens are spectacular with their terraces and Italianate style a marked contrast to the wildly beautiful landscape. A shuttle bus runs to the castle from the visitor centre, but the 3.6km walk is a better way to soak up the scenery.

THE DRIVE: Head west on the R251, an exhilarating, bouncing drive through cinematic scenery: the Derryveagh Mountains tower to your left, and the fast-approaching peak of Mt Errigal fills your windscreen

PHOTO OPPORTUNITY

Mountainous Glengesh Pass for a 'Did I really drive that?' snap.

ahead. At the hamlet of Dunlewey (*Dún Lúiche*, 16km), turn left to the lake.

04 Dunlewey

Simply stepping out of your car in this mountain hamlet provides an insight into the isolated way of life this high in the hills. It's underlined at the **Dunlewey Centre** *(Ionad Cois Locha; dunleweycentre.com)*, where the 30-minute tour of a thatched weaver's cottage reveals a huge loom, spartan bedroom (complete with chamber pot under the iron bedstead) and snug lounge warmed by a peat fire.

THE DRIVE: The R251, then the N56, begin a slow descent south, bumping past crags and sudden loughs and bogs. Shortly after heritage-town Ardara turn right, following brown signs to Glengesh Pass. It's an ear-popping ascent up hairpin bends and past wayside shrines. Near the top, 60km from Dunlewey, turn right into the walled parking bay.

DETOUR

Loughrea Peninsula

Start: 04 Dunlewey

This leg's scenery is beautiful enough, but if you fancy some sandy shores with your mountains, try this detour. Around 20km south of Dungloe, at Maas, instead of swinging left on the N56 to Glenties, peel right onto the coastal R261, which winds deep into beautiful Loughrea Peninsula. Next, take a minor road right to **Narin**, following signs to the beach *(trá)*, a 4km-long, spectacular, dune-backed, sandy stretch, where you can walk out to tiny **Iniskeel Island** at low tide.

Post-stroll, continue on the shoreside road, past Portnoo and Rossbeg, rejoining the R261, then the N56 at Ardara.

Glengesh Pass, Donegal
GABRYSBL/SHUTTERSTOCK

05 Glengesh Pass

Glengesh Pass provides one of Donegal's most spectacular mountain views, and this parking spot is the place to take that holiday snap. A V-shaped valley sweeps away far below, while the Derryveagh Mountains line up far behind. The road you've just driven up is a tiny ribbon, snaking off into the distance. There's a picnic area immediately below the parking spot, ensuring an alfresco meal with a truly memorable view.

THE DRIVE: Edging over the pass, a cluster of wind turbines spins into view. Descend gradually, past unfenced grazing land (watch out for free-roaming sheep) and neat piles of drying peat. Suddenly, the sea around Glen Head appears. Head through Glencolumbcille (*Gleann Cholm Cille*, 16km) on the Malin Beg Rd; the folk village comes soon after.

06 Glencolumbcille

Glencolumbcille may feel like the middle of nowhere, but the three-pub village offers scalloped beaches, a strong sense of Irish identity and an insight into a fast-disappearing way of life. **Glencolmcille Folk Village** *(glenfolkvillage.com)* was set up in 1967 to freeze-frame traditional folk life for posterity. Its six thatched 18th- and 19th-century cottages are packed with everyday items, from beds and cooking pans to tools and open fires.

THE DRIVE: The R263 snakes south and soon reveals the massive mountain of Sliabh Liag. Edge past it to Carrick *(An Charraig)* then follow brown Sliabh Liag signs south beside the inlet to tiny Teelin (*Tieleann*, 9km).

07 Sliabh Liag

The Cliffs of Moher may be more famous, but the ones at Sliabh Liag (Slieve League) are taller – some of the highest in Europe, in fact. This 600m-high, multicoloured rock face seems stark and otherworldly as it rears up from the Atlantic Ocean. A diminutive 12-seater boat, the **Nuala Star** *(sliabhleagueboattrips.com)*, sets off from Teelin to the foot of the cliffs. The trips are weather dependent and have to be booked. If the sea is too rough, you can drive or walk to the cliffs.

THE DRIVE: The drive east from Carrick completes a gradual descent from wild, pitted hills to smoother urban life; remote homesteads give way to garden-fronted houses. The N56 skirts Donegal town, from where the N15 heads south to Sligo, 110km from Sliabh Liag.

DETOUR

Donegal Castle

Start: 07 Sliabh Liag

Midway between Sliabh Liag and Sligo, riverside **Donegal Castle** *(heritageireland.ie)* makes for a picturesque detour. The original 1474 castle was torched then rebuilt in 1623, along with a neighbouring Jacobean house. It's a deeply attractive spot: grassy lawns lead up to geometric battlements, and rooms are packed with fine furnishings and antiques.

The castle is in the centre of pretty Donegal town. Follow signs from the N56 and afterwards take the N15 to Sligo.

08 Sligo Town

An appealing overnight base, vibrant Sligo combines lively pubs and futuristic buildings with old stone bridges and a historic abbey. It also shines a spotlight on William Butler Yeats (1865–1939), Sligo's greatest literary figure and one of Ireland's premier poets.

Sligo County Museum *(sligolibrary.ie/museum)* showcases Yeats' manuscripts and letters, along with sepia photos, a copy of his 1923 Nobel Prize medal and a complete collection of his poetic works.

THE DRIVE: Take the N4 south then the N17 (signed Galway). Soon the R293 meanders left through Ballymote and a deeply agricultural landscape. Make for Gurteen (also spelt Gorteen), 32km from Sligo, following signs for the Coleman Irish Music Centre. It's the pink building right beside the main village crossroads.

09 Gurteen

You've just explored poetry, now for another mainstay of Irish culture: music. The **Coleman Irish Music Centre** *(colemanirishmusic.com)* champions melody and culture, south Sligo style, with multimedia exhibits on musical history, instruments, famous musicians and Irish dancing. The centre also provides tuition and sheet-music sales, and stages performances.

THE DRIVE: Continue south on the R293, an undulating ribbon of a road that deposits you in bustling Ballaghaderreen. There pick up the N5 west (signed Westport) for an effortless cruise through lowlands that are grazed by cattle and dotted with rounded hills. Some 55km later, signs point right for the National Museum of Country Life.

10 Castlebar

Your discovery of Ireland's heritage continues, this time with a celebration of the ingenuity and self-sufficiency of the Irish people. The **National Museum of Country Life** *(museum.ie)* explores everything from wickerwork to boat building, and herbal cures to traditional clothing. This historical one-stop shop is a comprehensive, absorbing depiction of rural

Spanish Arch and quay, Galway City

JOSE IGNACIO RETAMAL/SHUTTERSTOCK

☑ TOP TIP

PAY YOUR WAY

The M6 heading east out of Galway is a sleek, effortless drive. But, like all shiny new things, it has to be paid for: have your €2.30 ready for the toll booth 20km east of Athenry.

traditions and skills between 1850 and 1950.

THE DRIVE: From the outskirts of Castlebar, the N84 heads south (signed Galway), bouncing beside scattered settlements before dog-legging through appealing Ballinrobe. This hummocky landscape of fields and dry-stone walls is replaced by bogs edged with peat stacks as you near Galway city (80km).

11 Galway City

The biggest reason to stop in Galway city is simply to revel in its hedonistic, culture-rich spirit. Narrow alleys lead from sight to sight beside strings of pubs overflowing with live music.

Start explorations at the quayside **Spanish Arch** (1584), thought to be an extension of Galway's medieval walls. Next, walk a few paces to the **Galway City Museum** *(galwaycitymuseum.ie)*, where exhibits trace daily life in the city through history. Highlights include the smelly medieval era and photos of President John F Kennedy's 1963 visit to Galway. Then stroll a few metres to the **Hall of the Red Earl** *(galwaycivictrust.ie)*, the artefact-rich archaeological remains of a 13th-century power base.

You can't leave Galway without experiencing a music session, up Quay St and High St to Mainguard St and Tig Chóilí, a gem of a fire-engine-red pub that stages two *céilidhs* a day.

THE DRIVE: Join the M6 towards Dublin for the hour-long, smooth motorway cruise to Athlone. Follow signs to Athlone West/Town Centre. Soon the River Shannon, bobbing with houseboats and pleasure cruisers, eases into view. Park by Athlone Castle (80km), which appears straight ahead.

DETOUR

Athenry

Start: 11 Galway City

Most people sweep past Athenry, but it actually preserves one of Ireland's most intact collections of medieval architecture. This amiable town features a restored, box-like Norman castle *(heritageireland.ie)*, the medieval **Parish Church of St Mary's**, a 13th-century **Dominican Priory** (with superb masonry) and an original market cross.

Athenry sits beside the M6, and is signed off it.

12 Athlone

The thriving riverside town of Athlone is an enchanting mix of stylish modern developments and ancient, twisting streets. **Viking Ship Cruises** *(vikingtoursireland.ie)* runs trips from beside Athlone Castle, cruising the River Shannon aboard a replica Viking longship sailed by costumed crew. The best trip goes south to the stunning ruins at Clonmacnoise.

THE DRIVE: Continue through Athlone, picking up the minor N62, which rises and dips past grazing livestock to Birr (45km). Soon a boggy landscape takes over; look for the swathes of exposed soil left by industrial-scale peat harvesting. At Birr follow signs to the imposing, crenellated gateway of the Birr Castle Demesne.

13 Birr

Feel-good Birr is one of the Midlands' most attractive towns, with elegant pastel Georgian buildings and a spirited nightlife buzzing with live music. It also features **Birr Castle Demesne** *(birrcastle.com*; p90), where magnificent, 1000-species-strong gardens frame a large artificial lake. Don't miss the romantic Hornbeam cloister and the 12m-high box hedge, planted in the 1780s and now one of the world's tallest.

THE DRIVE: The N62 loops south through Roscrea, with the Silvermine Mountains' dark tops creeping up on the right. Then come Templemore's wide streets, before the N62 wiggles onto the M8 (head towards Cork); the Rock of Cashel (74km) is signed 13km later.

14 Rock of Cashel

The iconic and much-photographed **Rock of Cashel** *(heritageireland.ie)* is one of Ireland's true highlights – Queen Elizabeth II included it on her historic 2011 visit. The 'rock' is a fortified hill, the defences of which shelter a clutch of historic religious monuments.

The site has been a defensive one since the 4th-century and its compelling features include the towering 13th-century Gothic cathedral, a 15th-century four-storey castle, an 11th-century round tower and a 12th-century Romanesque chapel.

It's a five-minute stroll along Bishop's Walk from the appealing market town of Cashel.

THE DRIVE: As you head north up the M8 (signed Dublin) you'll notice rounded field-chequered hills, backed by a distant smudge of mountains. At Urlingford, take the R693 into central Kilkenny, 67km from Cashel.

15 Kilkenny

Kilkenny *(Cill Chainnigh)* is the Ireland of many people's

imaginations, with its gracious medieval cathedral, tangle of 17th-century passageways, old-fashioned shopfronts and ancient live-music pubs. Make for **Kilkenny Castle** *(kilkenny castle.ie)*, a late-12th-century stone affair built by the son-in-law of Richard de Clare, the Anglo-Norman conqueror of Ireland (graced with the sobriquet 'Strongbow'). Guided tours focus on the Long Gallery, an impressive hall with high ceilings, vividly painted Celtic and Pre-Raphaelite motifs and ranks of po-faced portraits.

THE DRIVE: Pick up the R700 southeast to New Ross. Hills feature again here, both in the rise and fall of the twisting road and in the blue-black ridge of the Blackstairs Mountains far ahead. At New Ross (42km) make for the quay and the three-masted sailing vessel.

16 New Ross

In Ireland's Great Famine of 1845–51 a staggering three million people died or emigrated, often to America and Australia. Many left in 'coffin ships', so called because of their appalling mortality rates. When you step aboard the replica **Dunbrody Famine Ship** *(dunbrody.com)* you 'become' a migrant: you're allocated a living space and rations, while actors around you vividly re-create life on board. Expect cramped conditions, authentic sounds and smells and often-harrowing tales.

THE DRIVE: Head onto the N30 to Enniscorthy, a gentle, rural leg punctuated by the frequent treat of roadside stalls selling sweet Wexford strawberries. As you head towards central Enniscorthy (32km), the National Rebellion Centre is a sharp left, up the hill.

17 Enniscorthy

Enniscorthy's warren of steep streets descends from Augustus Pugin's cathedral to a riverside Norman castle. But the town is most famous for some of the fiercest fighting of the 1798 uprising against British rule, when rebels captured the town. That story is told in the **National 1798 Rebellion Centre** *(1798centre.ie)*, where exhibits cover the French and American Revolutions that sparked Wexford's abortive revolt. It also chronicles what followed: the rebels' retreat and the massacre by English troops of hundreds of women and children.

THE DRIVE: Carry on through Enniscorthy, crossing the river to pick up the N11, south, to Wexford (22km). Then comes a long straight run, beside the River Slane and past more strawberry stalls, until the waters of Wexford Harbour glide into view.

18 Wexford Town

The sleepy port town of Wexford is a pleasing place to stroll through heritage-rich streets beside a wide estuary. Guided tours *(€5)* set out at 11am from Monday to Saturday (March to October) from the **tourist office** *(visitwexford.ie)* in the Wexford Arts Centre on Cornmarket; it also provides maps. Or explore by yourself: head up Harper's Lane to North Main St and the 18th-century St Iberius' Church (where Oscar Wilde's forebears were rectors). A left up George St leads to Abbey St and **Selskar Abbey** (Henry II did penance here after the murder of Thomas Becket); the 14th-century **Westgate** sits at the street's end.

THE DRIVE: Drive south along Wexford's boat-lined waterfront to join the R739, where you'll see more fruit stands and a gentle landscape of trees and rich pastures – it feels a world away from the harsh, high hills at your trip's start. Soon the thatched cottages of Kilmore Quay (23km) appear.

19 Kilmore Quay

This tiny, relaxed port is the perfect finish to your trans-Ireland trip. Seafood restaurants, fisher's pubs and B&Bs cluster around a boat-packed harbour. Just offshore, the **Saltee Islands** *(salteeislands.info*; p107) overflow with gannets, guillemots, kittiwakes and puffins; the **Saltee Ferry** *(threesisters.ie/saltee-ferry*; Kilmore Quay Harbour) runs from April to September (booking required).

If the weather scuppers that plan, stroll west from the quay to the 9km-long, wildlife-rich dunes of **Ballyteigue Burrow**, passing a memorial garden for those lost at sea, before reaching the Cull, a 4km-long sliver of land sheltering a slender inlet teeming with widgeons, oystercatchers, curlews and more.

Atlantic puffins, Saltee Islands, Wexford
NICOLA_K_PHOTOS/SHUTTERSTOCK

WHY I LOVE THIS TRIP

ISABEL ALBISTON, WRITER

It's not just dizzying clifftops, the wild Atlantic roaring and spraying below, and the only reminder of proximate civilisation drifting over in the scent of tangy peat smoke and the sound of bleating sheep; it's also vibrant cities packed with culture and buzzing with nightlife. From the stark mountains in the north to the gentle lowlands of the south, this trip is one heck of a drive.

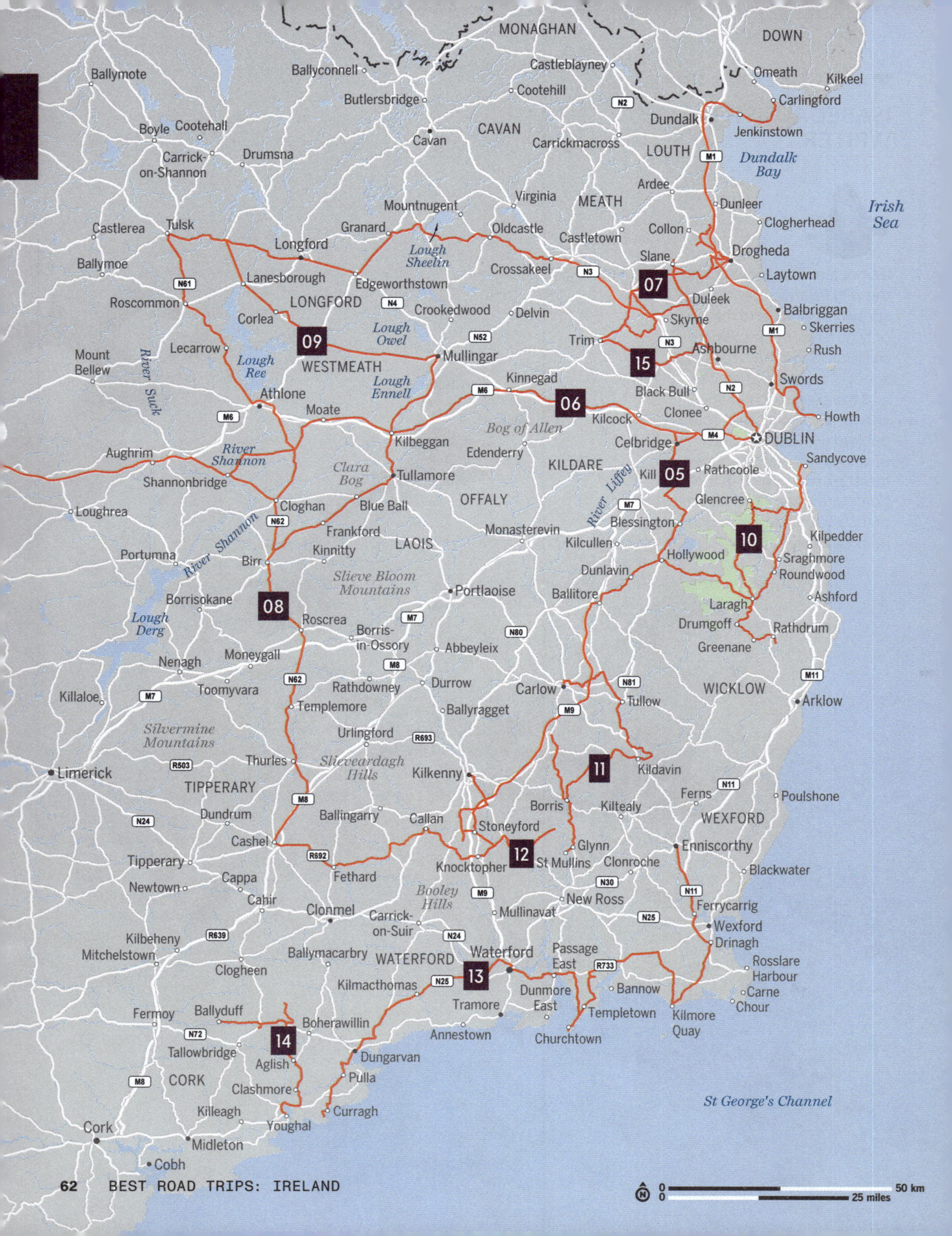
MONAGHAN
DOWN
Ballymote
Ballyconnell
Castleblayney
Omeath
Kilkeel
Cootehill
Carlingford
Butlersbridge
N2
Dundalk
Jenkinstown
Boyle
Cootehall
Cavan
CAVAN
Carrickmacross
LOUTH
M1
Dundalk Bay
Carrick-on-Shannon
Drumsna
Ardee
Virginia
MEATH
Dunleer
Irish Sea
Mountnugent
Clogherhead
Castlerea
Tulsk
Granard
Oldcastle
Castletown
Collon
Longford
Lough Sheelin
Slane
Drogheda
Ballymoe
Crossakeel
N3
Laytown
N61
Lanesborough
Edgeworthstown
07
Roscommon
LONGFORD
N4
Crookedwood
Delvin
Duleek
Balbriggan
Corlea
Skryne
M1
Skerries
Lough Owel
N52
Trim
N3
Mount Bellew
Lecarrow
09
Mullingar
15
Ashbourne
Rush
River Suck
Lough Ree
WESTMEATH
Kinnegad
N2
Swords
Lough Ennell
M6
06
Black Bull
Athlone
Moate
Clonee
Howth
M6
Kilcock
Bog of Allen
M4
DUBLIN
Kilbeggan
Celbridge
Aughrim
River Shannon
Edenderry
KILDARE
Sandycove
Clara Bog
Kill
05
Rathcoole
Shannonbridge
Tullamore
Loughrea
Cloghan
Blue Ball
OFFALY
River Liffey
Glencree
N62
N7
Blessington
Frankford
Monasterevin
10
Kilpedder
River Shannon
LAOIS
Kilcullen
Portumna
Kinnitty
Birr
Hollywood
Sraghmore
Dunlavin
Roundwood
Slieve Bloom Mountains
Portlaise
Ballitore
Ashford
Borrisokane
08
Laragh
Lough Derg
Roscrea
M7
Drumgoff
Rathdrum
Borris-in-Ossory
N80
Abbeyleix
Greenane
Nenagh
Moneygall
M8
N62
Rathdowney
Durrow
N81
Carlow
WICKLOW
M11
Killaloe
M7
Toomyvara
Tullow
Arklow
Templemore
M9
Ballyragget
Silvermine Mountains
Urlingford
R693
R503
Thurles
Slieveardagh Hills
11
Limerick
Kilkenny
Kildavin
TIPPERARY
N11
Poulshone
M8
Borris
Kiltealy
Ferns
N24
Dundrum
Ballingarry
Callan
WEXFORD
Stoneyford
Cashel
Glynn
Enniscorthy
R692
12
St Mullins
Clonroche
Tipperary
Knocktopher
Blackwater
Fethard
Cappa
N30
Newtown
Booley Hills
M9
N11
Cahir
New Ross
Clonmel
Mullinavat
Ferrycarrig
Carrick-on-Suir
N25
Wexford
Kilbeheny
R639
N24
Drinagh
Mitchelstown
Ballymacarbry
WATERFORD
Waterford
Passage East
Rosslare Harbour
Clogheen
R733
13
Kilmacthomas
N25
Dunmore East
Bannow
Carne
Chour
Fermoy
Ballyduff
Tramore
Templetown
Kilmore Quay
N72
Boherawillin
Annestown
Churchtown
Tallowbridge
14
Aglish
Dungarvan
M8
CORK
Pulla
Clashmore
St George's Channel
Killeagh
Curragh
Cork
Youghal
Midleton
Cobh
0
50 km
0
25 miles

365 FOCUS PHOTOGRAPHY/SHUTTERSTOCK

R675 route along the Copper Coast (p109), Waterford

DUBLIN & EASTERN IRELAND

EXPLORE

DUBLIN & EASTERN IRELAND

In Ireland, all roads lead to – and from – Dublin, Ireland's capital and its biggest city by far. From the city centre, a spider's web of motorways, national routes and narrow country lanes bring you into the heart of the country, but there's also so much to explore in the region surrounding the capital. Within just an hour's drive of Dublin, you can find yourself on a lonely mountain pass, visiting a grand Georgian mansion or transported back 3500 years to explore a passage tomb built before the pyramids were even a twinkle in the pharaohs' eyes.

Dublin

It's likely that your trip to Ireland will begin and end in Dublin, home to roughly a quarter of the population, the country's main airport and two seaports, for arrivals from Holyhead and Liverpool in the UK. You'll likely spend at least a couple of days in the capital, exploring its numerous attractions, sampling its many restaurants and going for a pint in one of its 1000-plus pubs.

Paid, on-street parking is available throughout the city, with rates classed by colour coding – the further you are from the city centre, the cheaper the parking is. Dublin is also where you'll find all of the provisions you'll need for your road trip, from every kind of personal item to anything you need for your car.

There's no shortage of accommodation options, either, but if you're planning to visit during summer or a big festival, advance bookings are a must. The city centre – on both sides of the River Liffey – is the most popular spot to base yourself, with options in all budget categories. Many places to stay don't have dedicated parking spaces but will have deals with nearby car parks for discounted rates. The near suburbs, particularly south of the city centre, are where you'll find a range of elegant guesthouses and boutique hotels, many of which do have dedicated car parks – usually free and available on a first-come, first-served basis.

WHEN TO GO

June to mid-September means the best weather but also the biggest crowds. Hotels in Dublin are usually full and at their most expensive. Easter to May and late September into October can be beautiful, with fewer visitors and lower accommodation rates. Winter is cold and usually wet, but accommodation rates are at their lowest.

Kilkenny

Kilkenny is a smallish city of around 25,000, but it's a well-developed tourist hub with a decent range of accommodation, both within and outside the tight medieval centre. Hotels just outside the city centre are bigger and have good parking. The city is famous for its castle and the warren of medieval streets that radiate from it, which are lined with great pubs and restaurants, as well as some of the best shops in the region. If you're looking for handicrafts to take home as souvenirs, you won't find better than the wares at Kilkenny Design Centre, just opposite the castle.

Waterford

If you're arriving on a ferry from the European mainland, you'll likely arrive in Rosslare, just a short drive from handsome Waterford city – Ireland's oldest city. It's a good base from which to explore the southeast, including the vestiges of its Viking and medieval origins, stored in three excellent museums. The outer fringes have plenty of hotels and B&Bs, while the city centre has a great selection of restaurants and pubs.

TRANSPORT

Dublin is ringed by the M50 motorway, from which seven motorways radiate to deliver traffic to the rest of the country. All motorways are tolled beyond the outlying suburbs. The M50 has barrier-free tolling between Junctions 6 and 7; most rental cars come with automatic trackers that will add the cost of the toll to your final payment; otherwise, you must pay online *(eflow.ie)* within 24 hours.

WHERE TO STAY

On the Waterford Greenway, **Mount Congreve Gate Lodge** is a stunningly refurbished 18th-century gate lodge.

Stauntons on the Green is a Georgian guesthouse hiding in plain sight on Dublin's elegant St Stephen's Green. Recently refurbished, it's replete with gorgeous historical touches.

On the beach in Rosslare Harbour, **Kelly's Resort Hotel & Spa** is Ireland's premier family resort, with 130 years of family expertise behind it, and oodles of activities around it.

Behind the doors of the strikingly contemporary **Pillo Hotel** in Ashbourne, County Meath, is a strong commitment to the environment and the care of people with autism – the sensory room is amazing.

RESOURCES

- **Dublin Tourism**
  Official website of Dublin Tourism. *visitdublin.com*
- **Discover Ireland**
  Official website of Fáilte Ireland, Ireland's tourist board. *discoverireland.ie*
- **Lovin Dublin**
  What's happening in the city, updated daily. *lovindublin.com*
- **All the Food**
  Constantly updated guide to eating out in Dublin. *allthefood.ie*

WHAT'S ON

- **Cat Laughs Comedy Festival**
  Kilkenny draws world-renowned comedians for a fab comedy festival in early summer.
- **West Waterford Festival of Food**
  The southeast's abundant produce is celebrated over three sumptuous days in April.
- **Temple Bar TradFest**
  Dublin turns its attentions to traditional music in January, with performances taking place all over the city.

05

DUBLIN & EASTERN IRELAND

A LONG WEEKEND AROUND DUBLIN

DURATION: 3 DAYS

DISTANCE: 230KM / 143 MILES

GREAT FOR: FOOD & DRINK, HISTORY, OUTDOORS

BEST TIME TO GO: APRIL TO SEPTEMBER SEES BIG CROWDS, BUT THE SUN ALSO SHINES THE MOST THEN.

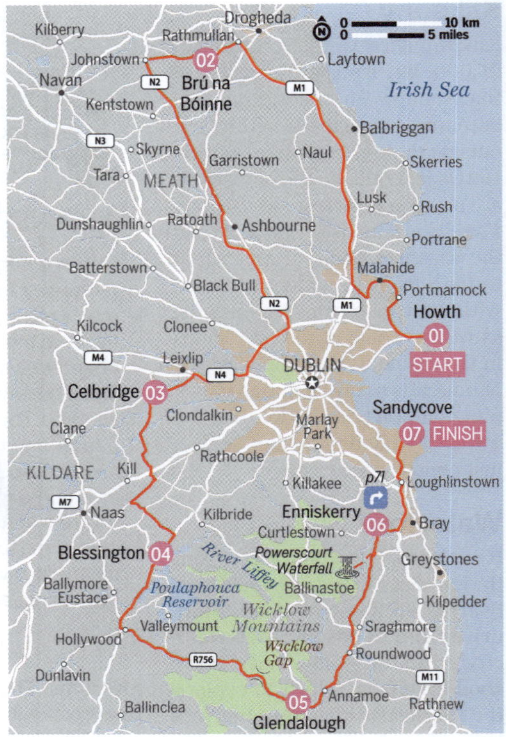

You can plunge into the very depths of Irish history, be awestruck by some of Ireland's most beautiful buildings and lose yourself in stunning countryside without ever being more than 50km from Dublin. This trip explores the very best of what the capital's environs have to offer – from coastal breaks to mountain retreats and a rip-roaring ride through 3500 years of history.

LINK YOUR TRIP

02 Ireland's Highlights
Dublin is the starting point of this classic trip that delivers the country's five-star attractions.

03 The Long Way Round
From Dublin, take a couple of weeks to explore the country.

01 Howth

The pretty little port town of Howth is built on steep streets running down to its small but busy harbour, which has transformed itself from shipping port to yachting and fishing hub. Only 11km north of Dublin's city centre, it has long been a desirable residential suburb.

Howth is essentially a very large hill surrounded by cliffs, and the summit (171m) has excellent views across Dublin Bay right down to Wicklow. From the peak you can walk to the top of the **Ben of Howth**, which has a cairn said to mark a 2000-year-old Celtic royal grave. The 1814 **Baily Lighthouse**, at the southeastern corner, is on the site of an old stone fort and can be reached by a dramatic clifftop walk. There was an earlier hilltop beacon here, in 1670.

Besides the views, the other draw is the busy **weekend market** and

DAWID K PHOTOGRAPHY/SHUTTERSTOCK

★ BEST FOR

CULTURE

Russborough House, a Palladian pile with a top-notch art collection.

Howth, Dublin

the collection of good seafood restaurants huddled around the harbour.

THE DRIVE: For the 56km trip, take the right at Sutton onto Harbour Rd (R105) towards Baldoyle; you'll have the Malahide estuary on your right and, on the spit of land beyond it, the famous Portmarnock Golf Links. Turn left onto Moyne Rd and take the M1 *(tolled; €2.30)* north, exiting at Junction 9 for Donore.

02 Brú na Bóinne

Pharaohs hadn't even conceived of the pyramids when the Neolithic pre-Celts built this vast necropolis on the banks of the River Boyne. Collectively known as Brú na Bóinne (the Boyne Palace), the passage tombs (and superb visitor centre) are one of the most extraordinary sights in Europe and shouldn't be missed.

THE DRIVE: Take Staleen Rd for 6.8km to the N2/M2. After 37km, merge onto the M50, taking the exit at Junction 7 for the N4 and go west for 7km as far as Junction 6. Follow the R403 as far as Celbridge. The 63km trip should take between 45 minutes and an hour.

03 Celbridge

The magnificent **Castletown House** *(castletown.ie)* simply has no equal. It is Ireland's largest and most imposing Georgian estate, and a testament to the vast wealth enjoyed by the Anglo-Irish gentry during the 18th-century.

Built between 1722 and 1732, the house was commissioned by Speaker of the Irish House of Commons William Conolly (1662–1729), who wanted a house commensurate with his position as Ireland's richest man.

The original 16th-century Italian palazzo design of the house was created by the Italian architect Alessandro Galilei (1691–1737) in 1718. In 1724 the project was entrusted to Sir Edward Lovett Pearce (1699–1733).

The house is full of Palladian touches, including the terminating pavilions and the superb Long Gallery, full of family portraits and fancy stucco work by the Italian

Francini brothers. Thomas Jefferson was such a fan of the style that much of Washington, DC is designed accordingly.

THE DRIVE: Drive southeast on the R409 for 1.6km. At the roundabout, take the first exit onto the R449. After 1.2km, take the R405 for 2.5km and take the Dublin Road south. After 22.2km turn right onto the N81. Russborough House is 3.9km away on your right. The whole drive is 34.4km.

04 Blessington

Dominating the one-street town of Blessington (pubs, shops, a handful of 17th- and 18th-century townhouses) is magnificent **Russborough House** *(russborough.ie)*, one of Ireland's finest stately homes, built for Joseph Leeson (1705–83), later the first Earl of Milltown and, later still, Lord Russborough. The Palladian pleasure palace was built between 1741 and 1751 to the design of Richard Cassels, who was at the height of his fame as an architect. Richard didn't live to see it finished, but the job was well executed by Francis Bindon. The house remained in the Leeson family until 1931. In 1952 it was sold to Sir Alfred Beit, the nephew of the cofounder of the de Beers diamond-mining company. Uncle Alfred was an obsessive art collector, and when he died, his impressive haul - which includes works by Velázquez, Vermeer, Goya and Rubens - was passed on to his nephew, who brought it to Russborough House.

The admission price includes a 45-minute tour of the house, which is decorated in typical Georgian style.

THE DRIVE: Follow the N81 south for 5.2km, take a left onto the R411 for 1.4km and then cut across the Wicklow Mountains on the R756 via the stunning Wicklow Gap. It's a 23.4km stretch to Laragh; Glendalough is only 3km further on.

PHOTO OPPORTUNITY

Sugarloaf Mountain, from the entrance drive to Powerscourt Estate.

05 Glendalough

Location, location, location. When St Kevin came to this spectacular glacial valley in the heart of the Wicklow Mountains in 498 to found a small monastic settlement, did he realise that the settlement would grow into one of Ireland's most important centres of learning and, 15 centuries later, one of the country's most popular tourist attractions? Probably not.

THE DRIVE: Head northeast on the R755 for 21km, skirting the eastern edge of Wicklow Mountains National Park, then follow the road signs for Enniskerry. Overall distance 28.9km.

06 Enniskerry

Backing onto the pretty village of Enniskerry is the expanse of **Powerscourt Estate** *(powerscourt.com)*, which gives contemporary observers a true insight into the style of the 18th-century super-rich. The main entrance is 500m south of the village square.

The estate has existed more or less since 1300, when the LePoer (later anglicised to Power) family built themselves a castle here. The property changed Anglo-Norman

Powerscourt Estate, Wicklow
PETER KROCKA/SHUTTERSTOCK

hands a few times before coming into the possession of Richard Wingfield, newly appointed Marshall of Ireland, in 1603. His descendants were to live here for the next 350 years. A fire in 1974 gutted most of the house, so the biggest draws of the whole pile are the magnificent 20-hectare formal **gardens** and the breathtaking views that accompany them.

THE DRIVE: Continue onto the M11 north and take the exit for Dun Laoghaire. The Wyattville Rd becomes Church Rd; keep going north and follow the road signs for Sandycove. It's 16.7km from Powerscourt to Sandycove.

DETOUR

Powerscourt Waterfall

Start: 06 Enniskerry

Signposted from the Powerscourt Estate is the 121m **Powerscourt Waterfall** *(powerscourt.com/waterfall)*. It's the highest waterfall in Britain and Ireland, and is most impressive after heavy rain. A nature trail has been laid out around the base of the waterfall, taking you past giant redwoods, ancient oaks, beech, birch and rowan trees. There are plenty of birds in the vicinity, including the chaffinch, cuckoo and willow warbler. It's also a popular 7km walk to the waterfall.

07 Sandycove

The handsome seaside town of Sandycove is now just part of greater Dublin, but it is renowned for its excellent restaurants, pretty beach and a Martello tower, built by British forces to keep an eye out for a Napoleonic invasion and now housing the **James Joyce Tower & Museum** *(joycetower.ie)*. This is where the action begins in James Joyce's epic novel *Ulysses*. The museum was opened in 1962 by Sylvia Beach, the Paris-based publisher who first dared to put the book into print, and has photographs, letters, documents, various editions of Joyce's work and two death masks of Joyce.

ESSEVU/SHUTTERSTOCK

Russborough House

RUSSBOROUGH HOUSE: THE TERRORISTS, THE THIEVES & THE ART LOVERS

In 1974 the Irish Republican Army (IRA) decided to get into the art business by stealing 16 paintings from Russborough House. They were eventually all recovered, but 10 years later the notorious Dublin criminal Martin Cahill (aka the General) masterminded another robbery from the Russborough House collection, this time for Loyalist paramilitaries. On this occasion, however, only some of the works were recovered, and of those, several were damaged beyond repair – a good thief does not a gentle curator make.

In 1988 the owner, Sir Albert Beit, decided to hand over the most valuable of the paintings to the National Gallery; in return, the gallery agreed to lend other paintings to the collection as temporary exhibits. The sorry story didn't conclude there. In 2001, two thieves drove a jeep through the front doors, making off with two paintings worth nearly €4 million, including a Gainsborough that had been stolen, and recovered, twice before.

To add abuse to the insult already added to injury, the house was broken into again in 2002, with the thieves taking five more paintings, including two by Rubens. Thankfully, all of the paintings were recovered after both attempts, but where a succession of thieves couldn't succeed, the cost of the upkeep did: in 2015 the owners announced they were going to auction off 10 of the paintings, a decision that caused much consternation as the family had always maintained that the collection was to be held in trust for the Irish people.

Sandycove, Dublin

RINALDS ZIMELIS/SHUTTERSTOCK

STAY AWHILE

DUBLIN

BY FIONN DAVENPORT

'Awhile' in Dublin could be a week, a month or the rest of your life – that's the kind of pull my hometown has. There's the obvious attractions: **Trinity College** *(visittrinity.ie)* and the core of Georgian streets and squares, the huge collection of museums – if I was to pick one that represents the city, I'd go for the **Little Museum of Dublin** *(littlemuseum.ie)* on St Stephen's Green – and, of course, the home of Guinness, which is the city's most popular paid-in attraction.

Some of the most interesting attractions are just outside the city centre – go west into Kilmainham for the **Irish Museum of Modern Art** *(imma.ie)* and, just beyond it, **Kilmainham Gaol** *(kilmainhamgaolmuseum.ie)*, where most of the leaders of the Easter Rising were executed.

But as much as Dublin provides ample distractions for every kind of tourism, Ireland's capital is really much more about local vibes. There's a fabulous dining scene – every kind of cuisine at every budget (my current favourite is **Comet**, *cometrestaurant.com*, just off Dawson St) – and a world-renowned pub scene. Picking a favourite is impossible, because it's all about mood. For a classic pint, there's **Mulligan's of Poolbeg St** or the **Long Hall** on Sth Great George's St, reputedly Springsteen's choice when he's in town. If I want more of a scene, then it's the pubs along Dawson St or the trendy pubs in Stoneybatter, one of the coolest neighbourhoods just north of the Liffey.

LINK YOUR TRIP

Many trips start in Dublin, including 02 **Ireland's Highlights** and 06 **East to West**, both of which take you into the west from the capital.

Left: Kilmainham Gaol; Right: The Long Hall

FROM LEFT: SALVADOR MANIQUIZ/SHUTTERSTOCK, GABRIEL12/SHUTTERSTOCK

PLACES TO STAY

Dublin has accommodation of every style and budget. Staying in the centre keeps you close to the action but comes with the highest prices.

- **Brooks Hotel**
  Boutique, family-run hotel in the city centre with exceptionally comfortable beds. *brookshotel.ie*

- **The Westbury**
  Just off Grafton St, this is five-star luxury in the heart of the city. *doylecollection.com*

- **Wilder Townhouse**
  Set in a striking red-brick building, the Wilder has a delightfully quirky vibe. *thewilder.ie*

- **Chancery**
  Quietly elegant hotel that blends modern comfort with low-key, luxe vibes. *thechanceryhotel.ie*

06

DUBLIN & EASTERN IRELAND

EAST TO WEST

DURATION: 7 DAYS

DISTANCE: 435KM / 270 MILES

GREAT FOR: HISTORY, OUTDOORS

BEST TIME TO GO: THE WARMER MONTHS (APRIL TO SEPTEMBER) ARE FESTIVAL TIME IN GALWAY.

★ BEST

TWO DAYS

From the Aran Islands back to Connemara and down to County Clare and The Burren.

Dunguaire Castle (p76), Galway

Go west! As you quit Dublin's suburban sprawl the landscape continues to soften and before you know it you're in Galway, gateway to beautiful, brooding Connemara, where the mountainous landscape is punctuated by brown bog and shimmering lakes. Explore one of the country's most magnificent spots before looping south into The Burren of County Clare, the spiritual home of Irish traditional music.

LINK YOUR TRIP

23 Best of the West
In Galway you can connect with this trip, which brings you from Sligo south to County Kerry.

29 County Clare
Explore the rest of lyrical County Clare by travelling the 40km from Doolin to Ennis.

01 Dublin

A day in the capital should give you enough time to take a walk and check out the city's big-ticket items. Culture buffs should definitely stroll through the archaeology and history branch of the **National Museum of Ireland** *(museum.ie)* – don't miss the Treasury's golden hoard of artefacts from the Bronze and Iron Ages as well as its eerily fascinating collection of preserved 'bog bodies'.

THE DRIVE: The 123km drive to Clonmacnoise is largely uneventful, courtesy of the convenient M4/M6 tolled *(€2.30)* motorway, from which you see fields and little else. Take exit 7 towards Moate and get on the R444 – Clonmacnoise is signposted as you go.

02 Clonmacnoise

Straddling a hill overlooking a bend in the Shannon, Clonmacnoise *(heritageireland.ie)* is

PATRYK KOSMIDER/SHUTTERSTOCK

one of the main reasons Ireland gained the moniker 'land of saints and scholars'.

THE DRIVE: From Clonmacnoise, take the R357 for 18km towards Ballinasloe, Galway's county town and the first town you'll come to as you enter the county across the River Suck. Here you can rejoin the M6; it's 63km to Galway city.

DETOUR

The Man Who Really 'Found' America?

Start: 02 Clonmacnoise

About 21km southeast of Ballinasloe along the R355 is the 12th-century **Clonfert Cathedral**, built on the site of a monastery said to have been founded in 563 by St Brendan 'the Navigator', who is believed to be buried here.

Although the jury is out on whether St Brendan reached America's shores in a tiny *currach* (rowing boat), there are carvings of Ogham (the earliest form of writing in Ireland) in West Virginia that date from as early as the 6th century, suggesting an Irish presence in America well before Columbus set foot there. The marvellous six-arch Romanesque doorway, adorned with surreal human heads, is reason enough to visit.

03 Galway City

Galway is the long-established, self-proclaimed and generally accepted capital of bohemian Ireland, with a long-standing tradition of attracting artists, musicians and other creative types to its pub- and cafe-lined streets.

THE DRIVE: The N59 cuts through the heart of the region – in the distance you'll see Connemara's mountain ranges, the Maumturks and the Twelve Bens.

After about 58km, just before Recess, take a 5km detour north along the R344 and take in the majesty of the Lough Inagh Valley before rejoining the road and continuing towards Clifden, 28km further on.

04 Clifden

Connemara's principal town is a genteel Victorian-era fishing port that makes a good stopover, especially during the summer months, when it casts off its wintry covers and offers visitors a nice taster of what drew 19th-century tourists to it. You can amble about its narrow streets or stare at the sea from the head of the narrow bay, into which falls the River Owenglin.

THE DRIVE: The R341 coast road goes to Roundstone, but cut through the Roundstone Bog from Ballinaboy for some fine scenery. Rejoin the R341 at Toombeola and turn left onto the N59 before turning right onto the R340 for the ferry to Inishmore from Rossaveal or a flight from Minna. From Clifden, it's 57km to Rossaveal, 64km to Minna.

05 Inishmore

Do not doubt that the effort you made to get here wasn't worth it, for a visit to the largest of the Aran Islands (indeed, any of the three) is one of the more memorable things you'll do in Ireland. The big draw is the spectacular Stone Age fort of **Dun Aengus** *(Dún Aonghasa; heritageireland.ie)*, but don't forget to explore some of the island's other ruins, scattered about the place like so much historical detritus. There's also a lovely beach at **Kilmurvey** (west of Kilronan), while up to 50 grey seals sun themselves and feed in the shallows of **Port Chorrúch**.

PHOTO OPPORTUNITY

Dun Aengus just before sunset.

THE DRIVE: You'll have to go back to Minna or Rossaveal to pick up your car. On your way back along the R336 to Galway, stop off in Spiddal, in the heart of Connemara's Gaeltacht (Irish-speaking) heartland. Beyond Galway city, turn off the N18 and go 10km along the N67 to Kinvara.

06 Kinvara

The small stone harbour of Kinvara (sometimes spelt Kinvarra) sits smugly at the southeastern corner of Galway Bay, which accounts for its Irish name, Cinn Mhara (Head of the Sea). It's a posh little village, the kind of place where all the jeans have creases in them. It makes a good pit stop between Galway and Clare.

Dominating one end of the harbour is the chess-piece-style **Dunguaire Castle** *(shannonheritage.com)*, erected around 1520 by the O'Hynes clan and in excellent condition following extensive restoration. It is widely believed that the castle occupies the former site of the 6th-century royal palace of Guaire Aidhne, the king of Connaught. Dunguaire's past owners have included Oliver St John Gogarty (1878–1957) – poet, writer, surgeon and inspiration for James Joyce's fictional Buck Mulligan, one of the cast of *Ulysses*.

The least authentic way to visit the castle is to attend a medieval banquet. Stage shows and shtick provide diversions while you plough through a big group meal.

THE DRIVE: The N67 from Kinvara skirts along the western edge of The Burren; this particularly desolate-looking (but no less beautiful) landscape is in evidence beyond Ballyvaughan, about 20km on. Doolin is a further 23km away; just past Lisdoonvarna, take a right onto the R476.

07 Doolin

Only 6km north of the Cliffs of Moher is Doolin, whose reputation as a terrific spot to spend a couple of days isn't just down to its proximity to one of the bona fide stars of the Irish tourist trail. It helps, sure, but Doolin's popularity is largely due to its pubs, or, rather, to the musicians who play in them: the area is full of talented performers who play almost every night. There are lots of pubs to choose from, but if we had to pick one, it'd be **McGann's** *(mcgannspubdoolin.com)*, complete with turf fires, dartboard and great grub.

THE BURREN

Stretching across northern Clare, from the Atlantic coast to Kinvara in County Galway, The Burren is a striated limestone landscape shaped beneath ancient seas, then forced high and dry by a great geological cataclysm. Land and sea seem to merge into one vast, moody, rocky and at times fearsome space beneath huge skies, accented with ancient burial chambers and medieval ruins.

Oyster farm, Kilcolgan, Galway
BARTOSZ LUCZAK/SHUTTERSTOCK

CLARINBRIDGE OYSTER FESTIVAL

South of Galway, Clarinbridge *(Droichead an Chláirin)* and Kilcolgan *(Cill Cholgáin)* are at their busiest during the **Clarenbridge Oyster Festival** *(galwaytourism.ie/event/clarenbridge-oyster-festival)*, held during the second weekend of September. However, the oysters are actually at their best from May through the summer.

Oysters are celebrated year-round at **Paddy Burkes Oyster Inn** *(paddyburkesgalway.com)*, a thatched inn by the bridge dishing up heaped servings in a roadside location.

Moran's Oyster Cottage *(moransoystercottage.com)* is a thatched pub and restaurant with a facade as plain as the inside of an oyster shell. Find a seat on the terrace overlooking Dunbulcaun Bay, where the oysters are reared before they arrive on your plate. It's a well-marked 2km west of the noxious N18, in a cove near Kilcolgan.

07

★ BEST FOR

CULTURE

Trim's imposing castle is a monument to medieval power.

DUBLIN & EASTERN IRELAND

THE BOYNE VALLEY

DURATION: 2 DAYS

DISTANCE: 76KM / 47 MILES

GREAT FOR: HISTORY, OUTDOORS

BEST TIME TO GO: THE SUN DOESN'T SET UNTIL AFTER 10PM BETWEEN JUNE AND JULY, BUT SEPTEMBER OFTEN GETS THE BEST WEATHER.

Trim Castle, Meath

Only 112km long, the River Boyne isn't especially impressive, but its valley can lay claim to being Ireland's most significant historical stage. The breathtaking prehistoric passage tomb complex of Brú na Bóinne is the main highlight, but the remnants of Celtic forts, Norman castles and atmospheric monasteries are but the most obvious clues to the area's rich and long-standing legacy.

LINK YOUR TRIP

08 Ancient Ireland
Connect to this trip from Brú na Bóinne and continue time travelling through Ireland's historic past.

03 The Long Way Round
From Monasterboice, head north on the M1 to Belfast and this hugely rewarding two-week trip.

01 Trim

Remarkably preserved **Trim Castle** (King John's Castle; *heritageireland.ie*) was Ireland's largest Anglo-Norman fortification and is proof of Trim's medieval importance. Hugh de Lacy founded Trim Castle in 1173, but Rory O'Connor, said to have been the last high king of Ireland, destroyed this motte-and-bailey castle within a year. The building you see today was begun around 1200 and has hardly been modified since, although it was badly damaged by Cromwellian forces when they took the town in 1649.

THE DRIVE: It's only 15km from Trim to Tara. Located 7.3km northeast of Trim, along the R161, is 12th-century Bective Abbey, built in the lush farmland still in evidence today on both sides of the road as you drive.

02 Hill of Tara

The Hill of Tara is Ireland's most sacred stretch of turf, an

ADAM. BIALEK/SHUTTERSTOCK

entrance to the underworld, occupying a place at the heart of Irish history, legend and folklore. It was the home of the mystical druids, the priest-rulers of ancient Ireland, who practised their particular form of Celtic paganism under the watchful gaze of the all-powerful goddess Maeve *(Medbh)*. Later it was the ceremonial capital of the high kings – 142 of them in all – who ruled until the arrival of Christianity in the 6th-century. It is also one of the most important ancient sites in Europe, with a Stone Age passage tomb and prehistoric burial mounds that date back 5000 years. Although little remains other than humps and mounds of earth on the hill, its historic and folkloristic significance are immense.

The **Tara Visitor Centre** *(heritageireland.ie)* is housed within a former Protestant church (with a window by artist Evie Hone) and screens a 20-minute audiovisual presentation about the site.

THE DRIVE: From Tara, the 31km drive to Brú na Bóinne takes you through the county town of Navan, the crossroads of the busy Dublin road (M3/N3) and the Drogheda–Westmeath road (N51). If you stop here, Trimgate St is lined with restaurants and pubs. Two kilometres south of the centre is the relatively intact 16th-century Athlumney Castle.

03 Brú na Bóinne

The vast Neolithic necropolis known as Brú na Bóinne (the Boyne Palace) is one of the most extraordinary sites in Europe and shouldn't be missed. A thousand years older than Stonehenge, it's a powerful and evocative testament to the mind-boggling achievements of prehistoric humans – for which it was designated a UNESCO World Heritage Site.

The area consists of many different sites; the three principal ones are Newgrange, Knowth and Dowth, but only the first two are open to visitors, and then only as part of an organised tour, which departs from the **Brú na Bóinne Visitor Centre** *(heritageireland.ie)*, from where a bus will take you to the tombs. The centre houses an extraordinary series of interactive exhibits on prehistoric Ireland and its passage tombs, and has an excellent book and souvenir shop.

THE DRIVE: The 7km drive from Brú na Bóinne is along a tiny rural road that takes you through the village of Donore. The battle site is 5km north of Donore, on the southern bank of the River Boyne.

04 Battle of the Boyne Site

More than 60,000 soldiers of the armies of King James II and King William III fought on this patch of farmland on the border of Counties Meath and Louth in 1690. In the end, William prevailed and James sailed off to France.

Today, the **battle site** *(battleoftheboyne.ie)* is part of the Oldbridge Estate farm. At the visitor centre you can watch a short show about the battle, see original and replica weaponry of the time, and explore a laser battlefield model.

THE DRIVE: It's only 5km to Drogheda; almost immediately you'll find yourself driving from fecund landscape into suburban sprawl as you approach Drogheda's outlying expanse.

05 Drogheda

Across the river from the main town of Drogheda is **Millmount**, which may have once been a prehistoric burial ground but is now home to a Martello tower and army barracks.

Part of the barracks is now the **Millmount Museum**, which has interesting displays about the town and its history. Exhibits include three wonderful late-18th-century guild banners, perhaps the last in the country. There's also a room devoted to Cromwell's brutal siege of Drogheda and the Battle of the Boyne. Across the courtyard, the **Governor's House** opens for temporary exhibitions.

THE DRIVE: The rich pastureland that drew the early Irish here has largely disappeared beneath the suburban sprawl, but, after 2km, as you go left off the N1 onto the N51, you'll get a better sense of classic Irish farmland (even though you'll drive over the M1 motorway!). As you get to the Boyne, go right onto Glen Rd until you get to Mellifont. The whole drive is 9.5km long.

DETOUR

Drogheda to Castlebellingham via the Coast Road

Start: 05 Drogheda

Most people just zip north along the M1 motorway, but if you want to meander along the coast and see a little of rural Ireland, opt for the R166 from Drogheda north along the coast.

The picturesque little village of **Termonfeckin** was, until 1656, the seat and castle of the primate of Armagh. The 15th-century castle, or tower house, is tiny and worth a five-minute stop.

About 2km further north is the busy seaside and fishing centre of **Clogherhead**, with a good, shallow Blue Flag beach at Lurganboy. Squint to ignore the caravan parks and take in the lovely views of the Cooley and Mourne Mountains instead.

The 33km route comes to an end in **Castlebellingham**. The village grew up around an 18th-century crenellated mansion, and generations of mud farmers served the landlord within. From here you can come back on the M1; it's only 29km from Castlebellingham to Drogheda.

06 Mellifont Abbey

In its Anglo-Norman prime, this **abbey** *(heritageireland.ie)* was the Cistercians' first and most magnificent centre in the country. Although the ruins are highly evocative and well worth exploring, they still don't do real justice to the site's former splendour.

Mellifont's most recognisable building, and one of the finest pieces of Cistercian architecture in Ireland, is the lavabo, an octagonal washing house for the monks. It was built in the early 13th-century and used lead pipes to bring water from the river. A number of other buildings would have surrounded this main part of the abbey.

The visitor centre describes monastic life in detail. The ruins themselves are always open and there's good picnicking next to the rushing stream. The abbey is about

CROMWELL'S DROGHEDA INVASION

Oliver Cromwell (1599–1658) may be lauded as England's first democrat and protector of the people, but he didn't have much love for the Irish, dismissing them as a dirty race of papists who had sided with Charles I during the Civil War. So when 'God's own Englishman' landed his 12,000 troops in Dublin in August 1649, he set out for Drogheda, determined to set a brutal example to any other town that might resist his armies.

Over a period of hours, an estimated 3000 people were massacred, mostly royalist soldiers but also priests, women and children. The defenders' leader, Englishman and royalist Sir Arthur Aston, was bludgeoned to death with his own wooden leg. Of the survivors, many were captured and sold into indentured servitude in the Caribbean.

Cromwell defended his action as God's righteous punishment of treacherous Catholics, and was quick to point out that he had never ordered the killing of non-combatants: it was the 17th-century's version of 'collateral damage'.

MATGO/SHUTTERSTOCK

📷 PHOTO OPPORTUNITY

The round tower at Monasterboice at sunset.

Round tower at Monasterboice, Louth

1.5km off the main Drogheda–Collon road (R168).

THE DRIVE: The easiest way to get to Monasterboice from Mellifont Abbey is to take Old Mellifont Rd; after 1.6km, turn left onto the R168; after 1.5km, turn right onto Drogheda Rd. Follow it for 1.6km and turn left at the signpost for Monasterboice, from where it's a further 1.7km. The total distance is just 6.4km.

07 Monasterboice

Crowing ravens lend an eerie atmosphere to Monasterboice, an intriguing monastic site containing a cemetery, two ancient church ruins, one of the finest and tallest round towers in Ireland, and two of the best high crosses.

The **high crosses** of Monasterboice are superb examples of Celtic art. The crosses had an important didactic use, bringing the gospels alive for the uneducated, and they were probably brightly painted originally, although all traces of colour have long disappeared.

Come early or late in the day to avoid the crowds.

08

★ BEST FOR

CULTURE

The passage graves at Brú na Bóinne.

DUBLIN & EASTERN IRELAND

ANCIENT IRELAND

DURATION: 4 DAYS

DISTANCE: 529KM / 329 MILES

GREAT FOR: HISTORY, OUTDOORS

BEST TIME TO GO: APRIL TO SEPTEMBER FOR THE LONG DAYS AND BEST WEATHER.

Eastern passage of Knowth, Brú na Bóinne, Meath

This trip transports you from the Neolithic era to the last days of the first millennium, via the signposts of Ireland's astonishing history: the prehistoric treasure trove of Cruachan Aí; the ancient passage graves of Brú na Bóinne and Loughcrew; the ancient Celtic capital atop the Hill of Tara; and the rich monastic settlements of Clonmacnoise, Glendalough and Cashel – some of the most important early medieval universities in Europe.

LINK YOUR TRIP

12 Kilkenny's Treasures
It's 20km from Jerpoint Abbey to Kilkenny, the first stop in the trip dedicated to the county.

22 The Holy Glen
In Cashel you can connect to this trip exploring the very best of County Tipperary.

01 Brú na Bóinne

A thousand years older than Stonehenge, the extensive Neolithic necropolis known as Brú na Bóinne (the Boyne Palace) is simply breathtaking, even if at first glance it just looks like a handful of raised mounds in the fecund fields of County Meath.

The largest artificial structures in Ireland until the construction of the Anglo-Norman castles 4000 years later, the necropolis was built to house VIP corpses. Only two of the passage graves are open to visitors (Newgrange and Knowth) and they can only be visited as part of a carefully controlled organised tour departing from the Brú na Bóinne Visitor Centre.

THE DRIVE: Follow the signposts for Slane and the N2 as you wend your way across the Meath countryside for 8km or so; the Hill of Slane is 1km north of the village.

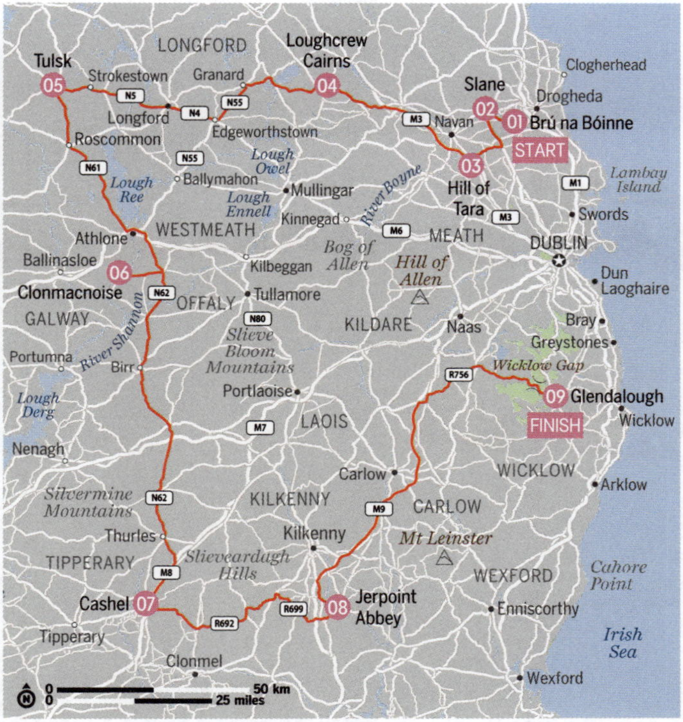

02 Slane

The fairly plain-looking **Hill of Slane** stands out only for its association with a thick slice of Celto-Christian mythology. According to legend, St Patrick lit a paschal (Easter) fire here in 433 to proclaim Christianity throughout the land.

It was also here that Patrick supposedly plucked a shamrock from the ground, using its three leaves to explain the paradox of the Holy Trinity – the union of the Father, the Son and the Holy Spirit in one.

THE DRIVE: Go south on the N2 for 11km and turn right onto the R153. After 2km, take the left fork and keep going for 7.5km before turning left on the R147. After 2km, turn right and drive 1.3km to the Hill of Tara (23.7km all up).

03 Hill of Tara

The Hill of Tara *(Teamhair)* has occupied a special place in Irish legend and folklore for millennia, although it's not known exactly when people first settled on this gently sloping hill with its commanding views over the plains of Meath. Tara's remains are not visually impressive. Only mounds and depressions in the grass mark where the Iron Age hillfort and surrounding ringforts once stood, but it remains an evocative, somewhat moving place, especially on a warm summer's evening. To make sense of it all, stop by the **Tara Visitor Centre** *(heritageireland.ie)*.

THE DRIVE: Head north and take the M3, which becomes the N3 at Kells. Keep going for 3.7km and at the roundabout take the first exit onto the R163. Follow it for 8km; it eventually morphs into the R154. The cairns are along here, just west of Oldcastle. The drive is 44km altogether.

04 Loughcrew Cairns

There are 30-odd tombs here but they're hard to reach and relatively few people ever bother, which means you can enjoy this moody and evocative place in peace.

Like Brú na Bóinne, the graves were all built around 3000 BCE, but unlike their better-known and better-excavated peers, the Loughcrew tombs were used at least until 750 BCE. As at Newgrange, larger stones in some of the graves are decorated with spiral patterns. Some of the graves look like large piles of stones, while others are less obvious, their cairn having been removed.

Nearby is the **Loughcrew Megalithic Centre** *(loughcrewmegalithiccentre.com)*, with a small but absorbing museum.

THE DRIVE: The 87km between Loughcrew and Tulsk takes you through the heart of middle Ireland, past small glacial lakes and low-lying hills. Head 28km west and turn left onto the N55 at Granard to Edgeworthstown and take the N4 to Longford. Take the N5 as far as handsome Strokestown, where you should stop for an amble; Tulsk is 10km west along the same road.

05 Tulsk

Anyone with an interest in Celtic mythology will be enthralled by the area around the village of Tulsk in County Roscommon, which contains 60 ancient national monuments, including standing stones, barrows, cairns and fortresses, making it the most important Celtic royal site in Europe.

The **Cruachan Aí Visitor Centre** *(Rathcroghan; rathcroghan.ie)* has audiovisual displays and informative panels and maps that explain the significance of the sites.

According to the legend of *Táin Bó Cúailnge* (Cattle Raid of Cooley), Queen Maeve *(Medbh)* had her palace at Cruachan Aí. The Oweynagat Cave (Cave of the Cats), believed to be the entrance to the Celtic other world, is also nearby.

THE DRIVE: As you drive the 73km south to Clonmacnoise along the N61, you'll have Lough Ree on your left for much of the drive. Many of the lake's 50-plus islands were once inhabited by monks and their ecclesiastical treasures. These days, it's mostly anglers, sailors and birdwatchers who frequent it.

PERSPECTIVES/GETTY IMAGES

Birr Castle

A NIGHT IN BIRR

Feel-good Birr, County Offaly, is one of the most attractive towns in the Midlands, with elegant pastel Georgian buildings lining its streets, a magnificent old castle, an excellent choice of accommodation and spirited nightlife with great live music. Despite its appeal, Birr remains off the beaten track and you can enjoy its delights without jostling with the crowds.

For more about Birr, see p90.

06 Clonmacnoise

Ancient Ireland is sometimes referred to as the 'land of saints and scholars', and one of the reasons why was the monastic city of Clonmacnoise, one of Europe's most important centres of study between the 7th and 12th centuries. It was a top university before Oxford was a glint in the scholar's eye.

Founded in 548 by St Ciarán, the monastery (whose name in Irish is *Cluain Mhic Nóis*, which means 'Meadow of the Sons of Nós') that became a bustling city is in remarkably good condition: enclosed within a walled field above a bend in the River Shannon is a superb collection of early churches, high crosses, round towers and graves, including those of the high kings of Ireland.

THE DRIVE: It's 107km along the N62 to Cashel; overnighting in handsome Birr (which has great accommodation and nightlife) is recommended.

07 Cashel

Straddling a green hill above the town, the **Rock of Cashel** *(heritageireland.ie)* is one of Ireland's most important archaeological sites and one of the most evocative of all ancient monuments.

It had been a prominent Celtic power base since the 4th-century; most of what remains today dates from when it was gifted to the Church in 1101. Over the next 400 years, various bishops ordered the construction of the 13th-century

Hill of Tara (p83), Meath
MNSTUDIO/SHUTTERSTOCK

cathedral, a wonderfully complete round tower, the finest Romanesque chapel (1127) in the country and the sturdy walls that surround it all. Although it's a collection of religious buildings, the rock here was heavily fortified; the word 'cashel' is an Anglicisation of the Irish word *caiseal*, which means 'fortress'.

Scattered throughout are monuments, panels from 16th-century altar tombs and coats of arms. If you have binoculars, look for the numerous stone heads on capitals and corbels high above the ground.

THE DRIVE: Tipperary and western Kilkenny are classic examples of good Irish farmland; as you wend your way east along the R692 and R690, you'll pass stud farms and cattle ranches. Ten kilometres northeast of Cottrellstown via the R697 is the 29m-high Kilree round tower and, next to it, a 9th-century high cross. The drive to Jerpoint Abbey from Cashel is 60km.

08 Jerpoint Abbey

One of Ireland's finest Cistercian ruins, **Jerpoint Abbey** *(heritageireland.ie)* near Thomastown was established in the 12th century and has been partially restored. The tower and cloister date from the late 14th or early 15th century. The 45-minute tours are worthwhile, as the guides flesh out the abbey's fascinating history.

THE DRIVE: As you come off the M9 and take the R756 east towards Glendalough, you'll climb into the wildest parts of the Wicklow Mountains, eastern Ireland's most scenic spectacle. Just before Glendalough you'll drive through the Wicklow Gap, between Mt Tonelagee (816m) to the north and Table Mountain (700m) to the southwest. Total distance to Glendalough: 117km.

09 Glendalough

Of all Ireland's monastic cities, none has the secluded beauty and isolated majesty of Glendalough, whose impressive ruins are more than rivalled by their setting: two dark glacial lakes at the foot of a forested valley that remain, despite the immense popularity of a visit, a profoundly peaceful and spiritual place.

In 498 the solitude-seeking St Kevin went to live in a Bronze Age tomb on the south side of the **Upper Lake**, but most of what you see dates from the 9th-century onwards, when Kevin's settlement rivalled Clonmacnoise as one of Ireland's premier universities: huddled around the eastern end of the **Lower Lake** are Glendalough's most fascinating buildings, including a roofless cathedral, a couple of churches, a gatehouse and a round tower.

The **Glendalough Visitor Centre** *(heritageireland.ie)* has a 20-minute audiovisual presentation called Ireland of the Monasteries.

Rock of Cashel (p85), Tipperary

DAWID K PHOTOGRAPHY/SHUTTERSTOCK

TOP TIP

THE CASHEL SHOT

Cashel looks good from pretty much every angle, but the most atmospheric photo is from the ruins of Hore Abbey, set in flat farmland less than 1km west of Cashel.

09

★ BEST FOR

CULTURE

Explore Ireland's tormented history at Strokestown Park.

DUBLIN & EASTERN IRELAND

MONASTERIES, MOUNTAINS & MANSIONS

Castletown House, Celbridge, Kildare

DURATION: 3 DAYS

DISTANCE: 278KM / 172 MILES

GREAT FOR: FOOD & DRINK, HISTORY, OUTDOORS

BEST TIME TO GO: LATE SPRING AND EARLY AUTUMN ARE IDEAL: WITH SMALLER CROWDS AND GOOD WEATHER.

This is a journey through Irish heritage, much of it overlapping with Ireland's ancient east: handsome towns like Birr and Strokestown may not attract star billing but are all the better for it, while better-known attractions like Clonmacnoise and Castletown House are outstanding examples of monastic splendour and Georgian extravagance, respectively. And did we mention whiskey? How about a visit to the home of the smoothest Irish whiskey of all?

LINK YOUR TRIP

33 Northwest on Adrenaline
Explore the northwest's heart-racing activities with an easy 61km drive from Strokestown to Sligo.

23 Best of the West
At trip's end, head west to Westport and pick up this western extravaganza.

01 Celbridge

Celbridge, County Kildare, is now a satellite town serving Dublin, only 20km to the east, but in the 18th-century it was known as the location for Ireland's most magnificent Georgian pile, **Castletown House** *(castletown.ie)*, which simply has no peer.

The house was built between the years 1722 and 1732 for William Conolly (1662–1729), speaker of the Irish House of Commons and, at the time, Ireland's richest man.

The job of building a palace fit for a prince was entrusted to Sir Edward Lovett Pearce (1699–1733). Inspired by the work of Andrea Palladio, Pearce enlarged the original design of the house and added the colonnades and terminating pavilions. In the US, Thomas Jefferson became a Palladian acolyte and

much of official Washington, DC, is in this style.

A highlight of the opulent interior is the Long Gallery, replete with family portraits and exquisite stucco work by the Francini brothers.

THE DRIVE: It's 85km to Tullamore from Celbridge, and most of the route is along the painless and featureless M4 and M6 motorways; at Junction 11 on the M4, be sure to take the left-hand fork onto the M6 towards Galway and Athlone. Exit the M6 at Junction 5; Tullamore is a further 11km along the N52.

02 Tullamore

Offaly's county town is a bustling but workaday place with a pleasant setting on the Grand Canal. It's best known for Tullamore Dew Whiskey, which was distilled in the town until 1954, when operations moved to Clonmel, County Tipperary.

In 2014 this all changed again, when the distillery opened a new factory on the edge of town. You can't visit it, but you can explore the town's distilling history in the refurbished **Tullamore Dew Visitor Centre** *(tullamoredew.com)*, located in a 19th-century canal-side warehouse. At the end of the tour you'll get to sample some produce and, inevitably, be encouraged to buy it for friends and family.

THE DRIVE: It's only 36km from Tullamore to Birr. As you drive the N52 south towards Birr, you'll skirt the northern edge of the Slieve Bloom Mountains, which rise suddenly from the great plain of middle Ireland.

DETOUR

Slieve Bloom Mountains

Start: 02 Tullamore

Although the Slieve Bloom Mountains aren't as spectacular as some Irish ranges, their sudden rise from a great plain and the absence of visitors make them highly attractive. You'll get a real sense of being away from it all as you tread the deserted blanket bogs, moorland, pine forests and isolated valleys.

For leisurely walking, **Glenbarrow**, southwest of Rosenallis, has an interesting trail by the cascading River Barrow. Other spots are

Glendine Park, near the Glendine Gap, and the **Cut mountain pass**.

For something more challenging, you could try the **Slieve Bloom Way**, a 70km signposted trail that does a complete circuit of the mountains, taking in most major points of interest. The recommended starting point is the car park at Glenbarrow, 5km from Rosenallis, from where the trail follows tracks, forest firebreaks and old roads around the mountains. The trail's highest point is at Glendine Gap (460m).

03 Birr

The main reason to visit handsome Birr is to explore the attractions and gardens of **Birr Castle Demesne** *(birrcastle.com)*, built in 1620 by the Parsons family, who still own it to this day. The Parsons were a remarkable family of pioneering Irish scientists, and their work is documented in the **historic science centre**. Exhibits include the massive telescope built by William Parsons in 1845, for 75 years the largest in the world. It was used to make innumerable discoveries, including the spiral galaxies, and to map the moon's surface.

Otherwise, the 50-hectare castle grounds are famous for their magnificent **gardens** set around a large artificial lake. They hold over 1000 species of plants from all over the world; something always seems to be in bloom. Look for one of the world's tallest box hedges, planted in the 1780s and now standing 12m high, and the Hornbeam cloister.

THE DRIVE: You'll see mostly fields of cows as you drive the 33km to Clonmacnoise along the N62; at Cloghan, turn left onto the slightly narrower and lonelier R357. You'll have the River Shannon on your left-hand side when you turn onto the R444 for the last 7.5km, via Shannonbridge's 16-arch limestone bridge dating from 1757.

PHOTO OPPORTUNITY

Immortalise the gardens of Birr Castle demesne.

04 Clonmacnoise

One of the most important monastic sites in Ireland, the marvellous ruins of Clonmacnoise are also one of the most popular tourist attractions in the country, so be prepared to share your visit with other awestruck tourists and busloads of curious schoolkids.

THE DRIVE: Rejoin the M6 19km north of Clonmacnoise. At Junction 4, take the N52 north towards Mullingar; on your left, keep an eye out for Lough Ennell: the far side is home to Lilliput House, which was frequently used by Jonathan Swift and gave him the name he used in *Gulliver's Travels*. In total, the drive is 62km long. Detour to Athlone, 25km from Clonmacnoise, for a Thai meal.

05 Belvedere House & Gardens

About 5.5km south of Mullingar, overlooking Lough Ennell, is **Belvedere House** *(belvedere-house.ie)*, an immense 18th-century hunting lodge set in 65 hectares of gardens. More than a few skeletons have come out of Belvedere's closets: the first earl, Lord Belfield, accused his wife and younger brother Arthur of adultery. His wife was placed under house arrest here for 30 years, and Arthur was jailed in London for the rest of his life. Meanwhile, the earl lived a life of decadence and debauchery. On his death, his wife emerged dressed in the fashion of three decades earlier, still protesting her innocence.

THE DRIVE: Mullingar, just north, has a couple of good hotels and restaurants. From there, drive northwest into County Longford, whose low hills have few tourist sights but are a haven for anglers who come for the superb fishing around Lough Ree and Lanesborough. From Belvedere House, the drive to Corlea along the R392 is 42km.

06 Corlea Trackway

Longford's main attraction is the magnificent **Corlea Trackway** *(heritageireland.ie)*, an Iron Age bog road near Keenagh that was built in 148 BCE. An 18m stretch of the historic track has now been preserved in a humidified hall at the visitor centre, where you can join a guided tour that details the bog's unique flora and fauna, and fills you in on how the track was discovered and the methods used to preserve it. Wear a windproof jacket as the bog land can be blowy.

THE DRIVE: Strokestown is 29km northwest of Corlea along the R392 as far as Lanesborough, after which you'll cut through the green, lush countryside along the R371. After 11km, take a left onto the N5, which will take you right into Strokestown, 4.5km further on.

MICHAEL CASH PHOTOGRAPHY/SHUTTERSTOCK

Belvedere House & Gardens, Westmeath

DETOUR

One of Ireland's Best Traditional Pubs

Start: 06 Corlea Trackway

About 10km east of Lanesborough is the tiny hamlet of Killashee, which is home to **Magan's**, a delightful old bar, grocery and hardware store that seems stuck in aspic, completely oblivious to the pull and push of modern life. It's well off the beaten track, and is rarely frequented by anyone other than locals, which makes it an even better destination for a pint.

07 Strokestown

Roscommon's most handsome town is, for nonresidents, all about Strokestown Park and the **National Famine Museum** *(strokestownpark.ie)*, the entrance to which is through the three Gothic arches at the end of Strokestown's main avenue.

Admission to the beautifully preserved **Palladian house** is by a 50-minute guided tour, taking in a galleried kitchen with state-of-the-art clockwork machinery, and a child's bedroom complete with 19th-century toys and fun-house mirrors.

In direct and deliberate contrast to the splendour of the house and its grounds is the harrowing museum, which sheds light on the devastating 1840s potato blight. There's a huge amount of information to take in, but you'll emerge with an unblinking insight into the starvation of the poor, and the ignorance, callousness and cruelty of those who were in a position to help. Allow at least half a day to see the house, museum and gardens.

10

DUBLIN & EASTERN IRELAND

WICKLOW MOUNTAINS

★ BEST FOR

CULTURE

Glendalough: 1500 years of monastic history beautifully nestled in a glacial valley.

Round tower, Glendalough (p94)

DURATION: 3 DAYS

DISTANCE: 70KM / 43 MILES

GREAT FOR: HISTORY, OUTDOORS

BEST TIME TO GO: FROM LATE AUGUST TO SEPTEMBER, THE CROWDS THIN OUT AND THE HEATHER IS IN BLOOM.

This drive takes you down the spine of the Wicklow Mountains, whose dramatic scenery and weather-whipped bleakness make up for what they lack in height. Along the way, you'll visit fine Palladian mansions and a beautiful monastic site nestled at the foot of a glacial valley – be prepared to pull over and gawp at the scenery that unfolds.

LINK YOUR TRIP

08 Ancient Ireland
At Glendalough you can start this trip through Ireland's ancient heritage...in reverse.

05 A Long Weekend Around Dublin
From Enniskerry, hook up with this trip exploring the best of Dublin's surrounds.

01 Enniskerry

If you're coming from Dublin, Enniskerry is a handsome village at the top of the R117, aka the '21 Bends', but its pretty shops and cafes are merely a prelude to a visit to the superb 64-sq-km **Powerscourt Estate**, whose workers' domestic needs were the very reason Enniskerry was built in the first place.

Due to a fire, you can't visit the Palladian mansion, apart from the ground-floor cafe and outlet of the popular Avoca handicrafts store, but it's the gardens that will have you in thrall. Laid out (mostly) in the 19th century, they are a magnificent blend of landscaped gardens, sweeping terraces, statuary, ornamental lakes, secret hollows, rambling walks and walled enclosures containing with more than 200 types of trees and shrubs, all beneath the stunning natural backdrop of the Great Sugarloaf Mountain to the southeast.

THE DRIVE: The narrow, twisting L1011 cuts 9.7km through the northern edge of the mountains,

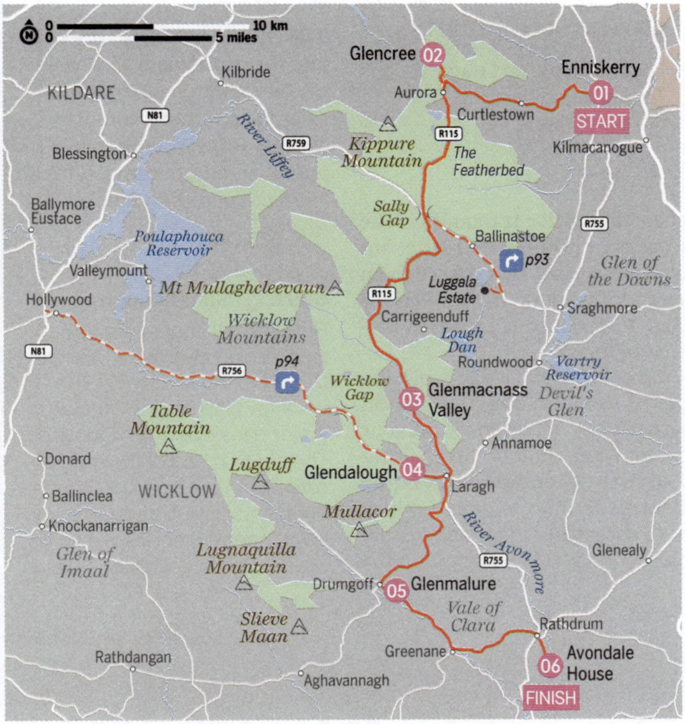

VINCENT MACNAMARA/SHUTTERSTOCK

with only a hint of what's to come further on. As you approach Glencree you'll pass through mostly forest.

02 Glencree

Glencree is a leafy hamlet set into the side of the valley of the same name, which opens east to give a magnificent view down to Great Sugarloaf Mountain and the sea.

The valley floor is home to the **Glencree Oak Project**, an ambitious plan to reforest part of Glencree with the native oak vegetation that once covered the majority of the country, but now only covers 1% of Ireland's land mass.

The village, such as it is, has a tiny shop and a hostel but no pub. There's a poignant German cemetery, **Deutscher Soldatenfriedhof** (German Military Cemetery), dedicated to the 134 German servicemen who died in Ireland during WWI and WWII. Just south of the village, the former military barracks are a retreat house and reconciliation centre for people of different religions from the Republic and the North.

THE DRIVE: At Glencree you'll join Wicklow's loveliest, loneliest road, the Old Military Rd (R115), which cuts through a desolate valley of gorse and brown bog and gets more desolate as you go south. After 8.4km, you'll reach the Sally Gap crossroads; turn right onto the R759 for the gap itself or continue for another 5km to the Glenmacnass Valley.

DETOUR

Luggala

Start: 02 Glencree

If you turn right (east) at the Sally Gap crossroads onto the R759, you'll be on the Sally Gap, one of the two main east–west passes across the Wicklow Mountains and a stretch of road surrounded by some spectacular countryside. About 5km on, the narrow road passes above the dark and dramatic **Lough Tay**, whose scree slopes slide into Luggala (Fancy Mountain). This almost-fairy-tale estate was owned by Garech de Brún of the Guinness family, but in 2019 was sold to an Italian billionaire. You can't visit the estate itself, but there's a popular looped walk that circles it from a height. The small River Cloghoge links Lough Tay with Lough Dan just to the south. You can continue on the R759 for another 3km or so, turning right onto the R755 for Roundwood, or double-back onto the Old Military Rd and make your way south via Glenmacnass.

03 Glenmacnass Valley

Desolate and utterly deserted, the Glenmacnass Valley, a stretch of wild bogland between the Sally Gap crossroads and Laragh, is one of the most beautiful parts of the mountains, although the sense of isolation is quite dramatic.

The highest mountain to the west is Mt Mullaghcleevaun (848m), and the River Glenmacnass flows south and tumbles over the edge of the mountain plateau in a great foaming cascade. There's a car park near the top of the Glenmacnass Waterfall. Be careful when walking on rocks near the waterfall, as a few people have slipped to their deaths. There are fine walks up

Mt Mullaghcleevaun or in the hills to the east of the car park.

THE DRIVE: Beyond the Glenmacnass Valley, the Old Military Rd descends for 13km into Laragh, a busy crossroads village that serves as a supply point for nearby Glendalough. It's a good spot to stop and eat or buy provisions. Glendalough is 2km west of here.

04 Glendalough

Wicklow's most visited attraction and one of the country's most important historic sites is the collection of ruined churches, buildings, shelters and a round tower that make up the ancient monastic city of Glendalough, founded in 498 by St Kevin, who came to the (then) desolate valley looking for a spot of contemplative tranquillity. The ruins are certainly evocative, but it's their setting that makes them special: two dark and mysterious lakes tucked into a deep valley covered in forest.

You could spend a day exploring the ruins and taking in the local scenery, but whatever you do, your exploration should start with a visit to the **Glendalough Visitor Centre** *(heritageireland.ie)*, which has a decent 20-minute audiovisual presentation called Ireland of the Monasteries.

PHOTO OPPORTUNITY

Looking down on Lough Tay and Luggala from the Sally Gap.

THE DRIVE: As you go deeper into the mountains southwest of Glendalough along the R755, near the southern end of the Military Rd, everything gets a bit wilder and more remote. It's an 11km drive to Glenmalure.

DETOUR

The Wicklow Gap

Start: 04 Glendalough

Between Mt Tonelagee (816m) to the north and Table Mountain (700m) to the southwest, the Wicklow Gap (R756) is the second major pass over the mountains. The eastern end of the road begins just to the north of Glendalough and climbs through some lovely scenery northwestwards up along the Glendassan Valley.

Lough Tay (p93), Wicklow

NA. KNOE/SHUTTERSTOCK

It passes the remains of some old lead and zinc workings before meeting a side road that leads south and up Turlough Hill, the location of Ireland's only pumped-storage power station. You can walk up the hill for a look over the Upper Lake. The western end of the gap meets the N81, from which it's only a few kilometres north to Blessington and Russborough House.

05 Glenmalure

Beneath the western slopes of Wicklow's highest peak, Lugnaquilla Mountain (924m), is Glenmalure, a dark and sombre blind valley flanked by scree slopes of loose boulders. After coming over the mountains into Glenmalure, you turn northwest at the Drumgoff bridge. From there it's about 6km up the road beside the River Avonbeg to a car park where trails lead off in various directions.

THE DRIVE: The tiny rural road to Rathdrum is called Riverside; it takes you down out of the mountains through some lush forest for 12km into Rathdrum for Avondale House.

JURAJ KAMENCKY/SHUTTERSTOCK

Glendalough Valley

GLENDALOUGH VALLEY WALKS

The Glendalough Valley is all about walking and clambering. There are nine marked walkways in the valley, the longest of which is about 10km, or about four hours' walking. Before you set off, drop by the **National Park Information Office** *(wicklowmountains nationalpark.ie)* and pick up the relevant leaflet and trail map *(each around €1)*.

A word of warning: don't be fooled by the relative gentleness of the surrounding countryside or the fact that the Wicklow Mountains are really no taller than big hills. The weather can be merciless here, so be sure to take the usual precautions, have the right equipment and tell someone where you're going and when you should be back.

For Mountain Rescue call 999.

06 Avondale House

The quiet village of Rathdrum at the foot of the Vale of Clara comprises little more than a few old houses and shops. However, it's not what's in the town that's of interest to visitors, but what's just outside it.

Avondale House *(heritageireland.com)* is a fine Palladian mansion surrounded by a marvellous 209-hectare estate, which was the birthplace and Irish home of the 'uncrowned king of Ireland', Charles Stewart Parnell (1846–91), champion of the struggle for Home Rule and one of the key figures of the Irish independence movement. Designed by James Wyatt in 1779, the house has many highlights, including a stunning vermilion-hued library and beautiful dining room.

On the grounds is the superb **Beyond the Trees** *(beyondthetreesavondale.com)*, a 1.4km spiral treetop walkway built on timber pylons with fab views over the top of, well, everything.

11

DUBLIN & EASTERN IRELAND

CARLOW BACK ROADS

DURATION: 3 DAYS

DISTANCE: 118KM / 73 MILES

GREAT FOR: HISTORY, OUTDOORS

BEST TIME TO GO: CARLOW'S FLOWER FESTIVALS TAKE PLACE THROUGHOUT JULY AND SEPTEMBER.

Strings of quietly picturesque villages wind through Carlow, Ireland's second-smallest county. The scenic Blackstairs Mountains dominate the southeast, while the region's most dramatic chunk of history is Europe's biggest dolmen, just outside quiet Carlow town. A ruined Gothic mansion and a reputedly haunted castle form the backdrop to two of the county's best flower-filled gardens.

LINK YOUR TRIP

12 Kilkenny's Treasures
From Borris, it's only 10km to Graiguenamanagh, from where you can explore County Kilkenny.

04 Tip to Toe
Travel 14km from St Mullins south to New Ross, where you can join this classic north-to-south trip.

01 Carlow Town

Carlow town's narrow streets and lanes are quiet these days, a far cry from 25 May 1789, when several hundred Irish insurgents were ambushed and executed by British troops during a ferocious battle in the middle of town. The dead were buried in gravel pits on the far side of the River Barrow, at Graiguecullen.

Built by William de Marshall on the site of an earlier Norman motte-and-bailey fort, the 13th-century **Carlow Castle** (*heritageireland.ie*; Mill Lane) survived Cromwell's attentions but was later converted into a lunatic asylum. The evocative portion that survives is a part of the keep flanked by two towers.

Other notable sights include the 19th-century **Cathedral of the Assumption** (*carlowcathedral.ie*) and the **Carlow County Museum** (*carlowmuseum.ie*).

INALEX/SHUTTERSTOCK

★ BEST FOR

GARDENS

The Altamont Gardens are the most spectacular of Carlow's beautiful gardens.

Altamont Gardens (p98), Carlow

THE DRIVE: Take the Athy road (R417) north for 2km; the Delta Sensory Gardens are on your left.

02 Delta Sensory Gardens

Located in an incongruous industrial estate on the northern edge of Carlow town are these remarkable **gardens** *(deltasensorygardens.com)*. Some 16 interconnecting, themed gardens cover one hectare and span the five senses – from a sculpture garden to a formal rose garden, a water and woodland garden, a willow garden and a musical garden with mechanical fountains. Admission proceeds benefit the adjoining Delta Centre, which provides services and respite for adults with learning disabilities.

THE DRIVE: Take the N80 for 2.2km, then the R726 for 2.4km heading east from Carlow town. You'll have to park the car and walk 300m to the dolmen field.

03 Browne's Hill Dolmen

Ireland's largest portal dolmen (tomb chamber) sits in a field and, from the road, doesn't look that impressive. But as you get closer you'll begin to appreciate the enormity of this 5000-year-old monster. The entrance to the chamber is flanked by two large upright stones (known as orthostats or megaliths) topped by a granite capstone that alone weighs well over 100 tonnes.

It's unclear how the stones got here in the first place, but experts have narrowed it down to two possibilities: they were deposited here during the Ice Age, or Stone Age people ate a hell of a lot of spinach and figured out a way of carrying them to the field.

THE DRIVE: It's 6km to Duckett's Grove. Continue southeast on the R726 for 700m before turning left on the L1009. The house is 5km ahead on your right (pass over the M9 en route).

ARTISANAL GLASS

About 3km east of Kells, in the neighbouring county of Kilkenny, is the small village of Stonyford. The local highlight, the nationally renowned **Jerpoint Glass Studio** *(jerpointglass.com)*, is housed in a rural stone-walled farm building 1km south of town, where you can watch workers craft molten glass into exquisite artistic and practical items.

04 Duckett's Grove

Until the main building burnt down in 1933, the Gothic fantasy that was Duckett's Grove was Carlow's most impressive building, the centrepiece of an estate that once spread across five counties. The house, which dates from the late 17th-century, was transformed into a Gothic mansion in 1830 and was used as a training camp for the IRA during the War of Independence.

The ruins are still impressive, and surrounding them are the original high brick garden walls that frame two sprawling, interconnected formal gardens.

THE DRIVE: Start the 18km drive by heading southeast on the R418 to Tullow before continuing south along the N81. After 7km, take a right for the Altamont estate.

05 Altamont Gardens

Generally considered to be the jewel in the Irish gardening crown, **Altamont Gardens** *(heritageireland.ie)* covers 16 hectares and is made up of informal and formal gardens, including a walled garden with carefully selected plantings arranged in naturalistic, idealised settings.

The estate's main avenue is lined with trees, including imported species such as red oaks and swamp cypresses, and it leads down to an artificial lake.

THE DRIVE: Take the N80 south for 3.5km and then the signposted left for Clonegal.

06 Clonegal

The idyllic village of Clonegal has a tiny little centre out of a nursery rhyme, with an arched stone bridge over a river that boasts swans and water flowers.

Huntington Castle *(huntingtoncastle.com)* is a spooky, dusty old keep built in 1625 by the Durdin-Robertson family, who still own it and live here today. The family conduct guided tours of the property, which, they claim, is haunted by two ghosts. The house features a mural of a mouse created in the 1920s by Walt Disney. The gardens combine the formal with rural fantasy. There's also a B&B and tearoom here.

THE DRIVE: The R724 cuts across southern County Carlow; Borris is 29km away.

07 Borris

Handsome Borris is a seemingly untouched Georgian village, strung out like a string bean down the side of a hill, with a dramatic mountain backdrop. That's Mt Leinster, site of an excellent scenic drive.

THE DRIVE: It's 15km from Borris to St Mullins, mostly along the R729 with the Blackstairs Mountains to your east.

Duckett's Grove, Carlow
MNSTUDIO/SHUTTERSTOCK

CARLOW IN BLOOM

County Carlow is renowned for its gardens, 21 of which form part of Ireland's first dedicated **garden trail** *(carlowgardentrail.com)*:

- Delta Sensory Gardens (p97)
- Huntington Castle's Gardens
- Duckett's Grove
- Kilgraney House Herb Gardens (p101)
- Altamont Gardens

DETOUR

Mt Leinster Scenic Drive

Start: 07 Borris

The highest peak in the Blackstairs Mountains, Mt Leinster (796m) has magnificent views of Counties Waterford, Carlow, Kilkenny and Wicklow from the top.

From Borris, drive south along the R702 and almost immediately take the signposted left for Mt Leinster. Keep going and take the left for Bunclody at the T-junction.

Continue around, keeping the mountain on your right; you'll arrive at the car park at Corribut Gap. The ground falls away steeply, offering stunning views of the Coolasnaghta valley to the north.

This is also the spot favoured by those taking advantage of Ireland's best hang-gliding – if you fancy taking off from the mountain, contact the **Irish Hang Gliding & Paragliding Association** *(ihpa.ie)* for further information.

DETOUR

Kilgraney House Herb Gardens

Start: 07 Borris

Herbs as you've never seen them grow in orderly profusion in **Kilgraney House Herb Gardens** *(kilgraneyhouse.com)*, which boasts a heady cocktail of medicinal and kitchen plants and also serves as a source of food for the inn and restaurant here. The recreated medieval monastic herb garden is a favourite. It's off the R705 halfway between Borris and Bagenalstown.

Route from Mt Leinster

SEMMICK PHOTO/SHUTTERSTOCK

PHOTO OPPORTUNITY

Immortalise the Black Castle from the banks of the Barrow.

08 St Mullins

Tranquil little St Mullins sits 6km downstream from Graiguenamanagh, which is in County Kilkenny. The village is the maternal home of Michael Flatley of *Riverdance* fame. Sure enough, the river snakes through here in the shadow of Brandon Hill, as does the River Barrow towpath from Borris. From the river, a trail winds uphill to the ruined hulk of an old **monastery** surrounded by the graves of 1798 rebels. A 9th-century Celtic cross, badly worn down over the centuries, still stands beside the monastery. Nearby, **St Moling's Well** is a holy well that seems to attract spare change.

THE DRIVE: It's 27km from St Mullins to Bagenalstown via Borris. The 12km stretch of the R705 from Borris to Bagenalstown follows the scenic River Barrow Valley, one of the nicest bits of road in all of Carlow.

09 Bagenalstown

About 12km north of Borris is Bagenalstown, which isn't quite as handsome, but is home to the O'Hara's **Carlow Brewing Company** *(carlowbrewing.com)*, a microbrewery that offers tours of its O'Hara's-brand beers. Its award-winning Irish stout bursts with flavour and certainly holds its own against that other Irish stout.

THE DRIVE: Leighlinbridge is 4km on along the R705.

10 Leighlinbridge

Leighlinbridge would be just another Carlow town if it weren't for the ominous ruins of the **Black Castle** on the banks of the Barrow. Dating from 1181, this was one of the first Norman castles built in Ireland and it was bequeathed to John de Claville by Henry II's lieutenant, Hugh de Lacy. The present castle was built by Sir Edward Bellingham in 1547, but was demolished by Cromwell's army in 1650.

12

DUBLIN & EASTERN IRELAND

KILKENNY'S TREASURES

DURATION: 3 DAYS

DISTANCE: 54KM / 34 MILES

GREAT FOR: HISTORY, OUTDOORS

BEST TIME TO GO: SPRING AND AUTUMN ARE IDEAL: THE WEATHER'S GOOD BUT THERE ARE FEWER VISITORS THAN IN THE SUMMER.

★ BEST FOR

CRAFTS

The exquisitely made artisanal crafts at the Nicholas Mosse Irish Country Shop.

Potter Nicholas Mosse

The enduring gift of the Normans, Kilkenny mesmerises visitors with its medieval alleys and castle, ruined abbeys and outstanding nightlife. Beyond the city limits, tiny roads navigate the beautiful valleys past the mementos of 800 years of Irish history, picture-postcard villages and a dynamic contemporary craft industry whose reputation is admired countrywide.

LINK YOUR TRIP

08 Ancient Ireland
From Kilree or Jerpoint Abbey you can connect to this trip that visits some of ancient Ireland's most important sites.

04 Tip to Toe
Kilkenny is one of the main stops on the classic Tip to Toe trip, which explores Ireland from north to south.

01 Kilkenny

Kilkenny *(Cill Chainnigh)* is the Ireland of many visitors' imaginations. Its majestic riverside castle, tangle of 17th-century passageways, rows of colourful, old-fashioned shopfronts and centuries-old pubs with traditional live music all have a timeless appeal, as does its splendid medieval cathedral.

Kilkenny's architectural charm owes a huge debt to the Middle Ages, when the city was a seat of political power. It's also sometimes called the 'marble city' because of the local black limestone, used on floors and in decorative trim all over town.

You can cover pretty much everything on foot in half a day but sampling its many delights will take much longer.

CHRISTOPHER HILL/ALAMY STOCK PHOTO

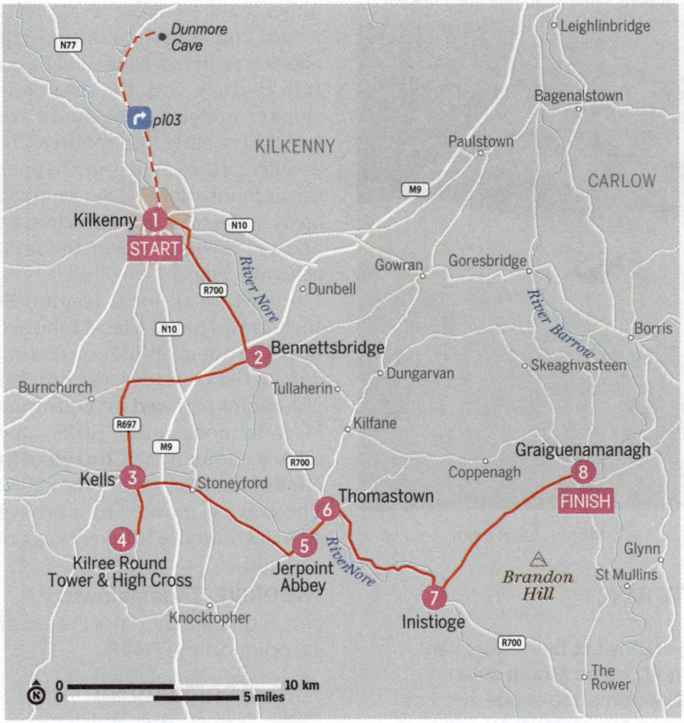

THE DRIVE: Drive southeast with the castle and the Nore on your immediate left along the Bennettsbridge Rd, which becomes the R700. It's only a short 8km drive to Bennettsbridge.

DETOUR

Dunmore Cave

Start: 01 Kilkenny

Just 6km north of Kilkenny on the Castlecomer road (N78) are the striking calcite formations of **Dunmore Cave** *(heritage ireland.ie)*. In 928 marauding Vikings killed 1000 people at two ringforts near here. When survivors hid in the caverns, the Vikings tried to smoke them out by lighting fires at the entrance. It's thought that they then dragged off the men as slaves and left the women and children to suffocate. Excavations in 1973 uncovered the skeletons of at least 44 people, mostly women and children. They also found coins dating from the 10th century.

Admission to the cave is via a compulsory – but highly worthwhile – guided tour. Although well lit and spacious, the cave is damp and cold; bring warm clothes.

02 Bennettsbridge

Bennettsbridge is an arts-and-crafts treasure chest, although these treasures are scattered throughout the town, rather than within a concentrated area.

In the big mill by the river west of town, the **Nicholas Mosse Irish Country Shop** *(nicholasmosse.com)* specialises in handmade spongeware – ceramics decorated with sponged patterns – which is exported worldwide to retail outlets such as Tiffany & Co. Short audiovisual displays explain the manufacturing process. The cafe here is renowned for its scones, and is the best choice locally for lunch.

Established in 1999, the workshop **Moth to a Flame** *(mothtoaflame.ie)* creates beautifully coloured and textured candles of all sizes, from bedside-table to church-altar scale.

THE DRIVE: The 12km drive to Kells takes you across the flat, luscious green plain of central Kilkenny. Follow Annamult Rd, cross over the N10, then turn left on the R697.

03 Kells

Kells (not to be confused with Kells in County Meath) is a mere hamlet with a fine stone bridge on a tributary of the Nore. However, in **Kells Priory**, the village has one of Ireland's most impressive and romantic monastic sites. This is the best sort of ruin, where visitors can amble about whenever they like, with no tour guides, tours, set hours or fees.

At dusk on a vaguely sunny day, the old priory is simply beautiful. Most days you stand a chance of exploring the site alone (apart from bleating and pooping sheep).

The ruins are 500m east of Kells on the Stonyford road.

THE DRIVE: Kilree is only 2.5km south of Kells along a small country road.

BETOFOTO/SHUTTERSTOCK

Mount Juliet's golf course

TEEING OFF IN THOMASTOWN

Just 6km from Thomastown heading southwest, high-flyers can tee off at the Jack Nicklaus–blessed golf course **Mount Juliet** *(mountjuliet.ie)*. Set over 600 wooded hectares, the estate also has its own equestrian centre, a gym and spa, two restaurants, wine masterclasses, and posh rooms catering to every whim, right down to the pillow menu *(accommodation from €150)*.

04 Kilree Round Tower & High Cross

Standing in an overgrown graveyard is a 29m-high **round tower** that has lost its cap. It was built sometime between the 8th and 11th centuries, and served as a bell tower, although it was also a handy place of refuge for locals looking to escape the unwelcome attention of invaders.

Next to it, standing more than 2m tall, is a simple early **high cross** that was long believed to be the grave of a 9th-century Irish high king, Niall Caille, who drowned in the nearby river in 847 while attempting the rescue of a servant or soldier, even though experts now reckon the cross is older than that. Still, Niall's resting place lies beyond the church grounds because he wasn't a Christian.

THE DRIVE: The 11km drive will have you doubling back towards Kells, but then taking a right on the Stonyford road, past Kells Priory. You'll pass Mt Juliet on your left. Turn left on the R448, and Jerpoint Abbey is a further 700m on your right.

05 Jerpoint Abbey

Ireland has an abundance of church ruins, but few are quite as magnificent as those of Jerpoint Abbey, a fine exemplar of Cistercian power and church-building. The abbey was first established in the 12th century, with the tower and cloister added sometime in the late 14th or early 15th century. The excellent 45-minute tours happen throughout the day. Set yourself apart in the remains of the cloisters and see if you can hear the faint echo of a chant.

According to local legend, St Nicholas (or Santa Claus) is buried near the abbey. While retreating during the Crusades, the knights of Jerpoint removed his body from Myra in modern-day Turkey and reburied him in the **Church of St Nicholas** to the west of the abbey. The grave is marked by a broken slab decorated with a carving of a monk.

THE DRIVE: Thomastown is only a quick 2.5km northeast of Jerpoint on the R448.

06 Thomastown

Named after Welsh mercenary Thomas de Cantwell, Thomastown has some fragments of a medieval wall and the partly ruined 13th-century **Church of St Mary**. Down by the bridge, **Mullin's Castle** is the sole survivor of the 14 castles once here.

Like the rest of Kilkenny, the area has a vibrant craft scene. Look out for **Clay Creations** *(bridlyons ceramics.com)*, displaying the quixotic ceramics and sculptures of local artist Brid Lyons.

THE DRIVE: The 8.5km drive south to Inistioge along the R700 is a splendidly scenic one through the valley of the River Nore; keep an eye out for the views of the ruined 13th-century Grennan Castle on your right as you go.

FOTOGRO/SHUTTERSTOCK

Graiguenamanagh

TOWN OF BOOKS

Graiguenamanagh's narrow streets spill over with booksellers, authors and bibliophiles during the three-day **Town of Books Festival** *(graiguenamanaghtownofbooks.ie)*. There are a couple of good used and antiquarian bookshops open year-round as well.

07 Inistioge

The little village of Inistioge (in-ish-teeg) is a picture. Its 18th-century, 10-arch **stone bridge** spans the River Nore and vintage shops face its tranquil square.

About 500m south of the village is the heavily forested **Woodstock Gardens and Arboretum** *(woodstock.ie)*, a beauty of a park with expansive 19th-century gardens, picnic areas and trails. The panorama of the valley and village below is spectacular. Coming from town, follow the signs for Woodstock Estate and enter the large gates (despite appearances, it's a public road), then continue along the road for about 1.5km until you reach the car park (parking costs €4 in coins).

THE DRIVE: It's 11km from Inistioge to Graiguenamanagh on the Graigue road, aka the L4209, so narrow that you'll wonder if there's room for oncoming traffic (there is).

08 Graiguenamanagh

Graiguenamanagh (greg-na-muh-na; known locally simply as Graigue) is the kind of place where you could easily find yourself staying longer than planned. Spanning the River Barrow, an ancient six-arch stone bridge is illuminated at night and connects the village with the smaller township of Tinnahinch on the County Carlow side of the river (look for the darker stones on the Carlow side – a legacy from being blown up during the 1798 rebellion).

The big attraction in town is the **Cistercian Duiske Abbey**, once Ireland's largest and still very much a working parish church (thanks to 800 years of changes and additions). To the right of the entrance look for the Knight of Duiske, a 14th-century, high-relief carving of a knight in chain mail who's reaching for his sword. On the floor nearby, a glass panel reveals some of the original 13th-century floor tiles, now 2m below the present floor level.

13

DUBLIN & EASTERN IRELAND

WEXFORD & WATERFORD

★ BEST FOR

CULTURE

Learn about bloody Irish history at the National 1798 Rebellion Centre.

Reenactment of the 1798 Battle of Enniscorthy, Enniscorthy, Wexford

DURATION: 5 DAYS

DISTANCE: 164KM / 102 MILES

GREAT FOR: HISTORY, FOOD & DRINK, OUTDOORS

BEST TIME TO GO: APRIL TO SEPTEMBER FOR THE LONG DAYS AND BEST WEATHER.

Collectively labelled the 'sunny southeast', Wexford and Waterford get less rainfall and more sunshine than anywhere else in Ireland, but the southeastern counties are about more than resort towns and pretty beaches. There's history aplenty round here, some stunning inland scenery and a vibrant foodie scene that mightn't be as well known as that in neighbouring Cork, but is just as good.

LINK YOUR TRIP

14 Blackwater Valley Drive
It's only 5km from Ardmore to Youghal and the start of the Blackwater Valley Drive.

04 Tip to Toe
You can hook up to this long country-length trip in Kilmore Quay.

01 Enniscorthy

Busy Enniscorthy *(Inis Coirthaidh)* is an attractive hilly town on the banks of the River Slaney in the heart of County Wexford, 20km north of Wexford town. For the Irish, its name is forever linked to some of the fiercest fighting of the 1798 rebellion, when rebels captured the town and castle and set up camp nearby at **Vinegar Hill** *(vinegarhill.ie)*.

Before climbing the hill (a 2km drive east of town), acquaint yourself with the story of the rebellion with a visit to the **National 1798 Rebellion Centre** *(1798centre.ie)*, which tells the tale of Wexford's abortive uprising against British rule in all its gory, fascinating detail. The rebels were inspired by the French and American Revolutions, but were beaten back by English troops, who then massacred

NIALL CARSON/ALAMY STOCK PHOTO

hundreds of women and children as reprisal for the uprising.

If you want to walk up Vinegar Hill, from Abbey Sq head out of town along Mill Park Rd or south along the river.

THE DRIVE: It's 43km to Kilmore Quay. You'll skirt around Wexford town on your way south along the N11; beyond the town, follow the directions for Rosslare and take the N25. Turn right onto the R739 to Kilmore Quay. The last stretch of road is the most scenic, as the countryside opens up in front of you.

02 Kilmore Quay

Straight out of a postcard, peaceful Kilmore Quay is a small village on the eastern side of Ballyteige Bay, noted for its lobsters and deep-sea fishing. Lining the attractive main street up from the harbour are a series of pretty whitewashed thatched cottages. The harbour is the jumping-off point for the Saltee Islands, home to Ireland's largest bird sanctuary, clearly visible out to sea.

The four-day **Kilmore Quay Seafood Festival** *(kilmorequayseafoodfestival.com)* in the second week of July involves all types of seafood tastings, music and dancing.

THE DRIVE: It's 31km from Kilmore Quay to the ruins of Tintern Abbey along the narrow R733. The promontory east of the Hook Peninsula, signposted as the Bannow Drive, is littered with Norman ruins, while Bannow Bay is a wildfowl sanctuary. As you cross Wellington Bridge onto the Hook Peninsula, keep an eye out for the remains of medieval Clonmines to the southwest.

DETOUR

Saltee Islands

Start: 02 Kilmore Quay

Just 4km offshore and accessible from Kilmore Quay via local boat (depending on the weather), the **Saltee Islands** *(salteeislands.info)* constitute one of Europe's most important bird sanctuaries, home to over 220 recorded species, principally the gannet, guillemot, cormorant, kittiwake, puffin and Manx shearwater. It's a noisier but more peaceful existence than its past as the favoured haunt of privateers and smugglers. The islands are also where you'll find some of the oldest rocks in Europe, dating back 2000 million years or more; findings also suggest that the islands were inhabited by the pre-Celts as long ago as 3500 to 2000 BCE.

The best time to visit is the spring and early-summer nesting season. The birds leave once the chicks can fly; by early August it's eerily quiet.

To get here, try **Eamon Hayes** at Kilmore Quay *(visitkilmorequay.ie/angling-cruises)*, but be sure to book in advance. You can park your car in town.

03 Tintern Abbey

In better structural condition than its Welsh counterpart, from where its first monks hailed, Ireland's moody **Tintern Abbey** *(heritageireland.ie)* is secluded amid 40 hectares of woodland. William Marshal, Earl of Pembroke, founded the Cistercian abbey in the early 13th-century after he nearly perished at sea and swore to establish a church if he made it ashore.

The abbey is 1.5km from the town of Saltmills, among wooded trails, lakes and idyllic streams. The grounds are always open, and a walk here is worth the trip at any time.

THE DRIVE: The 10km route across the Hook Peninsula along the R733 is the quickest way to Arthurstown, but the most scenic route is the 35km circumference of the peninsula, passing villages like Slade, where the most activity is in the swirl of seagulls above the ruined castle and harbour. Beaches include the wonderfully secluded Dollar Bay and Booley Bay, just beyond Templetown. Don't forget to spot the world's oldest working lighthouse, right at Hook Head.

04 Arthurstown

Chef Kevin Dundon is a familiar face on Irish TV, and the author of cookbooks *Full On Irish* and *Great Family Food*. His **Dunbrody Country House Hotel** *(dunbrodyhouse.com)*, in a period-decorated 1830s Georgian manor on 120-hectare grounds, is the stuff of foodies' fantasies, with a gourmet restaurant and cookery school *(one-day courses from €175)*.

Beside the R733, some 6km north of Dundon's pile, the ruined

Dunbrody Abbey, Wexford

IRISH DRONE PHOTOGRAPHY/SHUTTERSTOCK

Dunbrody Abbey *(dunbrodyabbey.com)* is a remarkably intact Cistercian abbey founded by Strongbow in 1170 and completed in 1220. A combined ticket includes a museum with a huge doll's house, minigolf and a very fun yew-hedge maze made up of over 1500 trees.

THE DRIVE: Instead of going the long way around, cut out a lengthy detour around Waterford Harbour and the River Barrow by taking the five-minute car ferry between Ballyhack in County Wexford and Passage East in County Waterford. Then follow the R683 to Waterford city. This way is only 12km long.

DETOUR

Passage Coast Road

Start: 04 Arthurstown

A little-travelled 11km-long coast road wiggles south between Passage East and Dunmore East to the south. At times single-vehicle width and steep, it offers mesmerising views of the ocean and undulating fields that you won't see from the main thoroughfares. Follow the R708 north to Waterford city.

05 Waterford City

Inhabited since 914 CE, Waterford *(Port Láirge)* is Ireland's oldest city, and much of the centre's street plan has retained its medieval feel.

Waterford's 1000-year history is told in wonderful fashion in a trio of museums collectively known as the **Waterford Museum of Treasures** *(waterfordtreasures.com)* that comprise **Reginald's Tower**, the oldest complete building in Ireland; the **Bishop's Palace**, home to a superb interactive museum; and the engrossing **Medieval Museum**, which tells the story of Waterford life before 1700.

PHOTO OPPORTUNITY

Look down on Ardmore Bay from St Declan's Church.

Since 1783 the city has been famous for its production of high-quality crystal. However, the factory closed in 2009 and all that's left is the **House of Waterford Crystal** *(waterfordvisitorcentre.com)*, a flashy showroom where you can see some pieces of crystal being blown, although most of the stuff you buy in the shop is made in Eastern Europe.

THE DRIVE: Follow the southern bank of the River Suir and take the N25 to get to Dungarvan, 45km away. Or travel south and take the R675 coastal route along the stunning **Copper Coast**, where you'll meet cerulean skies, azure waters, impossibly green hills and ebony cliff faces along the way.

06 Dungarvan

It isn't enough that Dungarvan has the looks: pastel-coloured houses huddled around a boat-filled port at the mouth of the River Colligan make it one of the southeast's prettiest towns. It now has the charm, in the form of a foodie reputation that makes it a must-stop destination for anyone looking to sample the best of Irish cuisine.

At the heart of the town is the Norman **castle** *(heritageireland.ie)*, which is slowly being restored to its once impregnable glory. But the real draws are culinary: Paul Flynn's **Tannery Cookery School** *(tannery.ie)*, adjoining a fruit, veg and herb garden, is one of Ireland's best. The annual **West Waterford Festival of Food** *(westwaterfordfestivaloffood.com)* celebrates the area's abundant fresh produce.

THE DRIVE: It's an easy 23km drive along the N25 to the turn-off for Ardmore, which then becomes the very rural R673 as you move south to the coast. This is rural Ireland at its most pristine, with farmhouses the only interruption to a stretch of undulating fields and stone walls.

07 Ardmore

The enticing seaside village of Ardmore may look quiet these days, but it's claimed that St Declan set up shop here between 350 and 420. This brought Christianity to southeast Ireland long before St Patrick arrived from Britain.

In a striking position on a hill above town, the ruins of **St Declan's Church** stand on the site of St Declan's original monastery alongside an impressive cone-roofed, 29m-high, 12th-century round tower, one of the best examples of these structures in Ireland.

If you're looking for a bit of beautiful seclusion, you'll find it on **Ballyquin beach**, home to tide pools, fascinating rocks and sheltered sand. It's 1km off the R673, 4km northeast of Ardmore. Look for the small sign.

STAY AWHILE

ARDMORE

BY FIONN DAVENPORT

Of all the seaside resorts of the southeast, Ardmore is the one that feels furthest removed from everything else. It's not on the main N25, but at the end of an 8km road that leads nowhere beyond itself. I don't arrive here by accident; I come because I've decided to. At first glance, it's almost modest, but Main St draws me down toward the strand, a broad, 2km sweep of sand tucked into a sheltered bay that seems designed for slowing down.

Off to the right, I follow Main St as it rises past the little pier and climbs the hill to **Ardmore Pottery & Gallery** *(ardmorepottery.com)*. Two generations of the Lincoln family have shaped this place, and as I move through it, the work on the shelves feels inseparable from the landscape outside.

A short distance further, beyond the Cliff House Hotel, I reach **St Declan's Well and Church**, regarded as Ireland's oldest Christian site. It's believed St Declan brought Christianity here in the 5th century, before St Patrick, and standing here, I'm at the start of Ardmore's finest experience: the 4km **cliff walk**.

The path carries me along the coastline past the rusting hulk of the *Samson* crane barge, wrecked here in 1987, and on to the watchtower at **Ardmore Head**. From there I loop inland, returning through fields and quiet lanes to the old cemetery, where **Ardmore Cathedral**, a tiny oratory and a 30m round tower stand watch over the village and sea.

LINK YOUR TRIP

The scenic 13 **Wexford & Waterford** trip ends in Ardmore, while the 14 **Blackwater Valley Drive** starts in nearby Youghal.

Left: Round tower, Ardmore Cathedral; Right: View of the *Samson* barge from the Ardmore cliff walk

FROM LEFT: PAUL KELLY/SHUTTERSTOCK, TOMASZ OCHOCKI/SHUTTERSTOCK

PLACES TO STAY

There isn't a huge amount of choice in Ardmore, but it includes one of Ireland's finest hotels.

- **Cliff House Hotel**
  Built into the cliff overlooking Ardmore Bay, this is one of Ireland's top coastal retreats. Its Michelin-starred restaurant is exceptional, but the terrace, with sweeping sea views, is just as special for a drink. Self-catering options suit families and range from basic to very luxurious. *cliffhousehotel.com*

- **Round Tower Hotel**
  This family-run hotel has 12 comfortable rooms in a characterful 1920s building, just below St Declan's Monastery and close to the village centre. It's a well-located base for exploring Ardmore. *roundtowerhotel.ie*

14

DUBLIN & EASTERN IRELAND

BLACKWATER VALLEY DRIVE

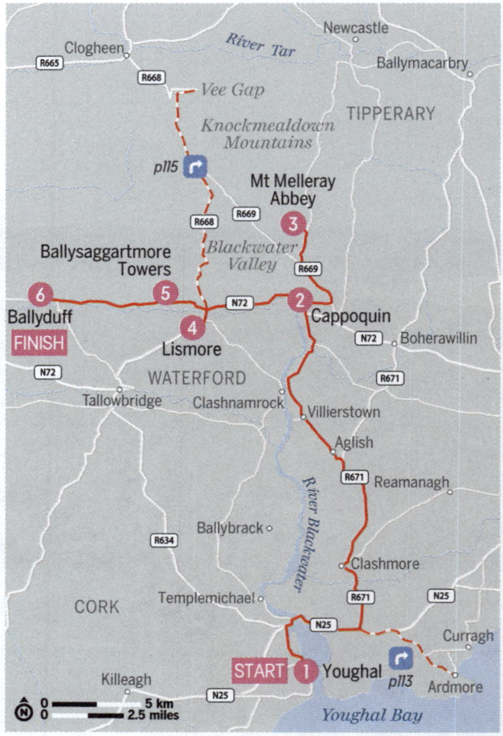

DURATION: 2 DAYS

DISTANCE: 65KM / 40 MILES

GREAT FOR: HISTORY, FAMILY

BEST TIME TO GO: JULY AND AUGUST FOR TRADITIONAL MUSIC.

This short drive takes you through one of the most scenic and historic stretches of southern Ireland. From the mouth of the River Blackwater in Youghal (where you can take to the river by boat), explore the river valley northwards as far as historic Lismore before turning west with the river to find traditional villages, beautiful mountain passes and one of the country's best centres for traditional music and dancing.

LINK YOUR TRIP

13 Wexford & Waterford
From Youghal it's only 5km to Ardmore, from which you can explore the sunny southeast.

22 The Holy Glen
Head 42km north from Lismore to Clonmel and explore some of Ireland's most important monastic sites.

01 Youghal

The ancient seaport of Youghal (*Eochaill*; pronounced yawl), at the mouth of the River Blackwater, was a hotbed of rebellion against the English in the 16th-century. Youghal was granted to Sir Walter Raleigh during the Elizabethan Plantation of Munster, and he spent brief spells living here in his house, **Myrtle Grove**. Oliver Cromwell spent the winter here in 1649.

Award-winning **Aherne's Seafood Bar & Restaurant** is a great choice for a meal in town, where seafood is the star.

Youghal has two Blue Flag beaches, ideal for building sandcastles modelled after the 1777 **Clock Gate**. **Claycastle** (2km) and **Front Strand** (1km) are both within walking distance of town, off the N25. Claycastle has summer lifeguards.

THE DRIVE: Start the 33km drive by taking the N25 east towards Dungarvan and then go

★ BEST FOR

FOODIES

Aherne's Seafood Bar & Restaurant in Youghal.

COURTESY AHERNE'S SEAFOOD BAR & RESTAURANT/RUTH CONNOLLY

Aherne's Seafood Bar & Restaurant, Youghal

north along the R671 (direction Clonmel). Take the turn for Villierstown and follow the route to Cappoquin through the tree-lined Dromana Woods. At the bridge over the River Finisk is a remarkable Hindu-Gothic gate, inspired by the Brighton Pavilion in England and unique to Ireland.

DETOUR

Ardmore

Start: 01 Youghal

Just 5km east of Youghal and south off the N25 is the beautifully isolated seaside village of Ardmore, whose setting and heritage are unmatched – St Declan brought Christianity here a good century before St Patrick showed up. The ruins of St Declan's Church stand on the site of the original **St Declan's Monastery**, next to one of Ireland's best examples of a 12th-century round tower.

Ardmore is also home to one of the country's best hotels, the **Cliff House Hotel**, which has a Michelin-starred restaurant. From the hotel, there's a lovely, 5km-circular **walk** that takes you past St Declan's Well, Ireland's oldest Christian ruin; the wreck of a crane ship that blew ashore in 1987; and a WWII lookout post.

02 Cappoquin

With the picturesque Blackwater Valley to the west, the small market town of Cappoquin sits neatly on a steep hillside at the foot of the rounded, heathery Knockmealdown Mountains.

Cappoquin House and Gardens *(cappoquinhouseandgardens.com)* is a magnificent 1779-built Georgian mansion and two hectares of formal gardens overlooking the River Blackwater. The entrance to the house is just north of the centre of Cappoquin; look for a set of huge black iron gates.

Cappoquin is also a good spot for anglers, as the town is right at the head of the Blackwater estuary, where there's some of the best game and coarse fishing in the country. The fishing season runs from the beginning of February to the end of September; in order to fish for salmon you'll have to purchase a state licence *(one day/21 days €36/50)* and a day permit *(€64)*; you can buy both at the **Titelines Tackle & Gift Shop**.

THE DRIVE: It's only 8km to Mt Melleray. Just right off the R669 to Mt Melleray is a signpost for Glenshelane Park, which has lovely forest walks and picnic spots that are popular with locals.

03 Mt Melleray Abbey

A fully functioning monastery that is home to two dozen Cistercian (Trappist) monks, the beautiful 19th-century **Mt Melleray Abbey** *(mountmellerayabbey.org)* in the Knockmealdown foothills welcomes visitors looking for quiet contemplation. There are tearooms (closed Monday) and a heritage centre. In 1954, six of the monks departed for New Zealand, where they founded the Abbey of Our Lady of the Southern Star in a remote location near Takapau, on the North Island.

THE DRIVE: You'll have to double-back to Cappoquin (8km) and then take the N72 west for 6km to Lismore. The Blackwater River will be on your left as you go.

04 Lismore

Over the centuries, political leaders and luminaries have streamed through quiet, elegant Lismore, the location of a great monastic university founded by St Carthage in the 7th century. King Alfred of Wessex attended the university, Henry II visited the papal legate Bishop Christian O'Conarchy here in 1171, and even Fred Astaire dropped by when his sister Adele married into the Cavendish family, who own the huge, 19th-century **castle** *(lismorecastlegardens.com)*. You can't visit inside (unless you rent it for an event) but you can access the three hectares of ornate and manicured gardens, thought to be the oldest in Ireland. There's a splendid yew walk where Edmund Spenser is said to have written *The Faerie Queene*.

Otherwise, pop into **St Carthage's Cathedral** (1679), deemed by William Thackeray to be one of the prettiest edifices he'd ever seen, and that was before the addition of the

Gate lodges, Ballysaggartmore Towers, Waterford

TRAVEL.LIFE/SHUTTERSTOCK

PHOTO OPPORTUNITY

The architectural folly at Ballysaggartmore Towers.

gorgeous Pre-Raphaelite Edward Burne-Jones stained-glass window.

THE DRIVE: Take the R666 Lismore–Fermoy road, signposted left over the bridge past Lismore Castle. The scenic drive overlooks the Blackwater; the 'towers' are signposted 3.5km out of Lismore on your right.

DETOUR

The Vee Gap

Start: 04 Lismore

The R668 north of Lismore cuts through the Knockmealdown Mountains and crosses the border into southern Tipperary. The road rises sharply through lush wooded countryside for 8km before emerging onto a beautiful upland plateau. A further 6km on, to your left, is Bay Lough, which makes for a nice amble. Beyond it is the Vee Gap, which cuts through the highest point of the mountains and offers superb views over three counties: Tipperary, Waterford and Limerick. Beyond the gap is the village of Clogheen, from where you can keep going to Clonmel.

KIERAN MOORE/SHUTTERSTOCK

Youghal, Cork

BLACKWATER CRUISE

If you want to explore the Blackwater River from the water, the jetty in Youghal is where you'll find the *Maeve*, which does 90-minute tours *(blackwatercruises.com)* of the river north to the remains of Templemichael Castle, about 8km north of Youghal. Captain Tony Gallagher is one of Youghal's best-known characters, as is his first mate, a dog named Pharaoh.

05 Ballysaggartmore Towers

One of the more breathtaking bits of architectural folly in southern Ireland, the Ballysaggartmore Towers are just off the R666 road to Fermoy, in the heart of a woodland that was once the demesne of Arthur Kiely-Ussher, an Anglo-Irish landlord with a reputation for harshness, ordering evictions of famine-stricken tenants for nonpayment of rent.

Still, he had a soft spot for his wife, who in 1834 demanded that he build her an estate to match that of her sister-in-law's, so he ordered the construction of two Gothic-style gate lodges (one of which serves as a bridge) as a prelude to a huge mansion. But Kiely-Ussher ran out of money and the house was never built, a bit of hubris that, given his treatment of his tenants, left locals to delight in his misfortune.

The lodges are free to visit at any time.

THE DRIVE: Continue west on the R666 to Ballyduff, with the River Blackwater on your left, a total distance of just 6km.

06 Ballyduff

This rural village (not to be confused with another Ballyduff in County Waterford) is a slice of traditional heaven: beautifully positioned on the Blackwater (the views are stunning), it goes about its business largely unperturbed by the demands of modern tourism.

During the summer, the big draw is **Booley House** *(thebooleyhouse.com)*, which since 1991 has been showcasing traditional Irish music, dancing and storytelling in its weekly show. **Lismore Heritage Centre** *(discoverlismore.com)* has details of upcoming shows.

The village's artistic tradition extends to amateur drama: companies from all over the country descend on St Michael's Hall for the annual **West Waterford Drama Festival** *(adci.ie)*, which runs for 10 days in March.

15

DUBLIN & EASTERN IRELAND

FAMILY FUN

DURATION: 3 DAYS

DISTANCE: 154KM / 96 MILES

GREAT FOR: HISTORY, FAMILY

BEST TIME TO GO: APRIL TO SEPTEMBER FOR THE LONG DAYS AND BEST WEATHER.

Within an hour's drive of Dublin is a wealth of child-friendly activities and distractions. The big draws are the interactive exhibits of Brú na Bóinne and the superb adventure centre in Carlingford, but there's plenty more in-between, including a popular farm where kids get to play with the animals, plus a fantastic amusement park.

LINK YOUR TRIP

30 The North in a Nutshell
From Carlingford, it's only 80km along the A1 to Belfast and the beginning of this trip.

08 Ancient Ireland
You can connect to this trip through time at Brú na Bóinne.

01 Dublin

A bit of interesting Dublin trivia: the original lion that roars at the beginning of all MGM films was Slats, born in the 28-hectare **Dublin Zoo** *(dublinzoo.ie)* in 1919. The zoo's other claim to fame is that it's one of the world's oldest, established in 1831. The lion-breeding program, begun in 1857, is another highlight, and you can see these tough cats – from a distance – on the 'African Plains', part of an expansion that saw the zoo double in size; other areas include 'World of Primates' and 'Fringes of the Arctic'.

Meet the Keeper is a big hit with kids, especially as they get a chance to feed the animals and participate in other activities. The City Farm is also excellent: it brings you within touching distance of chickens, cows, goats and pigs. There's also a zoo train and a nursery for infants.

THE DRIVE: The 29km drive to Emerald Park will take you northwest along the N2 to

★ BEST FOR

FAMILIES

You'll find animals and child-friendly activities at the revamped Dublin Zoo.

DESIGN PICS/THE IRISH IMAGE COLLECTION/GETTY IMAGES

Chimpanzees, Dublin Zoo

Ashbourne, where signs direct you left along the L50161 for the last 3.5km.

02 Emerald Park

Formerly called Tayto Park (after the Irish potato crisp brand Tayto) this popular **amusement park** *(emeraldpark.ie)* was renamed in 2023. It has attractions including Europe's largest wooden inverted roller-coaster, a 5D cinema (yes, 5D), a high-speed spinning Rotator and the stomach-churning Air Race ride. There's also a zoo, rock climbing, a zip line and a fantastic playground.

Admission includes zoo and playground entry; the wristband day pass is the most economical option for the rides.

THE DRIVE: Head southwest on the R125 for 12km, crossing over the M3 before turning right on the R154 for the remaining 15km to Trim (27km in all).

03 Trim

If you've watched the film *Braveheart*, Mel Gibson's 1995 epic about Scots rebel William Wallace, then you may recognise the remarkably preserved **Trim Castle**, which made a very acceptable stand-in for the castle at York.

Founded in 1173 by Hugh de Lacy, this was Ireland's largest Anglo-Norman fortification, but the original was destroyed by Rory O'Connor, Ireland's last high king, within a year of its construction: what you see here is the reconstruction, dating from 1200, and it's hardly changed since (despite a hell of a shellacking by Cromwellian forces in 1649).

THE DRIVE: Halfway along the 32km drive to Brú na Bóinne you'll hit the county town of Navan, which is pretty unremarkable except for the traffic – expect delays. Past Navan, the R147 is a classic rural road, with nothing but fields on either side and private houses.

04 Brú na Bóinne Visitor Centre

Bringing the Neolithic period to life, and putting the extraordinary accomplishments of Brú na Bóinne's constructors in remarkable and fascinating context, is this

NEWGRANGE FARM

One for the kids. A few hundred metres down the hill to the west of Newgrange tomb is a 135-hectare working farm. The truly hands-on, family-run **Newgrange Farm** *(newgrangefarm.com)* allows visitors to feed the ducks and lambs, and tour the exotic bird aviaries.

The owners keep things interesting, and demonstrations of threshing, sheepdog work and shoeing a horse are absorbing. Sunday at 3pm is a very special time when the 'sheep derby' is run. Finding jockeys small enough isn't easy, so teddy bears are tied to the animals' backs. Visiting children are made owners of their own sheep for the race.

excellent visitor centre. It explains in brilliant, interactive detail exactly how people lived 3500 years ago and how they managed to garner the mathematical genius to construct a passage tomb that allows for the precise alignment of the sun during the winter solstice.

A bus will take you from the visitor centre to the passage tomb itself, where a guide explains how it all came about. The tour finishes with a recreation of the winter solstice illumination: even with artificial light it's a pretty cool moment.

THE DRIVE: From Brú na Bóinne, you'll pass through farmland and the village of Donore, then the industrial outskirts of Drogheda, an 8km trip in all.

05 Drogheda

If the younger kids can stomach a little more history, the **Millmount Museum**, across the river from the main town of Drogheda, has 9000 years of it to tell. But it does so in an engaging, interactive way: the various collections touch on all aspects of the area's past, from geology to Cromwell's brutal siege of the town.

The cobbled basement is full of gadgets and utensils from bygone times, including a cast-iron pressure cooker and an early model of a sofa bed. A series of craft studios allow you to see the work of craftspeople working in a variety of mediums, from ceramics to silk.

THE DRIVE: Carlingford is 60km north of Drogheda along the M1 and, for the last 19km, the R173. Alternatively, you can take the longer but much more scenic coastal R166, which wends its way through the lovely villages of Termonfeckin and Clogherhead before rejoining the main road at Castlebellingham.

06 Carlingford

Amid the medieval ruins and whitewashed houses, this vibrant little village buzzes with great pubs, chic restaurants and upmarket boutiques, spirited festivals and gorgeous views of the mountains and across Carlingford Lough to Northern Ireland.

Besides the medieval ruins, attractions include an interesting **heritage centre** on the town's history, and the beginning of the 40km **Táin Trail**, which makes a circuit of the Cooley Peninsula through the

Trim Castle (p117), Meath

MONICAMI/SHUTTERSTOCK

PHOTO OPPORTUNITY

The medieval Trim Castle – memorable and impressive.

Cooley Mountains. The route is a mixture of surfaced roads, forest tracks and green paths.

We strongly recommend you check out the **Carlingford Adventure Centre** *(carlingfordadventure.com)*, which runs a wide range of activities, including sailing, kayaking, windsurfing, rock climbing and archery.

If you're here in mid-August, the **Carlingford Oyster Festival** *(carlingford.ie)* celebrates Carlingford's famous oysters with an oyster treasure hunt, fishing competition, music, food markets and a regatta on Carlingford Lough.

DETOUR

Flagstaff Viewpoint

Start: 06 Carlingford

Travelling along the Cooley Peninsula from Carlingford to Newry in Northern Ireland, a quick 3km detour rewards you with sweeping views of Carlingford Lough, framed by rugged, forested mountains, green fields and the glittering blue Irish Sea beyond. Flagstaff Viewpoint lies just over the border in County Armagh. Heading northwest along the coast road (the R173), follow the signs to your left onto Ferryhill Rd, then turn right up to the viewpoint's car park. The quickest way to reach Newry from here is to retrace your steps and rejoin the R173.

View from Flagstaff Viewpoint, Armagh

JASON RUDDY/SHUTTERSTOCK

MNSTUDIO/SHUTTERSTOCK

Newgrange

NEWGRANGE WINTER SOLSTICE

From the Brú na Bóinne Visitor Centre take the bus to Newgrange, where there lies the finest Stone Age passage tomb in Ireland. From here, at 8.20am on the winter solstice (between 18 and 23 December), the rising sun's rays shine through the roof box above the entrance, creep slowly down the long passage and illuminate the tomb chamber for 17 minutes. There is little doubt that this is one of the country's most memorable, even mystical, experiences (access is by lottery). There's a simulated winter sunrise for every group taken into the mound.

Galway
Galway Bay
Shannonbridge
Cloghan
OFFALY
Banagher
Birr
Monasterevin
Mountmellick
Portlaoise
Abbeyleix
Ballyragget
Freshford
Kilkenny
Kells
Callan
Carrick-on-Suir
Waterford
Tramore
Bunmahon
Dungarvan
Ring (An Rinn)
Laurencetown
Killimor
Portumna
Lough Derg
Borrisokane
Roscrea
Templemore
Urlingford
Thurles
Nenagh
TIPPERARY
Fethard
Cashel
Clonmel
Cahir
Bansha
Newtown
Kilbeheny
WATERFORD
Tallowbridge
Youghal
Youghal Bay
Rathcormack
Castletownroche
Fermoy
Midleton
Cloyne
Cobh
Carrigaline
Cork
Kinsale
Timoleague
Clonakilty
Rosscarbery
Bandon
Dunmanway
Drimoleague
Skibbereen
Baltimore
Cape Clear Island
Whitegate
Ballina
Limerick
Gort
CLARE
Bunratty
Shannon
Ennis
Corofin
Carron
New Quay
Inagh
Adare
LIMERICK
Kilmallock
Charleville
Buttevant
Mallow
Kanturk
CORK
Millstreet
Macroom
Newmarket
Rathkeale
Foynes
Labasheeda
Glin
Tarbert
Kilrush
Abbeyfeale
Listowel
Ballybunion
Castleisland
Farranfore
KERRY
Killarney
Killarney National Park
Kenmare
Glengarriff
Bantry
Durrus
Ballydehob
Goleen
Sheep's Head Peninsula
Mizen Head Peninsula
Adrigole
Lauragh
Eyeries
Allihies
Beara Peninsula
Bere Island
Caherdaniel
Sneem
Moll's Gap
Tralee
Tralee Bay
Castlemaine
Killorglin
Glenbeigh
Kells
Cahersiveen
Valentia Island
Waterville
Dingle Peninsula
Dingle
Cloghane
Maharees Islands
Reask
Dunquin
Great Blasket
Banna
Mouth of the Shannon
Kilkee
Carrigaholt
Kilbaha
Doonbeg
Liscannor
Inisheer
Inishmaan
Inishmore
Aran Islands
Kilmurvey
ATLANTIC OCEAN
N52
N62
M8
N24
M7
N18
M18
R473
N68
N69
N21
N20
N72
M8
N22
N25
N71
R585
R572
N70
R563
R487
16
17
18
19
20
21
22
0
50 km

ESSEVU/SHUTTERSTOCK

Gap of Dunloe (p131), Kerry

CORK & SOUTHWEST IRELAND

EXPLORE

CORK & SOUTHWEST IRELAND

The main draw of the southwest is simple: it's where you'll find some of Ireland's most iconic scenery. Three of the country's most famous peninsula drives are top of the list – the Ring of Kerry, the Dingle Peninsula and the Ring of Beara – which contain most of what you came to Ireland to experience.

While the scenery is unmatched, the shoal of charming fishing towns and villages have also helped establish the southwest as a gourmet heartland without parallel in Ireland – and that's before you explore Cork, which is Ireland's second city in size only.

Cork

Ireland's second city is first in every other respect, at least according to the locals, who are only half joking when they refer to it as the 'real capital of Ireland'. There's a good range of accommodation on the main island of the city, to the north in Shandon and around MacCurtain St. The biggest choice of B&Bs, however, is along Western Rd, which runs from the city centre to the large campus of University College Cork (UCC). Food is a big deal here, and the fine selection of restaurants is as good as you'll find anywhere in Ireland. There's a bunch of these in the narrow, pedestrianised streets of the Huguenot Quarter.

Limerick

Straddling the tidal basin of the mighty River Shannon, Limerick city is in the midst of a huge program of urban renovation, which has seen much of the city centre transformed, with the highlight being a rejuvenated waterfront complete with stylish boardwalk. There's plenty to keep you occupied here, including a handful of top-class sights, some fine restaurants

WHEN TO GO

Summer is peak season, with the biggest crowds and the highest accommodation rates. The peninsula drives are at their busiest, especially the Ring of Kerry. Easter to May and late September into October can be beautiful, with fewer visitors, although some accommodation closes earlier for winter. Winter is colder and much quieter. Many accommodations and attractions are closed.

and a decent selection of midrange accommodation. Staying in the centre means you're close to the action, but you'll have to plan for parking; otherwise, there's a number of hotels on the outskirts.

Killarney

You'd think Killarney was built for tourism, such is the abundance of shops, restaurants and accommodation whose sole concern is catering to visitors' needs. The town has some fine hostels and high-end hotels, as well as scores of generic hotels that cater to the stream of tour groups that flood the town in summer. There's a large cluster of B&Bs just outside town on Rock, Lewis and Muckross Rds, as well as a handful of campsites. There's no shortage of places to eat, either – from filling pub grub to high-end dining.

Dingle

Dingle is quaint in a sophisticated way. This colourful fishing port is full of superb pubs and some fabulous restaurants (seafood is obviously a big deal), while its collection of shops selling everything from artisanal homewares to locally roasted coffee is a telltale sign that this is a place with good taste. It's a small town, but there are plenty of hostels and midrange B&Bs, while a handful of pubs also offer accommodation. It's the only town of substance on the whole peninsula, so you're better off getting all your provisions here.

TRANSPORT

Cork and Limerick are on Ireland's motorway network, which links the two cities to Ireland's other major destinations. The N71 is a secondary road that skirts the coast between Cork and Killarney; the N72 cuts a more direct path between the two. There are good public transport links (train and bus) to the major towns, otherwise, driving is the best way to get around.

WHERE TO STAY

In the West Cork village of Rosscarbery, the **Celtic Ross Hotel** is a great option for families.

Just outside Skibbereen, **Liss Ard Estate** is an elegant country house with 26 superb rooms as well as the remarkable Sky Garden landscape artwork.

For a stay in beautiful isolation, you won't find anything nicer than the **Hidden Haven**, a luxury lodge tucked into the side of a remote mountain overlooking a small lake in West Cork.

Killarney's most luxurious accommodation is the **Europe Hotel & Resort**, a magnificent property overlooking the lake. It's a contender for best hotel in Ireland.

RESOURCES

- **Pure Cork**
  Top blog for all things Cork. *purecork.ie*
- **People's Republic of Cork**
  Indie website providing excellent info. *peoplesrepublicofcork.com*
- **Destination Killarney**
  News, info and stories from Killarney. *destinationkillarney.ie*
- **This is Limerick**
  A one-stop shop for all things Limerick. *limerick.ie*

WHAT'S ON

- **Cork Jazz Festival**
  October sees Cork welcome thousands of fans of jazz, blues and folk for a four-day extravaganza of music and drinking.
- **Dingle Food & Wine Festival**
  Held over four days in October, this fabulous foodie fest features a 'taste trail', with sampling at over 70 locations around the town.
- **Listowel Writers' Week**
  Bibliophiles flock to Listowel for five days of book-related fun in late May/early June.

16

CORK & SOUTHWEST IRELAND

RING OF KERRY

★ BEST FOR

WILDLIFE

Killarney National Park, home to Ireland's only wild herd of native red deer.

DURATION: 4 DAYS

DISTANCE: 202KM / 125 MILES

GREAT FOR: HISTORY, OUTDOORS

BEST TIME TO GO: LATE SPRING AND EARLY AUTUMN FOR TEMPERATE WEATHER FREE OF SUMMER CROWDS.

Red deer stags, Killarney National Park (p131)

You can drive the Ring of Kerry in a day, but the longer you spend, the more you'll enjoy it. The circuit winds past pristine beaches, medieval ruins, mountains, loughs (lakes) and the island-dotted Atlantic, with the coastline at its most rugged between Waterville and Caherdaniel in the peninsula's southwest. You'll also find plenty of opportunities for serene, starkly beautiful detours, such as the Skellig Ring and the Cromane Peninsula.

LINK YOUR TRIP

17 Dingle Peninsula
Another of Ireland's iconic peninsula drives, the picturesque Dingle Peninsula, is on Killarney's doorstep.

18 Southwest Blitz
Kick off from Killarney along the Ring of Kerry's coastline and continue into captivating County Cork.

01 Killarney

A town that's been in the business of welcoming visitors for more than 250 years, Killarney is a well-oiled tourism machine fuelled by the sublime scenery of its namesake national park, with competition helping keep standards high. Killarney nights are lively and most pubs put on live music.

Killarney and its surrounds have likely been inhabited since the Neolithic period, but it wasn't until the 17th-century that Viscount Kenmare developed the region as an Irish version of England's Lake District; among its notable 19th-century tourists were Queen Victoria and Romantic poet Percy Bysshe Shelley. The town itself lacks major attractions, but the landscaped grounds of nearby **Killarney House** and **Muckross House** *(muckross-house.ie)* frame photo-worthy panoramas of lake and mountain, while former

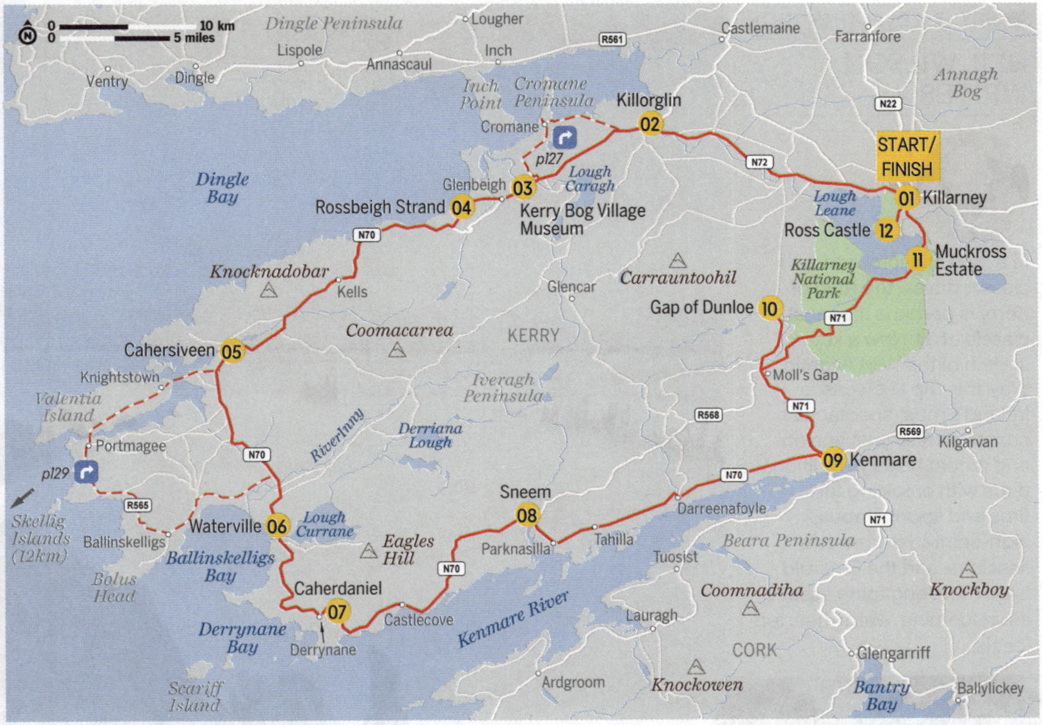

carriage drives around these aristocratic estates now serve as scenic hiking and biking trails open to all.

The town can easily be explored on foot in an hour or two, or you can get around by horse-drawn jaunting car.

THE DRIVE: From Killarney, head 22km west to Killorglin along the N72, with views south to Ireland's highest mountain range, Macgillycuddy's Reeks. The mountains' elegant forms were carved by glaciers, with summits buttressed by ridges of purplish rock. The name derives from the ancient Mac Gilla Muchudas clan; reek means 'pointed hill'. In Irish, they're known as *Na Crucha Dubha* (the Black Tops).

02 Killorglin

Killorglin *(Cill Orglan)* is quieter than the waters of the River Laune that lap against its 1885-built eight-arched bridge – except in mid-August, when there's an explosion of time-honoured ceremonies at the famous **Puck Fair** *(Aonach an Phuic; puckfair.ie)*, a pagan festival first recorded in 1603. A statue of King Puck (a goat) peers out from the Killarney end of the bridge.

Killorglin has some of the finest eateries along the Ring – **Bianconi** *(bianconi.ie)* and **Jack's Bakery** are both good spots for a late breakfast or early lunch.

THE DRIVE: Killorglin sits at the junction of the N72 and the N70; continue 13km along the N70 to the Kerry Bog Village Museum.

DETOUR

Cromane Peninsula

Start: 02 Killorglin

Open fields give way to spectacular water vistas and multi-hued sunsets on the Cromane Peninsula, with its tiny namesake village sitting at the base of a narrow shingle spit.

Cromane's exceptional eating place, **Jack's Coastguard Restaurant**, is a local secret and justifies the trip. Entering this 1866-built coastguard station feels like arriving at a low-key village pub, but a narrow doorway at the back of the bar leads to a striking, whitewashed contemporary space with lights glittering from midnight-blue ceiling panels, stained glass and metallic fish sculptures, and

♥ WHY I LOVE THIS TRIP

NEIL WILSON, WRITER

In a land crisscrossed with classic drives, the Ring of Kerry is perhaps the most classic of all. Now a key stretch of the Wild Atlantic Way, this trip showcases Ireland's most spectacular coastal scenery, its ancient and recent history, traditional pubs with crackling turf fires and spontaneous, high-spirited trad-music sessions, and the Emerald Isle's most engaging asset: its welcoming, warm-hearted locals.

huge picture windows looking out across the water. Seafood is the standout, but there's also steak, roast lamb and a veggie dish of the day.

Cromane is 9km from Killorglin. Heading southwest from Killorglin along the N70, take the second right and continue straight ahead until you get to the crossroads. Turn right; Jack's Coastguard Restaurant is on your left.

03 Kerry Bog Village Museum

Between Killorglin and Glenbeigh, the **Kerry Bog Village Museum** *(kerrybogvillage.ie)* recreates a 19th-century settlement typical of the small communities that carved out a precarious living in the harsh environment of Ireland's ubiquitous peat bogs.

You'll see the thatched homes of the turf cutter, blacksmith, thatcher and labourer, as well as a dairy, and meet rare Kerry Bog ponies.

THE DRIVE: It's less than 1km from the museum to the village of Glenbeigh; turn off here and drive 2km west to unique Rossbeigh Strand.

04 Rossbeigh Strand

This unusual beach is a 3km-long finger of shingle and sand protruding into Dingle Bay, with views of Inch Point and the Dingle Peninsula. On one side, the sea is ruffled by Atlantic winds; on the other, it's sheltered and calm.

THE DRIVE: Rejoin the N70 and continue 25km southwest to Cahersiveen.

Rossbeigh Strand
GREG FELLMANN/SHUTTERSTOCK

05 Cahersiveen

Cahersiveen's population – over 30,000 in 1841 – was decimated by the Great Famine and emigration to the New World. A sleepy outpost remains, overshadowed by the 688m peak of **Knocknadobar**. It looks rather dour compared with the peninsula's other settlements, but the atmospheric remains of 16th-century **Ballycarbery Castle**, 2.4km along the road to White Strand Beach from the town centre, are well worth a visit.

Along the same road are two stone ringforts. The larger, **Cahergall**, dates from the 10th century and has stairways on the inside walls, a clochán (circular stone building shaped like an old-fashioned beehive) and the remains of a house.

The smaller, 9th-century **Leacanabuile** has an entrance to an underground passage. Their inner walls and chambers give a strong sense of what life was like in a ringfort. Leave your car in the parking area next to a stone wall and walk up the footpaths.

THE DRIVE: From Cahersiveen you can continue 17km along the classic Ring of Kerry on the N70 to Waterville, or take the ultrascenic route via Valentia Island and the Skellig Ring, and rejoin the N70 at Waterville.

DETOUR

Valentia Island & the Skellig Ring
Start: 05 Cahersiveen

Crowned by Geokaun Mountain, 11km-long Valentia Island *(Oileán Dairbhre)* makes an ideal driving loop, with some lonely ruins that are worth exploring. Knightstown, the only town, has pubs, food and walks.

The **Skellig Experience** *(skelligexperience.com)* heritage centre, in a distinctive building with turf-covered barrel roofs, has informative exhibits on the offshore Skellig Islands. From mid-March to mid-October, it also runs two-hour cruises around the Skelligs *(no landing; adult/child €60/40, including museum entry)*.

If you're here between April and October, and you're detouring via Valentia Island and the Skellig Ring, a ferry service from Reenard Point, 5km southwest of Cahersiveen, provides a handy shortcut to Valentia Island. The five-minute crossing departs every 10 minutes. Alternatively, there's a bridge between **Portmagee** and the far end of the island.

Immediately across the bridge on the mainland, Portmagee's single street is a rainbow of colourful houses. On summer mornings the small pier comes to life with boats embarking on the choppy crossing to the Skellig Islands.

Portmagee holds **set-dancing workshops** over the May bank holiday weekend, with plenty of stomping practice sessions in the town's **Bridge Bar** *(moorings.ie/restaurant-and-bar)*, a friendly local gathering point that's also good for impromptu music year-round and more formal sessions in summer.

The wild and beautiful, 18km-long Skellig Ring road links Portmagee and Waterville via a Gaeltacht (Irish-speaking) area centred on Ballinskelligs *(Baile an Sceilg)*, with the ragged outline of Skellig Michael never far from view.

06 Waterville

A line of colourful houses on the N70 between Lough Currane and Ballinskelligs Bay, Waterville is charm-challenged in the way of many mass-consumption beach resorts. A statue of its most famous guest, Charlie Chaplin, beams from the seafront. The **Charlie Chaplin Comedy Film Festival** *(chaplinfilmfestival.com)* is held in August.

Waterville is home to world-renowned **Waterville Golf Links** *(watervillegolflinks.ie)*. At the north end of Lough Currane, Church Island has the ruins of a medieval church and beehive cell reputedly founded as a monastic settlement by St Finian in the 6th century.

THE DRIVE: Squiggle your way for 14km along the Ring's most tortuous stretch, past plunging cliffs, craggy hills and stunning views, to Caherdaniel.

> PHOTO OPPORTUNITY
>
> Ross Castle as you row a boat to Inisfallen.

07 Caherdaniel

The scattered hamlet of Caherdaniel counts two of the Ring of Kerry's highlights: **Derrynane National Historic Park**, the childhood home of the 19th-century hero of Catholic emancipation, Daniel O'Connell; and what is plausibly claimed as 'Ireland's finest view' over rugged cliffs and islands, as you crest the hill at **Beenarourke** (there's a large car park here).

Most activity here centres on the Blue Flag beach. **Derrynane Sea Sports** *(derrynaneseasports.com)* organises sailing, canoeing, surfing, windsurfing and waterskiing *(from €40 per person)*, as well as equipment hire *(around €20 per hour)*. **Eagle Rock Equestrian Centre** *(facebook.com/eaglerockequestrian)* offers beach, mountain and woodland horse treks for all levels.

THE DRIVE: Wind your way east along the N70 for 21km to Sneem.

08 Sneem

Sneem's Irish name, *An tSnaidhm*, translates as 'the knot', which is thought to refer to the River Sneem that twists and turns, knot-like, into nearby Kenmare Bay.

Take a gander at the town's two cute squares, then pop into the

Sneem

I WEI HUANG/SHUTTERSTOCK

Blue Bull, a perfect little old stone pub, for a pint.

THE DRIVE: Along the 27km drive to Kenmare, the N70 drifts away from the water to take in views towards the Kerry mountains.

09 Kenmare

The copper-covered limestone spire of **Holy Cross Church**, drawing the eye to the wooded hills above town, may make you forget for a split second that Kenmare is a seaside town. With rivers named Finnihy, Roughty and Sheen emptying into Kenmare Bay, you couldn't be anywhere other than southwest Ireland.

In the 18th-century Kenmare was laid out on an X-shaped plan, with a triangular market square in the centre. Today the inverted V to the south is the focus. Kenmare River (actually an inlet of the sea) stretches out to the southwest, and there are glorious mountain views.

Signposted southwest of the square is an early Bronze Age **stone circle**, one of the biggest in southwest Ireland. Fifteen stones ring a boulder dolmen, a burial monument rarely found outside this part of the country.

THE DRIVE: The coastal scenery might be finished but, if anything, the next 23km are even more stunning as you head north from Kenmare to the Gap of Dunloe on the narrow, vista-crazy N71, winding between crag and lake, with plenty of lay-bys to stop and admire the views (and recover from the switchback bends).

10 Gap of Dunloe

Just west of Killarney National Park, the Gap of Dunloe is ruggedly beautiful. In the winter

PATRYK KOSMIDER/SHUTTERSTOCK

Killarney National Park

KILLARNEY NATIONAL PARK

Designated a UNESCO Biosphere Reserve in 1982, **Killarney National Park** *(killarneynationalpark.ie)* is among the finest of Ireland's national parks. And while its proximity to one of the southwest's largest and liveliest urban centres (including pedestrian entrances right in Killarney's town centre) encourages high visitor numbers, it's an important conservation area for many rare species. Within its 102sq km is Ireland's only wild herd of native red deer, which has lived here continuously for 12,000 years, as well as the country's largest area of ancient oak woods and views of most of its major mountains.

Glacier-gouged Lough Leane (the Lower Lake or 'Lake of Learning'), Muckross Lake and the Upper Lake make up about a quarter of the park. Their crystal waters are as rich in wildlife as the surrounding land: great crested grebes and tufted ducks cruise the lake margins, deer swim out to graze on islands, and salmon, trout and perch prosper in a pike-free environment.

With a bit of luck, you might see white-tailed sea eagles, with their 2.5m wingspan, soaring overhead. The eagles were reintroduced here in 2007 after an absence of more than 100 years. There are now more than 50 in the park and they're starting to settle in Ireland's rivers, lakes and coastal regions. And like Killarney itself, the park is also home to plenty of summer visitors, including migratory cuckoos, swallows and swifts.

Keep your eyes peeled, too, for the park's smallest residents – its insects, including the northern emerald dragonfly, which isn't normally found this far south in Europe and is believed to have been marooned here after the last Ice Age.

it's an awe-inspiring mountain pass, squeezed between Purple Mountain and Macgillycuddy's Reeks. In high summer it's a magnet for the tourist trade, with buses ferrying countless visitors here for horse-and-trap rides through the Gap.

On the southern side, surrounded by lush, green pastures, is **Lord Brandon's Cottage**, accessed by turning left at Moll's Gap on the R568, then taking the first right, another right at the bottom of the hill, then right again at the crossroads (about 13km from the N71 all up). A simple 19th-century hunting lodge, it has an open-air cafe and a dock for boats from Ross Castle near Killarney. From here a (very) narrow road weaves up the hill to the Gap – theoretically you can drive this 8km route to the 19th-century pub **Kate Kearney's Cottage** and back but only outside summer. Even then walkers and cyclists have right of way and the precipitous hairpin bends are nerve-testing. It's worth walking or taking a jaunting car (or, if you're carrying two wheels, cycling) through the Gap: the scenery is a fantasy of rocky bridges over clear mountain streams and lakes. Alternatively, there are various options for exploring the Gap from Killarney.

THE DRIVE: Continue on the N71 north through Killarney National Park to Muckross Estate (32km).

11 Muckross Estate

The core of Killarney National Park is Muckross Estate, donated to the state by Arthur Bourn Vincent in 1932. **Muckross House** *(muckross-house.ie)* is a 19th-century mansion, restored to its former glory and packed with period fittings. Entrance is by guided tour.

The beautiful **gardens** slope down, and a building behind the house contains a restaurant, craft shop and studios where you can see potters, weavers and bookbinders at work. Jaunting cars wait to run you through deer parks and woodland to **Torc Waterfall** and **Muckross Abbey** *(about €20 each, return; haggling can reap discounts)*. The visitor centre has an excellent cafe.

Adjacent to Muckross House are the **Muckross Traditional Farms**. These reproductions of 1930s Kerry farms, complete with chickens, pigs, cattle and horses, recreate farming and living conditions when people had to live off the land.

THE DRIVE: Continuing a further 2km north through the national park brings you to historic Ross Castle.

12 Ross Castle

Restored **Ross Castle** *(heritageireland.ie)* dates back to the 15th-century, when it was a residence of the O'Donoghues. It was the last place in Munster to succumb to Cromwell's forces, thanks partly to its cunning spiral staircase, every step of which is a different height in order to break an attacker's stride. Access is by guided tour only.

You can take a motorboat trip *(around €15 per person)* from Ross Castle to **Inisfallen**, the largest of Killarney National Park's 26 islands. The first monastery on Inisfallen is said to have been founded by St Finian the Leper in the 7th century. The island's fame dates from the early 13th century when the *Annals of Inisfallen* were written here. Now in the Bodleian Library at Oxford, they remain a vital source of information on early Munster history.

Inisfallen shelters the ruins of a 12th-century oratory with a carved Romanesque doorway and a monastery on the site of St Finian's original.

THE DRIVE: It's just 3km north from Ross Castle back to Killarney.

Ross Castle

KEVIN M BROWN/SHUTTERSTOCK

TOP TIP

AROUND (AND ACROSS) THE RING

Tour buses travel anticlockwise around the Ring, and authorities generally encourage visitors to drive in the same direction to avoid traffic congestion and accidents. If you travel clockwise, watch out on blind corners, especially on the section between Moll's Gap and Killarney. There's little traffic on the Ballaghbeama Gap, which cuts across the peninsula's central highlands, with some spectacular views.

17

CORK & SOUTHWEST IRELAND

DINGLE PENINSULA

★ BEST FOR

HISTORY

Slea Head's astonishing concentration of ancient sites.

DURATION: 3–4 DAYS

DISTANCE: 185KM / 115 MILES

GREAT FOR: FOOD & DRINK, HISTORY, OUTDOORS

BEST TIME TO GO: JUNE TO AUGUST OFFER THE BEST BEACH WEATHER.

Ogham stone, Slea Head (p136)

As you twist and turn along this figure-of-eight drive, the coastline is the star of the show. The opal-blue waters surrounding the Dingle Peninsula provide a wealth of aquatic adventures and superbly fresh seafood, and you'll find that where the promontory meets the ocean – at wave-pounded rocks, secluded coves and wide, golden-sand beaches – Dingle's beauty is at its most unforgettable.

LINK YOUR TRIP

00 Ring of Kerry
From Tralee it's a quick 22km zip along the N22 to pick up Ireland's most famous driving loop in Killarney.

00 Southwest Blitz
Killarney is also the jumping-off point for another classic Irish road trip along the Ring of Kerry and a stunning swathe of County Cork.

01 Killarney

The lively tourist town of Killarney is an ideal place to kick off your trip, with a plethora of places to eat, drink and sleep. If you have time, the 102-sq-km **Killarney National Park** *(killarneynationalpark.ie)* immediately to its south, and the **Gap of Dunloe**, with its rocky terrain, babbling brooks and alpine lakes, are well worth exploring. On a tight schedule, however, you can still get a good overview of the area – and entertaining commentary, too – aboard a horse-drawn jaunting car, also known as a trap, which comes with a driver called a jarvey. The pick-up point, nicknamed 'the Ha Ha' or 'the Block', is on Kenmare Pl. Trips cost €40 to €80, depending on distance; traps officially carry up to four people.

THE DRIVE: The quickest route from Killarney to the peninsula is via the R563 to Milltown and

CYNTHIA SHIRK/SHUTTERSTOCK

Castlemaine. Turn west here onto the R561; you'll soon meet the coast before coming to the vast beach at Inch (41km).

02 Inch

Inch's 5km-long sand spit was a location for the movies *Ryan's Daughter* and *Playboy of the Western World*. Sarah Miles, a star of the former film, described her stay here as 'brief but bonny'.

The dunes are certainly bonny, a great spot for windswept walks, birdwatching and bathing. The west-facing Blue Flag beach (lifeguarded in summer) is also a hot surfing spot; waves average 1m to 3m. You can learn to ride them with **Offshore Surf School** *(facebook.com/OffshoreSurf School/)*.

Cars are allowed on the beach, but don't end up providing others with laughs by getting stuck.

Sammy's *(facebook.com/sammysinchbeach)*, at the entrance to the beach, is the nerve centre of the village. In addition to its beach-facing bar and restaurant, there's a shop, tourist information and trad music sessions during the summer.

THE DRIVE: Shadowing the coast, about 7km west of Inch, Annascaul (*Abhainn an Scáil*; also spelled Anascaul) is home to a cracking pub, the South Pole Inn, formerly run by Antarctic explorer Tom Crean in his retirement and now something of a Crean museum. Continuing 18km west of Annascaul brings you into Dingle town.

03 Dingle Town

Fanned around its fishing port, the peninsula's charming little capital is quaint without even trying. Dingle is one of Ireland's largest Gaeltacht towns (although locals have voted to retain the name Dingle, rather than go with the officially sanctioned Gaelic version *'An Daingean'*) and has long drawn runaways from across the world, making it a surprisingly cosmopolitan, creative place.

This is one of those towns whose very fabric is its attraction. Wander the higgledy-piggledy streets, shop for handcrafted jewellery, arts, crafts and artisan food and pop into old-school pubs. Two untouched examples are **Foxy John's** and **Curran's**, which, respectively, have old stock of hardware and outdoor clothing on display.

Boats leave Dingle's pier daily for one-hour **dolphin-spotting trips** *(dingledolphin.com)*. On land, the **Dingle Oceanworld** *(dingle-ocean world.ie)* aquarium has a fun walk-through tunnel.

Don't leave Dingle without catching traditional live music at pubs such as the **An Droichead Beag** (Small Bridge Bar; *androichead beag.com*), where sessions kick off at 9.30pm nightly, and standout seafood at its restaurant.

THE DRIVE: West of Dingle, along the R559, the signposted Slea Head Drive runs around the tip of the Dingle Peninsula. Driving clockwise offers the best views and although it's a mere 47km in length, doing this stretch justice requires a full day, at least.

04 Slea Head

Overlooking the mouth of Dingle Bay, Mt Eagle and Ireland's most westerly islands, the Blaskets, Slea Head has fine beaches and superbly preserved structures from Dingle's ancient past, including beehive huts, forts, inscribed stones and monastic sites.

The nearby village of **Ventry** *(Ceann Trá)*, 6km west of Dingle town, is idyllically set next to a wide sandy bay. Full-day boat trips to the Blasket Islands with **Blasket Island Eco Marine Tours** *(marinetours.ie)* depart from Ventry Harbour, with three hours ashore on Great Blasket; shorter trips are available. The **Celtic & Prehistoric Museum**, 4km southwest of the village, squeezes in an incredible collection of Celtic and prehistoric artefacts.

About 4.5km further west, the **Fahan beehive huts** sit on the on the inland side of the road. Fahan once had some 48 drystone *clochán* beehive huts dating from 500 CE, although the exact dates are unknown. Today five structures remain, including two that are fully intact. The huts are on the slope of Mt Eagle (516m), which still has an estimated 400-plus huts in various states of preservation.

THE DRIVE: Continuing north from Slea Head for just over 2km brings you to Dunmore Head, the westernmost point on the Irish mainland and the site of tiny but pretty Coumeenoole beach. From here it's around 3km to Dunquin.

05 Dunquin

Yet another pause on a road of scenic pauses, Dunquin is a scattered village beneath Mt Eagle and Croaghmarhin.

The Blasket Islands (now uninhabited) are visible offshore. Dunquin's **Blasket Centre** *(Ionad an Bhlascaoid Mhóir; blasket.ie)* is a wonderful interpretive centre with a floor-to-ceiling window overlooking the islands. Great Blasket Island's past community of storytellers and musicians is profiled, along with its literary visitors, such as John Millington Synge, writer of *Playboy of the Western World*. The practicalities of island life are covered by exhibits on shipbuilding and fishing. There's a cafe with Blasket views and a bookshop.

THE DRIVE: North from Dunquin is Clogher Head; a short walk takes you out to the head, with stunning views to Sybil Head and the Three Sisters. Follow the road another 500m around to the crossroads, where a narrow paved track leads to Clogher beach. Back on the loop road, head inland towards Ballyferriter (about 9km in all).

DETOUR

Dún an Óir Fort

Start: 05 Dunquin

En route between Dunquin and Ballyferriter, turn north 1km east of Clogher, from where narrow roads run to the east of the Dingle Golf Links course to Dún an Óir Fort (Fort of Gold), the scene of a hideous massacre during the 1580 Irish rebellion against English rule. All that remains is a network of grassy ridges, but it's a pretty spot overlooking sheltered Smerwick Harbour.

The fort is about 6km from Clogher. Return on the same road to just south of the golf course and turn east to rejoin the R559 and continue to Ballyferriter.

06 Ballyferriter

Housed in the 19th-century schoolhouse in the village of Ballyferriter *(Baile an Fheirtearaigh)*, the **Dingle Peninsula Museum** *(Músaem Chorca Dhuibhne; west kerrymuseum.com)* has displays on the peninsula's archaeology and ecology. Across the street there's a lonely, lichen-covered church.

The remains of the 5th- or 6th-century **Riasc Monastic Settlement** are an impressive, haunting sight, particularly the pillar with beautiful Celtic designs. Excavations have also revealed the foundations of an oratory first built with wood and later stone, a kiln for drying corn and a cemetery. The ruins are signposted as 'Mainistir Riaisc' along a narrow lane off the R559, about 2km east of Ballyferriter.

Connor Pass

JAN MIKO/SHUTTERSTOCK

CONNOR PASS

At 456m, Connor (or Conor) Pass is Ireland's highest motor road. On a foggy day you'll see nothing but the road just in front of you, but in fine weather it offers phenomenal views of Dingle Harbour to the south and Mt Brandon to the north. The road is in good shape, despite being very narrow and very steep on the north side (large signs portend doom for buses and trucks).

The car park at the pass yields views down to a scatter of lakes in the rock-strewn valley below, plus the remains of walls and huts where people once lived impossibly hard lives. When visibility is good, the 10-minute climb west to the summit of An Bhinn Dubh (478m) is well worthwhile for the kind of vistas that inspire mountain climbers.

THE DRIVE: The landscape around Ballyferriter is a rocky patchwork of varying shades of green, stitched by kilometres of ancient stone walls. Wind your way along the R559 some 2km east of the Riasc Monastic Settlement turn-off to reach an amazing dry-stone oratory.

07 Gallarus Oratory

The dry-stone **Gallarus Oratory** *(heritageireland.ie)* is quite a sight, standing in its lonely spot beneath the brown hills as it has done for some 1200 years. It has withstood the elements perfectly, apart from a slight sagging in the roof. Traces of mortar suggest that the interior and exterior walls may have been plastered. Shaped like an upturned boat, it has a doorway on the western side and a round-headed window on the east. Inside the doorway are two projecting stones with holes that once supported the door.

THE DRIVE: Pass back through Dingle town before cutting across the scenic Connor Pass to reach the northern side of the peninsula. About 6km before you reach Kilcummin, a narrow road leads north to the quiet villages of Cloghane (23km) and Brandon, and finally to Brandon Point overlooking Brandon Bay.

08 Cloghane

Cloghane *(An Clochán)* is another little piece of peninsula beauty. The village's friendly pubs nestle between **Mt Brandon** and Brandon Bay, with views across the water to the Stradbally Mountains. For many, the main goal is scaling 951m-high Mt Brandon *(Cnoc Bhréannain)*, Ireland's eighth-highest peak. If that sounds too energetic, there are plenty of coastal strolls.

> PHOTO OPPORTUNITY
>
> Snap a perfect panorama from Clogher Head viewpoint.

The 5km drive from Cloghane out to **Brandon Point** follows ever-narrower single-track roads wandered by sheep, culminating in cliffs with fantastic views south and east.

On the last weekend in July, Cloghane celebrates the ancient Celtic harvest festival **Lughnasa** with events – especially bonfires – both in the village and atop Mt Brandon. The **Brandon Regatta**, a traditional *currach* (rowing boat race), takes place in late August.

THE DRIVE: Retrace your route to Cloghane, head east to Kilcummin (7km) and continue a further 7km east to Castlegregory, the Dingle Peninsula's water-sports playground.

09 Castlegregory

A highlight of the quiet village of Castlegregory *(Caislean an Ghriare)* is the vista to the rugged hills to the south (a lowlight is the sprawl of philistine holiday homes).

However, things change when you drive up the sand-strewn road along the **Rough Point Peninsula**, the broad spit of land between Tralee Bay and Brandon Bay. Great underwater visibility makes this one of Ireland's best diving areas, where you can glimpse pilot whales, orcas, sunfish and dolphins. Professional dive shop **Waterworld** *(waterworld.ie)* is based at Harbour House in Fahamore. **Jamie Knox Watersports** *(jamieknox.com)* offers surf, windsurf, kitesurf, canoe and pedalo hire and lessons.

THE DRIVE: Continue east on the R560 for 4km then turn right and follow signs to one of the Dingle Peninsula's least-known gems, the Glanteenassig Forest Recreation Area.

10 Glanteenassig Forest Recreation Area

Encompassing 450 hectares of forest, mountains, lakes and bog, **Glanteenassig Forest Recreation Area** *(coillte.ie/site/glan teenassig)* is a magical, little-visited treasure. There are two lakes; you can drive right up to the higher lake, which is encircled by a plank boardwalk, though it's too narrow for wheelchairs or prams.

THE DRIVE: From Glanteenassig Forest Recreation Area, return to the main road and head east through the village of Aughacasla – home to the wonderful Seven Hogs inn – on the coast road (R560), which links up with the N86 to Blennerville (27km in total).

11 Blennerville

Blennerville, just over 1km southwest of Tralee on the N86, used to be the city's chief port, though the harbour has long since silted up. A 19th-century **windmill** *(blennerville-windmill.ie)* here has been restored and is the largest working flour mill in Ireland and Britain. Its modern visitor centre houses an exhibition on grain milling and on the thousands of emigrants who boarded 'coffin ships' from what was then Kerry's largest embarkation point.

ROBERT HARDING VIDEO/SHUTTERSTOCK

Gallarus Oratory

Admission includes a 30-minute guided windmill tour.

THE DRIVE: Staying on the N86 brings you into the heart of Tralee.

12 Tralee

Although Tralee is Kerry's county town, it's more engaged with the business of everyday life than the tourist trade. Elegant Denny St and Day Pl are the oldest parts of town, with 18th-century buildings, while the Square, just south of the Mall, is a pleasant, open contemporary space hosting **farmers markets** (liveliest on Saturday).

A 15-minute nature-safari boat ride is the highlight of a visit to Tralee's **wetlands centre** *(traleebaywetlands.org)*. You can also get a good overview of **Tralee Bay Nature Reserve's** 3000 hectares, encompassing saltwater and freshwater habitats, from the 20m-high viewing tower (accessible by lift/elevator), and spot wildlife from bird hides.

In Ireland and beyond, Tralee is synonymous with the **Rose of Tralee** *(roseoftralee.ie)* pageant, open to Irish women and women of Irish descent from around the world (the 'roses'). It takes place amid five days of celebrations in August.

An absolute treat is the **Kerry County Museum** *(kerrymuseum.ie)*, with excellent interpretive displays on Irish historical events and trends. The Medieval Experience recreates life (smells and all) in Tralee in 1450.

Ingeniously converted from a terrace house, **Roundy's** is Tralee's hippest little bar, spinning old-school funk, while **Baily's Corner** is deservedly popular for its traditional sessions.

STAY AWHILE

DINGLE

BY FIONN DAVENPORT

In December 2006, a 23-year-old Amy Winehouse delivered a mesmeric 20-minute set at St James' Church in Dingle for the Other Voices music series. The performance (look it up) went viral, and with it, Dingle's reputation as one of Ireland's most enticing towns. Framed by its fishing harbour and long a refuge for creative souls from around the world, it manages to feel both traditional – where some pubs double as shops and fishing boats still crowd the quay – and effortlessly cosmopolitan.

Dingle is one of those places where the town itself is the attraction. You can browse books at **Dingle Bookshop**, textiles from **Kerry Woollen Mills** *(kerrywoollenmills.ie)*, or watch master cutter Sean Daly at work in **Dingle Crystal** *(dinglecrystal.ie)*. **Brian de Staic's** *(briandestaic.com)* jewellery is internationally renowned, while **Dingle Surf Shop** *(dinglesurf.com)* equips those heading into the Atlantic. Between stops, the soundtrack is live traditional music drifting from classic pubs such as **Foxy John's**, **Dick Mack's**, **Curran's** and **John Benny's**, each with its own loyal following.

The food scene more than keeps pace. **Out of the Blue** *(outoftheblue.ie)* is arguably the best spot in town for superb seafood, while **Fish Box** *(thefishboxdingle.com)* serves the best fish and chips I've tasted. **Solas Tapas & Wine** *(solastapas.com)* brings a touch of Iberia to the west Kerry coast.

LINK YOUR TRIP

The Slea Head drive **(17 Dingle Peninsula)** begins just beyond the town, a compact loop filled with ancient sites and unforgettable coastal scenery.

MIN JING/SHUTTERSTOCK

LIV GAUNT/SHUTTERSTOCK

Left: Out of the Blue;
Right: John Benny's pub

PLACES TO STAY

Dingle has plenty of accommodation options, including some wonderful budget choices.

- **The Grapevine Hostel**
  Friendly hostel with a handy town-centre location, making it an ideal base for exploring Dingle.
  grapevinedingle.com

- **Rainbow Hostel & Camping**
  Set in spacious gardens 1.5km northwest of town, this relaxed hostel also offers camping and is the closest place to pitch a tent near Dingle.
  rainbowhosteldingle.com

- **Dingle Harbour Lodge**
  Overlooking the water, this comfortable guesthouse offers bright rooms, with upper-level options enjoying the best views and less street noise.
  dingleharbourlodge.com

- **Castlewood House**
  A short stroll from town, this elegant guesthouse is set in beautiful gardens.
  castlewooddingle.com

18

CORK & SOUTHWEST IRELAND

SOUTHWEST BLITZ

★ BEST FOR

FAMILIES

Ride the train or stroll around animal-filled Fota Wildlife Park.

DURATION: 4 DAYS

DISTANCE: 369KM / 229 MILES

GREAT FOR: FOOD & DRINK, HISTORY, OUTDOORS

BEST TIME TO GO: LATE SPRING AND EARLY AUTUMN FOR THE BEST WEATHER AND MANAGEABLE CROWDS.

Oryx, Fota Wildlife Park (p147), Cork

This drive around the country's stunning southwest conjures up iconic impressions of Ireland: soaring stone castles, dizzying sea cliffs, wide, sandy beaches, crystal-clear lakes, dense woodlands and boat-filled harbours. Villages you'll encounter en route spill over with brightly painted buildings, vibrant markets and cosy pubs with toe-tapping live music, perfectly poured pints and fantastic craic.

LINK YOUR TRIP

14 Blackwater Valley Drive
Youghal is the starting point for a glorious drive through the Blackwater Valley.

20 West Cork Villages
From Cork city, it's a quick 27km trip south to Kinsale to wind your way around West Cork's picturesque peninsulas.

01 Killarney

Killarney's biggest attraction, in every sense, is **Killarney National Park** *(killarneynationalpark.ie)*, with magnificent Muckross Estate at its heart. If you're not doing the classic Ring of Kerry route that brings you through the park, you should definitely consider a detour here. Right in town, there are pedestrian entrances to the park opposite **St Mary's Cathedral** *(killarneyparish.com)*, a superb example of neogothic architecture, built between 1842 and 1855.

Also worth a visit in the town centre is the 1860s **Franciscan Friary** *(franciscans.ie)*, with an ornate Flemish-style altarpiece, some impressive tilework and, most notably, stained-glass windows by Harry Clarke. The Dublin artist's organic style was influenced by art nouveau, art deco and symbolism.

Plunkett and College Sts are lined with pubs; on High St,

JACK BRZEZINSKI/SHUTTERSTOCK

behind leaded-glass doors, tiny traditional O'Connor's *(facebook.com/oconnorskillarney)* is one of Killarney's most popular haunts, with live music every night.

THE DRIVE: It's 22km west to Killorglin on the N72. To visit the too-gorgeous-for-words Gap of Dunloe, after 5km turn south onto Gap Rd and follow it for 3km to Kate Kearney's Cottage, where many drivers park in order to walk up to the Gap. You can also hire ponies and jaunting cars here (bring cash).

02 Killorglin

Unless you're here during mid-August's ancient Puck Fair, the main reason to pause at the pretty riverside town of Killorglin *(Cill Orglan)* is its excellent selection of eateries. These become rather more scarce on the Ring of Kerry coast road until you get to Kenmare, so consider picking up picnic fare here, too.

At smokery **KRD Fisheries** *(krdfisheries.com)* you can buy salmon direct from the premises. Nearby, Jack Healy bakes amazing breads and also makes pâté and beautiful sandwiches at **Jack's Bakery**.

THE DRIVE: It's 40km from Killorglin to Cahersiveen. En route, you'll pass the turn-off to the little-known Cromane Peninsula, with a truly exceptional restaurant, as well as the quaint and insightful Kerry Bog Village Museum and the turn-off to Rossbeigh Strand, with dazzling views north to the Dingle Peninsula.

03 Cahersiveen

The ruined **cottage** on the eastern bank of the Carhan River, on the left as you cross the bridge to Cahersiveen, is the humble birthplace of Daniel O'Connell (1775–1847). On the opposite bank there's a stolid bust of the man. Known as 'the Great Liberator', O'Connell was elected to the British Parliament in 1828, but as a Catholic he couldn't take his seat. The government was forced to pass the 1829 Act of Catholic Emancipation, allowing some well-off Catholics voting rights and the right to be elected as MPs. Learn more about it at the **Old Barracks Heritage Centre**

(theoldbarracks.net), housed in a tower of the former Royal Irish Constabulary (RIC). The barracks were burnt down in 1922 by anti-Treaty forces.

Ballycarbery Castle and ringforts are located here; Cahersiveen is also a jumping-off point for exploring Valentia Island and the Skellig Ring.

THE DRIVE: Continue from Cahersiveen for 17km along the N70 to Waterville. From Waterville the rugged, rocky coastline is at its most dramatic as the road twists, turns and twists again along the 12km stretch to Caherdaniel. At Beenarourke, the highest point of the road, you can stop to enjoy what is plausibly claimed to be 'Ireland's finest view', looking across the rocky coastline and scattered islands to Kenmare River, Bantry Bay and the rugged hills of the Beara Peninsula.

04 Caherdaniel

Hiding between Derrynane Bay and the foothills of Eagles Hill, Caherdaniel barely qualifies as a tiny hamlet. Businesses are scattered about the undergrowth like smugglers, which is fitting since this was once a haven for the same.

There's a Blue Flag beach, plenty of activities, good hikes and pubs where you may be tempted to break into pirate talk.

Sublime **Derrynane National Historic Park** *(derrynanehouse.ie)* incorporates Derrynane House, the ancestral home of Daniel O'Connell, whose family made money smuggling from their base by the dunes. Its gardens are astonishing, warmed by the Gulf Stream, with palms, 4m-high tree ferns, gunnera ('giant rhubarb') and other South American species. A walking track through the gardens leads to wetlands, beaches and cliff tops.

THE DRIVE: The N70 zigzags for 21km northeast to the quaint, colourful little village of Sneem. This area is home to one of the finest castle hotels in the country, the Parknasilla Resort and Spa. It's a further 27km drive along the N70 to Kenmare.

05 Kenmare

Set around its triangular market square, the sophisticated town of Kenmare is stunningly situated by Kenmare Bay.

Reached through the tourist office, the **Kenmare Heritage Centre** tells the history of the town from its founding as Neidín by the swashbuckling Sir William Petty in 1670. The centre also relates the story of the **Poor Clare Convent**, founded in 1861, which is still standing behind Holy Cross Church.

Local women were taught needlepoint lacemaking at the convent and their lacework catapulted Kenmare to international fame. Upstairs from the Heritage Centre, the **Kenmare Lace and Design Centre** has displays, including designs for 'the most important piece of lace ever made in Ireland' (in a 19th-century critic's opinion).

Star Outdoors *(staroutdoors.ie)* offers activities such as dinghy sailing *(from €65 per hour for up to six people; you'll need some prior experience)*, sea kayaking *(single/double per hour €22/38)* and hill walking for all levels.

Warm yourself with tea, coffee, rum and the captain's sea shanties on an entertaining two-hour voyage with **Seafari** *(seafariireland.com)* to spot Ireland's biggest seal colony and other marine life. Binoculars (and lollipops!) are provided.

THE DRIVE: Leave the Ring of Kerry at Kenmare and take the steep and winding N71 south for 44km to Bantry. For an even more scenic alternative, consider driving via the Ring of Beara, encircling the Beara Peninsula. If you don't have time to do the entire Ring, a shorter option is to cut across the Beara's spectacular Healy Pass Rd (R574).

06 Bantry

Framed by the craggy Caha Mountains, sweeping Bantry Bay is an idyllic inlet famed for its oysters and mussels. One kilometre southwest of the centre of bustling market town Bantry is **Bantry House** *(bantryhouse.com)*, the former home of Richard White, who earned his place in history when in 1798 he warned authorities of the imminent landing of patriot Wolfe Tone and his French fleet to join the countrywide rebellion of the United Irishmen. Storms prevented the fleet from landing, altering the course of Irish history. The house's **gardens** and the panoramic 'stairway to the sky' are its great glory, and it hosts the week-long **West Cork Chamber Music Festival** *(westcorkmusic.ie)* in June/July, when it closes to the public (the garden, craft shop and tearoom remain open).

THE DRIVE: Head north on the N71 to Bally-lickey and take the R584 and R585 to Crookstown, then the N22 through rugged terrain softening to patchwork farmland along the 86km journey to Cork city.

Caherdaniel, Kerry
DAVID YAWALKAR/SHUTTERSTOCK

DETOUR

Gougane Barra Forest Park
Start: 06 Bantry

Almost alpine in feel, **Gougane Barra** *(gouganebarra.com)* is a truly magical part of inland County Cork, with spectacular vistas of craggy mountains, silver streams and pine forests sweeping down to a mountain lake that is the source of the River Lee.

St Finbarre, the founder of Cork, established a monastery here in the 6th-century. He had a hermitage on the island in Gougane Barra Lake *(Lough an Ghugain)*, which is now approached by a short causeway. The small chapel on the island has fine stained-glass representations of obscure Celtic saints. A loop road runs through the park, with plenty of opportunities to walk the well-marked network of paths and nature trails through the forest.

The only place to air your hiking boots is the **Gougane Barra Hotel** *(gouganebarrahotel.com)*. There's an on-site restaurant, a cafe and a pub next door.

To reach the forest park, turn off the N71 onto the R584 about 6km north of Bantry and follow it northeast for 23km. Retrace your route to the N71 to continue back to Bantry and on to Cork city.

PHOTO OPPORTUNITY

The view from Beenarourke across rocky coastline and scattered islands.

07 Cork City

Ireland's second city is first in every important respect, at least according to the locals, who cheerfully refer to it as the 'real capital of Ireland'.

A flurry of urban renewal has resulted in new buildings, bars and arts centres and tidied-up thoroughfares. The best of the city is still happily traditional, though – snug pubs with regular live-music sessions, excellent local produce in an ever-expanding list of restaurants and a genuinely proud welcome from the locals.

Cork swings during **Guinness Cork Jazz** *(facebook.com/corkjazzfestival)*, with an all-star line-up in venues across town in late October.

Street musicians, Guinness Cork Jazz, Cork City

CABUSCAA/SHUTTERSTOCK

An eclectic week-long program of films from around the world screens in October/November during the **Cork Film Festival** *(corkfilmfest.org)*.

About 2km west of the city centre, faint-hearted souls may find the imposing former prison, **Cork City Gaol** *(corkcitygaol.com)*, grim but it's actually very moving, bringing home the harshness of the 19th-century penal system. An audio tour guides you around the restored cells, with models of suffering prisoners and sadistic-looking guards. The most common crime was simply poverty, with many of the inmates sentenced to hard labour for stealing loaves of bread. The prison closed in 1923, reopening in 1927 as a radio station.

THE DRIVE: Head east of central Cork via the N8 and N25, and take the turn-off to Cobh to cross the bridge to Fota Island and reach Fota Wildlife Park (18km).

DETOUR

Blarney Castle
Start: 07 Cork City

If you need proof of the power of a good yarn, join the queue to get into the 15th-century **Blarney Castle** *(blarneycastle.ie)*, one of Ireland's most inexplicably popular tourist attractions.

Queen Elizabeth I is said to have invented the term 'to talk blarney' out of exasperation with Lord Blarney's ability to talk endlessly without ever actually agreeing to her demands.

The clichéd **Blarney Stone** is perched at the top of a steep climb up a slippery spiral staircase. On the battlements, you bend backwards over a long, long drop (with safety grill and attendant to prevent tragedy) to kiss the stone (an act which is said to confer on you the gift of eloquence). Once you're upright, don't forget to admire the stunning views before descending.

If the throngs get too much, vanish into the Rock Close, part of the beautiful and often ignored gardens.

Head out of central Cork via Merchant's Quay and the N20; Blarney is about 10km northwest of the city.

08 Fota Wildlife Park

Kangaroos bound, monkeys and gibbons leap and scream on wooded islands, and cheetahs run without a cage or fence in sight at the huge outdoor **Fota Wildlife Park** *(fotawildlife.ie)*.

A tour train *(one way/return €1/2)* runs a circuit round the park every 15 minutes in high season, but the 2km circular walk offers a more close-up experience.

From the wildlife park, you can stroll to the Regency-style **Fota House** *(fotahouse.com)*. The mostly barren interior contains a fine kitchen and ornate plasterwork ceilings; interactive displays bring the rooms to life.

Attached to the house is the 150-year-old **arboretum**, which has a Victorian fernery, a magnolia walk and some beautiful trees, including giant redwoods and a Chinese ghost tree.

THE DRIVE: From Fota Wildlife Park, head south for 5km to Cobh.

09 Cobh

For many years Cobh (pronounced 'cove') was the port of Cork. During the Famine, some 2.5 million people left Ireland through the glistening estuary. In 1838 the Sirius, the first steamship to cross the Atlantic, sailed from Cobh, and the *Titanic* made its final stop here in 1912.

The original White Star Line offices, where 123 passengers embarked on the *Titanic's* final voyage, now houses the unmissable **Titanic Experience Cobh** *(titanicexperience cobh.ie)*. Admission is by tour, which is partly guided and partly interactive, with holograms, audiovisual presentations and exhibits.

Standing dramatically above Cobh, the massive French Gothic **St Colman's Cathedral** *(cobh cathedralparish.ie)* is out of all proportion to the town. Its 47-bell carillon, the largest in Ireland, weighs a stonking 3440kg.

In 1849 Cobh was renamed **Queenstown** after Queen Victoria paid a visit; the name lasted until Irish independence in 1921. Housed in the old train station, **Cobh Heritage Centre** *(cobhheritage.com)*

♥ WHY I LOVE THIS TRIP

NEIL WILSON, WRITER

Journeying from Killarney to Dungarvan, this trip not only incorporates all of Ireland's definitive elements but also plenty of unexpected ones, from the *Titanic's* fateful final port to exotic animals roaming free in an island-set zoo to a spine-tingling 9th-century prison – as well as countless opportunities for serendipitous detours (because, of course, serendipity is what makes a road trip a true classic).

tells the Queenstown story, with exhibits evoking the Famine tragedy, a genealogy centre and a cafe.

THE DRIVE: Travel north on the R624 then east on the N25 to Midleton (18km in total).

10 Midleton

The number-one attraction in Midleton is the former whiskey distillery now housing the **Jameson Experience** *(jamesonwhiskey.com)*, where you can learn how Irish whiskey is made. Attractive cafes, restaurants and a great farmers market make it worth stopping for a while.

THE DRIVE: Continue east on the N25 for the 28km drive to Youghal.

11 Youghal

The ancient seaport of Youghal (*Eochaill*; pronounced 'yawl'), at the mouth of the River Blackwater, was a hotbed of rebellion against the English in the 16th century. Oliver Cromwell wintered here in 1649 as he sought to drum up support for his war in England and quell insurgence from the Irish. Youghal was granted to Sir Walter Raleigh during the Elizabethan Plantation of Munster.

The curious **Clock Gate** was built in 1777 and served as a clock tower and jail concurrently; several prisoners taken in the 1798 Rising were hanged from its windows.

Main St has an interesting curve that follows the original shore; many of the shopfronts are from the 19th-century. Further up the street are six almshouses built by Englishman Richard Boyle, who bought Raleigh's Irish estates and became the first earl of Cork in 1616 in recognition of his work in creating 'a very excellent colony'. Across the road is the 15th-century tower house, **Tynte's Castle**, which originally had a defensive riverfront position before the River Blackwater silted up and changed course.

Built in 1220, **St Mary's Collegiate Church** incorporates elements of an earlier Danish church dating back to the 11th century. The churchyard is bounded by a fine stretch of the 13th-century town wall and one of the remaining turrets.

Beside the church, **Myrtle Grove** (not open to the public) is the former home of Sir Walter Raleigh, and a rare Irish example of a late medieval Tudor-style house.

THE DRIVE: Rejoin the N25 and cross the River Blackwater. Continue following the N25 northeast for the final run to Dungarvan, a 31km trip in all.

12 Dungarvan

One of Ireland's most enchanting coastal towns, pastel-shaded Dungarvan is best known for its foodie reputation, but there are some intriguing sights, too. On the waterfront, **Dungarvan Castle** *(heritageireland.ie)* dates back to the 12th-century. Admission is by (free) guided tour only.

Housed in a handsome building dating from the 17th-century, the **Old Market House Arts Centre** *(facebook.com/oldmarkethouse)* showcases contemporary art by local artists.

The **Waterford County Museum** *(waterfordmuseum.ie)* covers maritime heritage (with relics from shipwrecks), Famine history, local personalities and various other titbits, all displayed in an 18th-century grain store.

Cobh (p147), Cork

SUSANNE POMMER/SHUTTERSTOCK

19

CORK & SOUTHWEST IRELAND

SOUTHWESTERN PANTRY

★ BEST FOR

FOODIES

The English Market in Cork city showcases the county's tantalising bounty.

DURATION: 5 DAYS

DISTANCE: 165KM / 103 MILES

GREAT FOR: FOOD & DRINK, PHOTOGRAPHY

BEST TIME TO GO: PRODUCE IS AT ITS MOST ABUNDANT FROM SPRING ONWARDS.

English Market (p152), Cork City

Farmers markets, farmhouse cheeses, fishing fleets hauling in fresh seafood, the country's oldest smokehouse and its most famous black pudding, as well as icons such as Cork's mouth-watering English Market, Jameson's old whiskey distillery, the wonderful Ballymaloe House and its prestigious cookery school, and some of the nation's finest eateries are among the treats awaiting in Ireland's southwestern pantry. *Bain taitneamh as do bhéil (bon appétit)!*

LINK YOUR TRIP

14 Blackwater Valley Drive
Head 26km east along the N25 for more glorious food over the border in County Waterford.

20 West Cork Villages
Return to Kinsale to discover Cork's picturesque peninsulas.

01 Durrus

This little crossroads at the head of Dunmanus Bay has become something of a gourmet hotspot in recent years and earned an international reputation for the cheese produced by **Durrus Farmhouse** *(durruscheese.com)*. Its produce is sold all over Ireland and as far afield as America. You can visit by prior arrangement and watch the cheesemaking process through a viewing panel. To reach the farm, drive 900m out of Durrus along the Ahakista road, turn right at St James' Church and continue for 3km until you see the sign for the farm on the left.

THE DRIVE: From Durrus, zigzag 30km southeast through wooded hills on the N71 to Skibbereen.

02 Skibbereen

Try to time your journey through the busy market town of

GABRIEL12/SHUTTERSTOCK

Skibbereen *(Sciobairín)* to catch the **farmers market** *(facebook.com/p/Skibbereen-Farmers-Market)*. If you're in town in mid-September, don't miss the **Taste of West Cork Food Festival** *(atasteofwestcork.com)*, with a lively market and events at local restaurants.

Atlantic Sea Kayaking *(atlanticseakayaking.com)* runs guided sea-kayaking tours *(€75)* of Lough Hyne, 8km southwest of Skib – the nighttime ones are special due to the bioluminescent plankton.

THE DRIVE: It's 33km along the N71 from Skibbereen to Clonakilty; there are also slower but more scenic alternatives along the coast.

DETOUR

Baltimore
Start: 02 Skibbereen

Not only does Baltimore, 13km south of Skibbereen on the R595, have aquatic activities galore, but its seafood is sublime.

Over the last full weekend of May, **Baltimore's Seafood Festival** *(baltimoreseafoodfest.com)* sees jazz bands perform, wooden boats parade and pubs bring out free mussels and prawns.

The Lookout *(waterfrontbaltimore.ie)* restaurant, upstairs at the Waterfront hotel, enjoys elevated sea views and serves luscious shellfish platters containing lobsters, prawns, brown crabs, velvet crabs, shrimps and oysters. Check opening times online.

The beautiful gardens at the **Glebe Gardens & Café** *(westcorkhotel.com)* are an attraction in themselves. If you're dining, lavender and herbs add fragrant aromas that waft over the tables inside and out. Food is simple and fresh, and is sourced from the gardens and a list of local purveyors.

03 Clonakilty

Clonakilty is legendary as the birthplace of Michael Collins, commander-in-chief of the army of the Irish Free State that won independence from Britain in 1922.

It's also home to the most famous black pudding in the country.

The best place to buy the town's renowned blood sausage is **Edward Twomey** *(clonakiltyblackpudding.ie)*, with different varieties based on the original 1880s recipe. Look out for it too at Clonakilty's weekly **farmers market** *(facebook.com/clonmarket)*.

The state-of-the-art **Clonakilty Distillery** *(clonakiltydistillery.ie)* opened its doors to the public in 2019, producing triple-distilled single pot still Irish whiskey made with grain grown on the owners' family farm nearby.

THE DRIVE: Continue 42km northeast along the N71 through farming country interspersed with towns and villages to Kinsale (alternatively you can take the slower and more scenic coastal R600 road for 35km).

04 Kinsale

Harbour-set Kinsale *(Cionn tSáile)* is revered for its fine seafood restaurants thanks in large part to its busy fishing fleet. Tastings, meals and harbour cruises take place during Kinsale's two-day **Gourmet Festival** *(kinsalerestaurants.com)* in early October.

A weekly **farmers market** *(facebook.com/kinsalefarmersmarket)* takes place in Short Quay. Handmade chocolates and crystallised orange and ginger are among the enticing wares at artisan chocolatier **Koko Kinsale** *(kokokinsale.com)*.

Kinsale's roots in the wine trade are on display at the early-16th-century **Desmond Castle** *(heritageireland.ie)*, which houses a small wine museum.

> PHOTO OPPORTUNITY
>
> Kinsale's boat-filled harbour is a picture.

THE DRIVE: Head north for 27km on the R600 through patchwork farmland to Ireland's second-largest city.

05 Cork City

Cork's food scene is reason enough to visit. It sometimes seems you can't walk 100m through the city streets without bumping into a boutique coffee roaster, a farmhouse cheesemaker or an artisan baker.

Cork's English Market *(englishmarket.ie)* is a local – no, make that national – treasure. It could just as easily be called the Victorian Market for its ornate vaulted ceilings and columns. Scores of vendors sell some of the very best local produce, meats, cheeses and take-away food in the region. Favourites include **On the Pig's Back** *(onthepigsback.ie)*, serving house-made sausages and incredible cheeses.

On a mezzanine overlooking part of the market is one of Cork's best eateries. **Farmgate Café** *(farmgatecork.ie)* is an unmissable experience. Everything from the rock oysters to the ingredients for Irish stew and raspberry crumble is sourced from the market below. The best seats are at the balcony counter overlooking the passing parade of shoppers. On fine days, picnic in nearby **Bishop Lucey Park**.

The narrow, pedestrianised streets in Cork's Huguenot Quarter north of St Patrick's St throng with cafes and restaurants with outside tables; many serve till late. Don't leave Cork without sampling the heavenly Chocolatier's Hot Chocolate at confectioners **O'Conaill** *(oconaillchocolate.ie)*.

THE DRIVE: Some 19km east of Cork on the R624 towards Cobh is the feted Belvelly smokehouse.

06 Belvelly

No trip to County Cork is complete without a visit to an artisan food producer, and the effervescent Frank Hederman is more than happy to show you around **Belvelly** *(frankhederman.com)*, the oldest natural smokehouse in Ireland. Seafood and cheese are smoked here, but the speciality is fish – in particular, salmon. In a traditional process that takes 24 hours from start to finish, the fish is filleted and cured before being hung in the tiny smokehouse over beech woodchips. Phone or email Frank to arrange your visit.

THE DRIVE: It's just 14km from Belvelly to Midleton.

07 Midleton

Aficionados of fine Irish whiskey will know the main reason to linger in this bustling market town is to visit the restored 200-year-old building housing the **Jameson Experience**... and

CRISTIANMIHART/SHUTTERSTOCK

Harbour, Kinsale, Cork

purchase bottles of it, of course. Exhibits and tours explain the process of taking barley and creating whiskey (Jameson is today made in a modern factory in Cork).

Midleton's **farmers market**, behind the courthouse, is one of Cork's best markets, with bushels of local produce and producers who are happy to chat.

Next to the distillery, **Ferrit & Lee** *(ferritandlee.ie)* is a fine restaurant where whiskey plays a starring role, featuring in all kinds of dishes including the beef and the ice cream.

DETOUR

Ballymaloe House & Cookery School
Start: 07 Midleton

Drawing up at wisteria-clad **Ballymaloe House** *(ballymaloe.ie)*, 12km southeast of Midleton on the R629, you know you've arrived somewhere special. Rooms are period furnished and the beautiful grounds include a tennis court, swimming pool and shop. The menu at its celebrated restaurant is drawn up daily according to the produce available from Ballymaloe's extensive farms and other local sources. It also runs wine and gardening weekends.

Just over 3km further east (go through the village of Shanagarry and turn left opposite the church), TV personality Darina Allen runs the famous **Ballymaloe Cookery School** *(ballymaloecookeryschool.com)*. Book lessons, starting from half-day sessions *(€90 to €255)*, well in advance. There are pretty cottages for overnight students around the 40-hectare organic farm.

20

CORK & SOUTHWEST IRELAND

WEST CORK VILLAGES

★ BEST

AERIAL VIEWS

Take the cable car from the Beara Peninsula to tiny Dursey Island.

Cable car system to Dursey Island (p159)

DURATION: 7 DAYS

DISTANCE: 354KM / 220 MILES

GREAT FOR: FOOD & DRINK, HISTORY, OUTDOORS

BEST TIME TO GO: WEST CORK'S VILLAGES ARE LIVELIEST BETWEEN APRIL AND OCTOBER.

This trip contains one of Ireland's trinity of top peninsula drives: the spellbinding Beara Peninsula, straddling Counties Cork and Kerry. Beara's southern side, along Bantry Bay, harbours working fishing villages, while on the rugged northern side craggy roads cut in and out of nooks and crannies and tiny coves are like pearls in a sea of rocks.

LINK YOUR TRIP

16 Ring of Kerry
Head 27km north from Glengarriff to pick up the Ring of Kerry in Kenmare.

17 Dingle Peninsula
Killarney, 60km north of Glengarriff, is the gateway to the charming Dingle Peninsula.

01 Kinsale

Narrow, winding streets lined with artsy shops and a harbour full of bobbing fishing boats and pleasure yachts make Kinsale *(Cionn tSáile)* one of Ireland's favourite midsized towns. Its superb foodie reputation is a bonus.

The peninsula of Scilly is barely a 10-minute walk southeast, from where a lovely walking path continues 3km east to Summercove and the vast 17th-century, star-shaped **Charles Fort** *(heritageireland.ie)*.

THE DRIVE: At times you'll meet the coast as you wind 35km west along the R600 to Clonakilty.

02 Clonakilty

Cheerful Clonakilty is a bustling market town coursed by little waterways. It serves as a hub

PETER KROCKA/SHUTTERSTOCK

for the scores of beguiling little coastal towns that surround it.

Superb miniature models of the main towns in West Cork star at the **West Cork Model Railway Village** *(modelvillage.ie)*. A road train departs from the village on a 20-minute guided circuit of Clonakilty.

A visit to the **Michael Collins Centre and Museum** *(michael collinscentre.com)*, signposted off the R600 between Timoleague and Clonakilty, is an excellent way to make sense of the life of Clonakilty's most famous son, Irish Free State commander-in-chief Michael Collins. The main negotiator of the 1921 Anglo-Irish Treaty, Collins was forced to make major concessions, including the partition of the country, famously declaring that he was signing his own death warrant. He was tragically correct, as Civil War broke out in the treaty's aftermath. A tour reveals photos, letters and a reconstruction of the 1920s country lane, complete with armoured vehicle, where Collins was killed.

THE DRIVE: It's 33km along the N71 from Clonakilty to Skibbereen but it's possible to freelance along the coast the entire way. As a taster, at Rosscarbery, you can turn left onto the R597, which takes you past the pretty villages of Glandore *(Cuan Dor)* and Union Hall, and the turn-off to the Drombeg Stone Circle, rejoining the N71 at Leap.

03 Skibbereen

Weekending swells and yachties from Dublin descend on the busy market town of Skibbereen *(Sciobairín)*, which is as close to glitzy as West Cork gets. It's a far cry from the Famine, when Skibb was hit perhaps harder than any other town in Ireland, with huge numbers of the local population emigrating or dying of starvation or disease. **Skibbereen Heritage Centre** *(skibbheritage.com)* puts its history into harrowing perspective.

THE DRIVE: It's 16km along the N71 from Skibbereen to Ballydehob.

04 Ballydehob

The gateway to the Mizen Peninsula, Ballydehob is an emerging foodie hotspot. **Budd's** is a fabulous gourmet cafe, while across the street Michelin-starred **Chestnut** *(restaurantchestnut westcork.ie)* is one of the best in the county. Next door, **Levis** pub is a legendary watering hole.

THE DRIVE: From Ballydehob, continue along the N71 to the pretty village of Schull (pronounced 'skull'). Travelling on into the undulating countryside along the coastal road takes you through ever-smaller settlements to the village of Goleen. Ballydehob to Goleen is 23km.

05 Mizen Head Peninsula

The welcoming village of Goleen marks the start of the Mizen Head experience. Continue first to **Barleycove Beach**, with vast sand dunes hemmed in by two long bluffs dissolving into the surf. Then take the increasingly narrow roads to spectacular Mizen Head, Ireland's most southwesterly point. It's dominated by the **Mizen Head Signal Station** *(mizenhead.ie)*, completed in 1909 to warn ships off rocks that appear in the water around here like crushed ice in cola. From the visitors centre, various pathways lead to the station, culminating in the crossing of a spectacular arched bridge that spans a vast gulf in the cliffs.

Pints in the sunshine are the reward for venturing on the crooked road to the outpost of **Crookhaven** (if it's raining, make that 'pints by the fireplace...'). In its heyday Crookhaven's natural harbour was an important anchorage, and mail from America was collected here.

Leaving Crookhaven, you'll spot the turn-off to the left, marked **Brow Head** – the Irish mainland's southernmost point. Park at the bottom of the hill – the track is very narrow and there's nowhere to pull over should you meet a tractor coming the other way. After 1km the road ends and a path continues to the head.

THE DRIVE: Bear north to join the scenic coast road that follows the edge of Dunmanus Bay for most of the way to Durrus. Continue north to Bantry, 60km north of Goleen.

DETOUR

Sheep's Head Peninsula
Start: 05 Mizen Head Peninsula

At Durrus, one road heads for Bantry; take the other, which turns west to circumnavigate Sheep's Head Peninsula.

The least visited of Cork's three peninsulas, Sheep's Head has a charm all its own – and plenty of sheep. There are good seascapes from along most of the loop road.

Heading west from Durrus, the first hamlet you meet is **Ahakista** *(Atha an Chiste)*, which consists of a couple of pubs and a few houses stretched along the R591. The peninsula's other village is **Kilcrohane**, 6km to the southwest, beside a fine beach. You can get pub food in both villages.

From Kilcrohane, the **Goat's Path** road runs north over the western flank of Mt Seefin to Gortnakilly and offers terrific views. Alternatively, keep heading southwest to the tip of Sheep's Head, from where an excellent one-hour walk leads from the road end at Tooreen to the **Sheep's Head Lighthouse**. Rejoin the N71 at Bantry. For more information, visit *thesheepsheadway.ie*.

06 Bantry

The pleasant town of Bantry offers the chance to refuel at one of its excellent eateries, and to get a feel for the life of the 18th-century Irish aristocracy with a visit to impressive **Bantry House** *(bantryhouse.com)* and its glorious gardens, 1km southwest of the town centre on the N71.

THE DRIVE: Continue north on the N71 to Glengarriff and the Beara Peninsula. The contorted strata of the peninsula's underlying bedrock become evident as you drive west on the R572 towards Castletownbere, 50km from Bantry. On the highest hills – Sugarloaf Mountain and Hungry Hill – rock walls known as 'benches' snake backwards and forwards across the slopes.

07 Beara Peninsula

Encircling the Beara Peninsula, the Ring of Beara is, along with the Ring of Kerry and Dingle, one of Ireland's podium peninsula drives.

In the fishing town of **Castletownbere** *(Baile Chais Bhéara)*, you might recognise the front-cover photo of the late Pete McCarthy's 1998 bestseller, *McCarthy's Bar*, in three dimensions on Main St.

Barleycove Beach
D. RIBEIRO/SHUTTERSTOCK

Healy Pass Rd

BONN BONN FOTO/SHUTTERSTOCK

PHOTO OPPORTUNITY

Staggering sea cliffs at the far-flung Mizen Head Signal Station.

Tiny **Dursey Island**, at the end of the peninsula, is reached by Ireland's only **cable car** *(dursey island.ie)*, which sways 30m above Dursey Sound. After the thrill of the cable car ride, you can hike to the signal tower at the top of the island, and spot whales and dolphins in the surrounding waters.

It's 12km from the cable car to **Allihies** *(Na hAilichí)*. From here the beautiful R575 coast road, with hedges of fuchsias and rhododendrons, twists and turns for about 12km to **Eyeries**, a cluster of brightly coloured houses overlooking Coulagh Bay. From Eyeries you can forsake the R571 for the even smaller coast roads (lanes really) to the north and east, with views north to the Ring of Kerry.

At the crossroads of **Argroom** *(Ard Dhór)*, heading east towards Lauragh, look for signs pointing to the Bronze Age stone circle.

THE DRIVE: Cut across the spectacular **Healy Pass Rd** (R574) to Adrigole and return on the R572 to Glengarriff (32km). Alternatively, leaving Lauragh, you can skip Glengarriff a second time and take the R573, which hugs the coast, rejoining the more no-nonsense R571 at Tuosist for the 16km run east to Kenmare in County Kerry.

08 Glengarriff

Offshore from the village of Glengarriff, subtropical plants flourish in the rich soil and warm climate of the magical Italianate garden on **Garinish Island** *(garinishisland.ie)*. Ferry companies, including **Blue Pool Ferry** *(bluepoolferry.ie)*, leave every 30 minutes for the 15-minute boat trip past islands and seal colonies when the garden is open; fares exclude garden entry.

STAY AWHILE

CLONAKILTY

BY FIONN DAVENPORT

Cheerful, colourful Clonakilty – Clon to the locals – is my ideal base from which to explore West Cork. This is the town that perfected the art of black (blood) pudding – the secret recipe dates from the early 1800s and its story is told in all its interactive glory at the **Clonakilty Blackpudding Visitor Centre** *(clonakiltyblackpudding.ie)*. And if you're not keen on finding out how the proverbial sausage is made, you can pick some up (as well as a host of other ingredients for the classic Irish breakfast) from **Edward Twomey** on Main St.

Directly across the street is the other reason I love Clon. Three generations of the Barry family have witnessed **De Barra's** *(debarra.ie)* go from local pub with plenty of atmosphere to one of the country's best-known folk-music venues (without losing its traditional character). Jimi Hendrix's bass player, Noel Redding, moved here in the early 1970s and played here for the next 20 years, which inevitably drew hundreds of other musicians to its small stage, including David Bowie, Ed Sheeran and Christy Moore.

I also love the choice of restaurants here. On the edge of town, in the middle of a working farm, is **Field Kitchen** *(fieldkitchen.ie)*, where everything on the menu comes from the organic cattle farm and kitchen garden; a short walk from the middle of town is **Fernhill House** *(fernhillhousehotel.com)*, a Georgian country hotel with a terrific restaurant (they also make their own gin).

LINK YOUR TRIP

Clonakilty is on the epic **03 The Long Way Round** drive that ends in Donegal; you can also easily join the **20 West Cork Villages** drive.

CLIVE EVANS/ALAMY STOCK PHOTO

KEN WELSH/DESTINATIONS/ALAMY STOCK PHOTO

Left: Edward Twomey; Right: De Barra's

PLACES TO STAY

I love **Fernhill House** *(fernhillhousehotel.com)*, but when I'm in the area I always make a point of staying at **Inchydoney Island Lodge & Spa** *(inchydoneyisland.com)*, about 5km south of Clonakilty at the edge of one of my favourite beaches in Ireland. A superb seawater spa is at the heart of this sprawling property, which has echoes of New England decor, with airy spaces, painted white shutters, wicker shades and touches of blue, white and cream. There are two restaurants – the more casual Dunes Bistro where you can get elevated pub grub, and the fancier, French-inspired Gulfstream Restaurant.

21

CORK & SOUTHWEST IRELAND

SHANNON RIVER ROUTE

★ BEST FOR

DOLPHIN SPOTTING

Estuary-set Kilrush has a nature centre, dolphin trail and cruises.

Portumna Castle & Gardens, Galway

DURATION: 4 DAYS

DISTANCE: 296KM / 184 MILES

GREAT FOR: FOOD & DRINK, HISTORY, OUTDOORS

BEST TIME TO GO: EVEN IN HIGH SUMMER THERE ARE PLENTY OF CROWD-FREE ESCAPES.

Ireland's longest river provides a stunning backdrop to this route. It begins with gentle lake scenery around the boaters' paradise of Lough Derg, followed by fascinating historical sights in and around Limerick city. A visit to the world's only flying boat museum is followed by a short ferry trip across the Shannon Estuary to take in the sweeping white-sand beaches of Kilkee and the dramatic seacliffs of Loop Head.

LINK YOUR TRIP

25 Mountains & Moors
Head 70km northwest of Portumna to discover County Galway's romantic landscapes.

29 County Clare
It's just 25km north from Bunratty to Ennis for a tour of County Clare's cliff-framed coast, the otherworldly Burren and music-filled pubs.

01 Portumna

In the far southeastern corner of County Galway, the lakeside town of Portumna is popular for boating and fishing.

Impressive **Portumna Castle & Gardens** *(heritageireland.ie)* was built in the early 1600s by Richard de Burgo and boasts an elaborate, geometrical organic garden.

THE DRIVE: From Portumna, cross the River Shannon – also the county border – into County Tipperary. Take the N65 south for 7km then turn right onto the R493, winding through farmland. Briefly rejoin the N52 at the Nenagh bypass, then turn west on the R494, following it to Ballina (52km in all).

02 Ballina & Killaloe

Facing each other across a narrow channel, Ballina and Killaloe *(Cill Da Lúa)* are really one destination, even if they have different personalities (and counties).

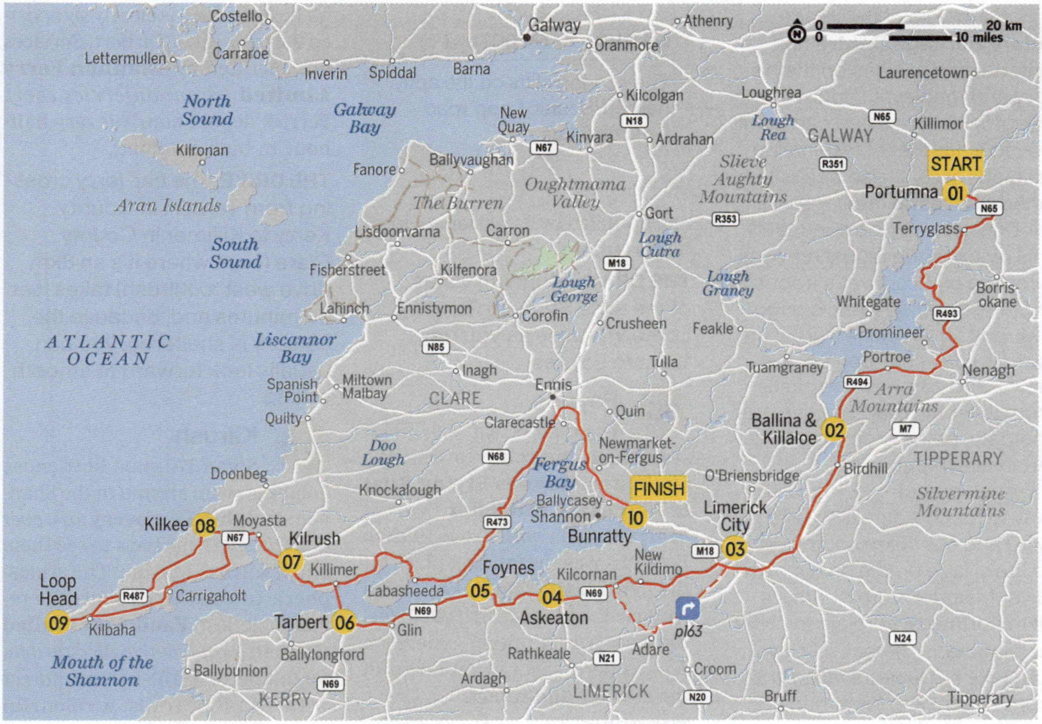

A fine 1770 13-arch one-lane bridge spans the river, linking the pair. You can walk it in five minutes or drive it in about 20 (a Byzantine system of lights controls traffic).

Ballina, in County Tipperary, has some of the better pubs and restaurants, while Killaloe typifies picturesque County Clare. It lies on the western banks of lower Loch Deirgeirt (the southern extension of Lough Derg), where it narrows at one of the principal crossings of the Shannon.

THE DRIVE: Continue following the R494 then the M7 southwest to Limerick city (about 24km).

03 Limerick City

Limerick city straddles the Shannon's broadening tidal stream, where the river runs west to meet the Shannon Estuary. Despite some unexpected glitz and gloss, it doesn't shy away from its tough past, as portrayed in Frank McCourt's 1996 memoir *Angela's Ashes*.

Limerick has an intriguing **castle** *(kingjohnscastle.com)*, built by King John of England between 1200 and 1212 on King's Island; the ancient **St Mary's Cathedral** *(saintmaryscathedral.ie)*, founded in 1168 by Donal Mór O'Brien, king of Munster; and the fabulous **Hunt Museum** *(huntmuseum.com)*, with the finest collection of Bronze Age, Iron Age and medieval treasures outside Dublin.

The dynamic **Limerick City Gallery of Art** *(gallery.limerick.ie)* is set in the city's Georgian area. Limerick also has a contemporary cafe culture, and renowned nightlife to go with its uncompromised pubs – as well as locals who go out of their way to welcome you.

THE DRIVE: The narrow, peaceful N69 follows the Shannon Estuary west from Limerick; 27km along you come to Askeaton.

DETOUR

Adare

Start: 03 Limerick City

Frequently dubbed 'Ireland's prettiest village', Adare centres on its clutch of perfectly preserved thatched cottages built by the 19th-century English landlord, the Earl of Dunraven, for workers constructing **Adare Manor** (now a palatial hotel). Today the cottages house craft shops and some of the region's finest restaurants.

In the middle of the village, **Adare Heritage Centre** has entertaining exhibits on the history and medieval context of the village's buildings and can point you to a number of fascinating religious sites. It also books tours of **Adare Castle** *(heritageireland.ie)*. Dating back to around 1200, this picturesque feudal ruin was wrecked by Cromwell's troops in 1657. Restoration work is ongoing; look for the ruined great hall with its early-13th-century windows. You can view the castle from the main road, the riverside footpath, or the grounds of the Augustinian priory.

From Limerick city, the fastest way to reach Adare is to take the M20 and N21 16km southwest to the village on the banks of the River Maigue. From Adare it's 9km northwest to rejoin the N69 at Kilcornan. Alternatively, you can take the less-travelled N69 from Limerick to Kilcornan and slip down to Adare.

04 Askeaton

Hidden just off the N69, evocative ruins in the pint-sized village of Askeaton include the mid-1300s **Desmond Castle**, a 1389-built **Franciscan friary**, and **St Mary's Church of Ireland** and **Knights Templar Tower**, built around 1829, as well as the 1740 **Hellfire gentlemen's club**. The ruins are undergoing a slow process of restoration that started in 2007. The town's **tourist office** *(askeatontouristoffice@gmail.com)* has details of ruins that you can freely wander (depending on restoration works) and can arrange free guided tours lasting about one hour, led by a passionate local historian.

PHOTO OPPORTUNITY

The soaring cliffs on the aptly named 'Scenic Loop' road west of Kilkee.

THE DRIVE: Stunning vistas of the wide Shannon Estuary come into view as you drive 12km to Foynes.

05 Foynes

Foynes is an essential stop along the route to visit the fascinating **Foynes Flying Boat & Maritime Museum** *(flyingboatmuseum.com)*. From 1939 to 1945 this was the landing place for the flying boats that linked North America with the British Isles. Big Pan Am clippers – there's a replica here – would set down in the estuary and refuel.

THE DRIVE: The most scenic stretch of the N69 is the 20km from Foynes to Tarbert in northern County Kerry, which hugs the estuary's edge.

06 Tarbert

The little town of Tarbert is where you'll hop on the car ferry to Killimer, in County Clare, saving yourself 137km of driving.

Before you do so, though, it's worth visiting the renovated **Tarbert Bridewell Jail & Courthouse** *(tarbertbridewell.com)*, which has exhibits on the rough social and political conditions of the 19th-century. From the jail, the 6.1km **John F Leslie Woodland Walk** runs along Tarbert Bay towards the river mouth.

The ferry dock is clearly signposted 2.2km west of Tarbert. Services are operated by **Shannon Ferry Limited** *(shannonferries.com)*. Ferries depart hourly (every half-hour in high summer).

THE DRIVE: The car-ferry crossing from Tarbert in County Kerry to Killimer in County Clare (from where it's an 8km drive west to Kilrush) takes just 20 minutes and, because the estuary is sheltered, you can usually look forward to smooth sailing.

07 Kilrush

Some 170-plus bottlenose dolphins swim around in the Shannon; **Dolphin Discovery** *(discoverdolphins.ie)* runs trips to see them out of Kilrush Marina. The atmospheric town also harbours the remarkable 'lost' **Vandeleur Walled Garden** *(vandeleurwalledgarden.ie)*, home to a 170-hectare forest with winding trails, a colourful array of plants and a beech maze.

THE DRIVE: Continue 14km west along the N67 to the beach haven of Kilkee.

08 Kilkee

The centrepiece of Kilkee *(Cill Chaoi)* is its wide, sheltered, crescent-shaped beach. The bay has high cliffs on the north end; to the south a coastal path leads to natural swimming pools known as the **Pollock Holes**. The waters are very tidal with sandy expanses replaced by waves in just a few hours.

Kilkee has plenty of guesthouses and B&Bs, though during high season, rates can soar and vacancies are scarce.

MAKASANA PHOTO/SHUTTERSTOCK

Loop Head

THE DRIVE: The 26.5km drive from Kilkee south to Loop Head ends in cliffs plunging into the Atlantic.

09 Loop Head

Capped by a working lighthouse, Loop Head *(Ceann Léime)* is County Clare's southernmost point, with breathtaking views as well as cycling, fishing and snorkelling opportunities.

THE DRIVE: On the R487, follow the 'Scenic Loop' (an understatement): you'll be struck by one stunning vista of soaring coastal cliffs after another. At Kilkee pick up the N67 east to just after Killimer, before continuing northeast on the looping, coastal R473. Next hop on M18/N18 south to Bunratty (110km all up).

10 Bunratty

Bunratty *(Bun Raite)* draws more tourists than any other place in the region. The namesake **castle** *(bunrattycastle.ie)* has stood over the area for centuries. In recent decades it's been spiffed up and swamped by attractions and gift shops. A theme park recreates a clichéd – and sanitised – Irish village of old.

With all the hoopla, it's easy to overlook the actual village, at the back of the theme park, which has numerous leafy spots to eat and sleep.

22

CORK & SOUTHWEST IRELAND

THE HOLY GLEN

★ BEST

CASTLE

Cahir Castle, like the quintessential beach sandcastle, with towers and moat.

DURATION: 2–3 DAYS

DISTANCE: 71KM / 45 MILES

GREAT FOR: HISTORY, OUTDOORS

BEST TIME TO GO: AUTUMN BRINGS GLORIOUS COLOURS AND A WALKING FESTIVAL

Cahir Castle, Tipperary

The landscapes viewed from your car windows are sublime, and it's easy to get out and about among them. The Glen of Aherlow is renowned for its walking. You will encounter varying terrain, from lush riverbanks on the Aherlow to whispering pine forests and windswept, rocky mountains that seem to stretch on forever.

LINK YOUR TRIP

12 Kilkenny's Treasures
Head 60km northeast of Cashel along the M8 and R693 to discover the medieval treasures of County Kilkenny.

14 Blackwater Valley Drive
Travel 87km south from Cashel to Youghal (County Cork), via Lismore, for the beautiful Blackwater Valley.

01 Clonmel

County Tipperary's largest and busiest town, Clonmel (*Cluain Meala*; 'Meadows of Honey') sits on the northern bank of the River Suir. Its historic buildings include the beautifully restored **Main Guard** *(heritageireland.ie)*; a **James Butler courthouse** dating from 1675; the 1802-built **County Courthouse**, where the Young Irelanders of 1848 were tried and sentenced to transportation to Australia; and the **Franciscan Friary** *(franciscans.ie)* – inside, near the door, a 1533 Butler-family tomb depicts a knight and his lady. There's some fine modern stained glass, especially in **St Anthony's Chapel**.

Informative displays on County Tipperary's history, from Neolithic times to the present, are covered at the well-put-together **South Tipperary County Museum** *(tipperarycoco.ie)*, which also hosts changing exhibitions.

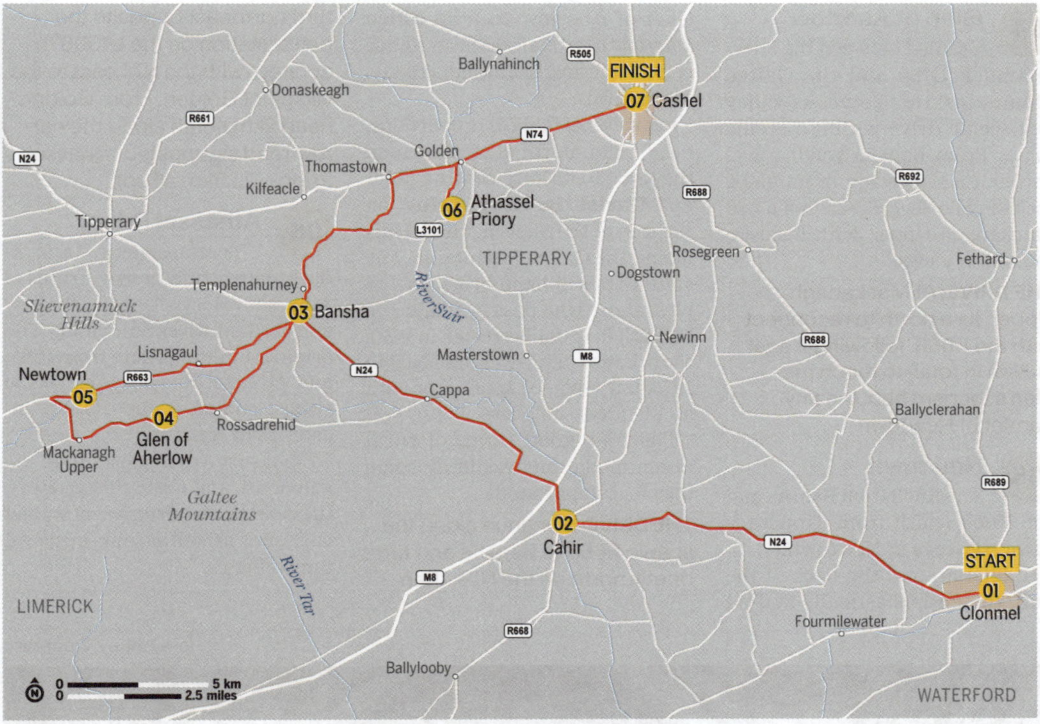

THE DRIVE: It's a quick 17km trip along the N24 west to Cahir.

02 Cahir

At the eastern tip of the Galtee Mountains, the compact town of Cahir (*An Cathair*; pronounced 'care') encircles the moated **Cahir Castle** *(heritageireland.ie)*, a feudal fantasy of rocky foundations, massive walls, turrets and towers, defences and dungeons. Founded by Conor O'Brien in 1142, it passed to the Butler family in 1375. In 1599 the Earl of Essex used cannons to shatter its walls, and it was surrendered to Cromwell in 1650. Its future usefulness may have discouraged the typical Cromwellian 'deconstruction' and it remains one of Ireland's largest and most intact medieval castles.

Walking paths follow the banks of the River Suir – a pretty path from behind the castle car park meanders 2km south to the thatched **Swiss Cottage** *(heritageireland.ie)*, surrounded by roses, lavender and honeysuckle. A lavish example of Regency Picturesque, it's more a sizeable house. The compulsory 30-minute guided tours are thoroughly enjoyable.

THE DRIVE: Drive northwest for 14km through farmland along the N24 (which, despite being a National Road, is narrow and twisting) to the village of Bansha, the jumping-off point for the Glen of Aherlow.

03 Bansha

The tiny village of Bansha (*An Bháinseach*, meaning 'a grassy place') sits at the eastern end of the Glen of Aherlow. Although Bansha itself has just a handful of facilities, it makes a good pit stop before embarking on the prettiest stretch of this trip.

THE DRIVE: From Bansha the 11km drive southwest takes in the best of County Tipperary's verdant, mountainous landscapes. Leave Bansha on the R663 and, after 500m, take the left fork (signposted 'Rossadrehid') in the road. Keep your eyes peeled for walkers and cyclists as you drive.

04 Glen of Aherlow

Cradled between the Slievenamuck Hills and the Galtee Mountains, this gorgeous valley is a scenic drive within a scenic drive. From Bansha you'll travel through a scattering of hamlets, including Booleen, Rossadrehid and Mackanagh Upper, with majestic mountain views.

THE DRIVE: At Mackanagh Upper, turn north to reconnect with the R663, following it east (4.2km in total) to reach the glen's tourism hub, the tiny hamlet of Newtown.

05 Newtown

The R663 from Bansha and the R664 south from Tipperary town converge at Newtown.

Hidden around the back of the pub, the enthusiastically staffed Glen of Aherlow **tourist office** (*aherlow.com*) is an excellent source of local information, including walking festivals.

For views of biblical proportions, head 1.6km north of Newtown on the R664 to its lofty viewing point and **Christ the King statue**, on the side of the Slievenamuck Hills facing the Galtee Mountains. The statue's raised hand is believed to bless those who pass by it and live beneath it. Initially erected in 1950, the original statue was damaged in 1975, but replaced soon after with an identical sculpture.

There's a good range of rural accommodation, including some bucolic campgrounds.

THE DRIVE: Continue along the scenic R663 to Bansha and turn briefly north on the N24, then turn northeast opposite the petrol station on the L4306 to connect with the N74 east to the village of Golden. From Golden, head 2km south along the narrow road signposted 'Athassel Priory' (23.5km all up).

06 Athassel Priory

The atmospheric – and, at dusk, delightfully creepy – ruins of Athassel Priory sit in the shallow and verdant River Suir valley. The original buildings date from 1205, and Athassel was once one of the richest and most important monasteries in Ireland.

What survives is substantial: the gatehouse and portcullis gateway, the cloister and stretches of walled enclosure, as well as some medieval tomb effigies.

Hore Abbey, Tipperary

MNSTUDIO/SHUTTERSTOCK

PHOTO OPPORTUNITY

The awe-inspiring Rock of Cashel from inside the Hore Abbey ruins.

Roadside parking is limited and very tight. The priory is reached across often-muddy fields.

THE DRIVE: Return to Golden and continue east along the N74 for 7km to the grand finale of the trip, Cashel, resplendently crowned by the Rock of Cashel.

07 Cashel

Rising from a grassy plain on the edge of the town, the **Rock of Cashel** *(heritageireland.ie)* is one of Ireland's most spectacular archaeological sites. The 'Rock' is a prominent green hill, banded with limestone outcrops, which bristles with ancient fortifications – the word 'cashel' is an Anglicised version of the Irish word *caiseal*, meaning 'fortress'.

Sturdy walls circle an enclosure that contains a complete round tower, a 13th-century Gothic cathedral and the finest 12th-century Romanesque chapel in Ireland. For more than a thousand years the Rock of Cashel was a symbol of power and the seat of kings and churchmen who ruled over the region.

It's a five-minute stroll from the town centre to the Rock; pretty paths include the **Bishop's Walk**. There are a couple of parking spaces for visitors with disabilities at the top of the approach road to the ticket office.

Just under 1km from the Rock, in flat farmland, is the formidable ruin of 13th-century **Hore Abbey**. Originally Benedictine and settled by monks from Glastonbury in England at the end of the 12th-century, it later became a Cistercian house.

Next to the car park below the Rock, heritage centre **Brú Ború** *(bruboru.ie)* offers an absorbing insight into Irish traditional music, dance and song.

Town museums include the engaging **Cashel Folk Village** *(cashelfolkvillage.com)*, exhibiting old buildings, shopfronts and memorabilia from around Cashel.

PIERRE LECLERC/SHUTTERSTOCK

Galtee Mountains

THE GALTEE MOUNTAINS

Extending west from Cahir for 23km, the Galtees stand slightly aloof from the other mountain groups in Ireland's south. They rise comparatively gradually from the sprawling 'Tipperary Plain' and much more steeply from beautiful Glen of Aherlow to the north.

The range's highest peak is Galtymore Mountain (919m), which towers over at least 12 other distinct summits. A prominent landmark far and wide, it stands proud of the rest of the range by almost 100m and is one of Ireland's 14 peaks or summits over 900m. Valleys bite deep into the main ridge, composed of purplish Devonian sandstone, so that the Galtees (pronounced with a short 'a' as in 'fact') are characterised by long spurs reaching out from the relatively narrow main ridge.

Tors, created by frost-shattering during the last ice age, are scattered along the ridge, notably forming a heap of conglomerate boulders known as O'Loughnan's Castle. The north face of the range is punctuated by corries – relics of the ice age that hide **Lough Muskry** and **Bohreen Lough**, impounded by massed moraine. The uplands of the range are largely covered with blanket bog, and conifer plantations are widespread across the lower slopes. The Glen of Aherlow tourist office in Newtown has walking information.

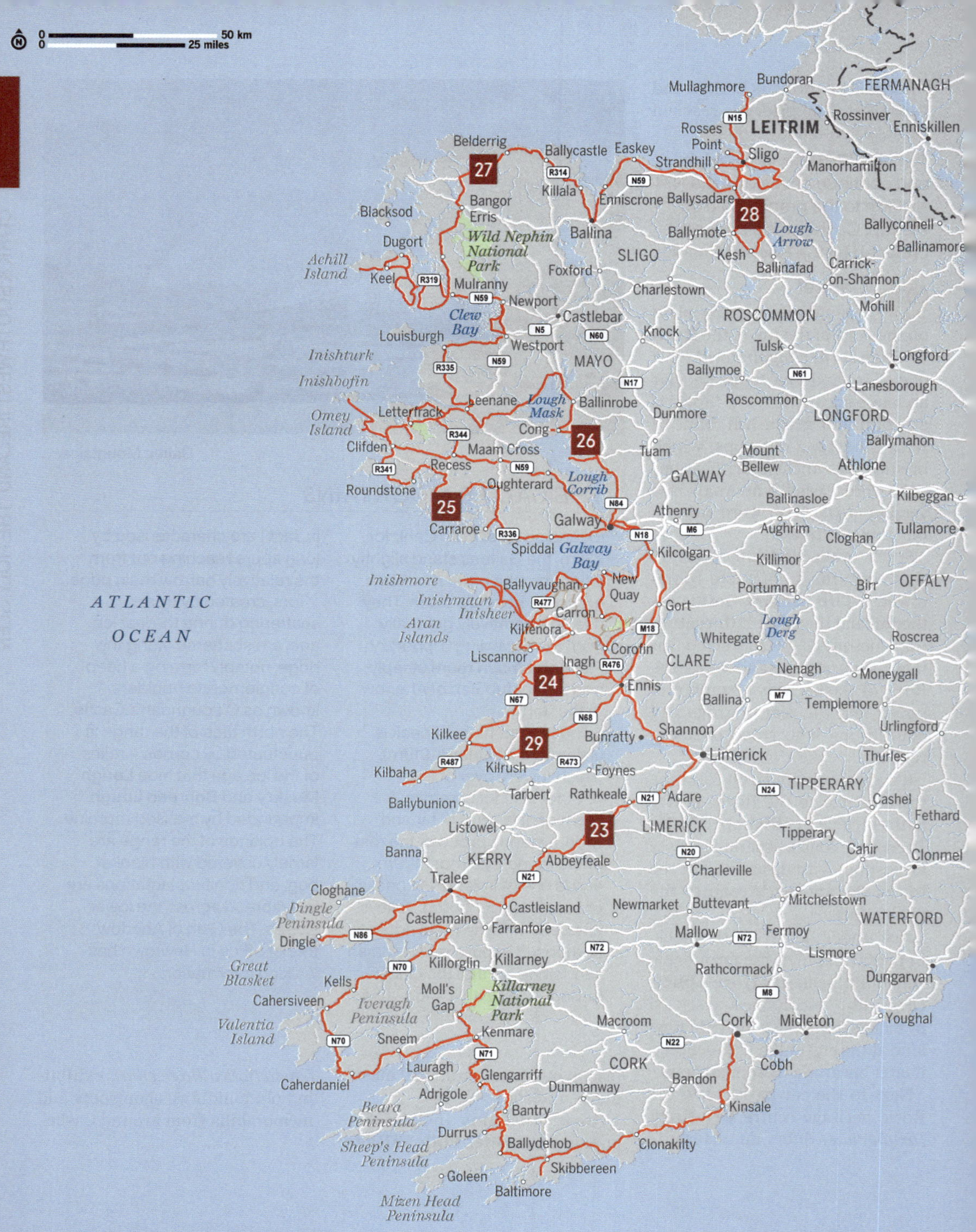
0 50 km
0 25 miles
ATLANTIC
OCEAN
LEITRIM
FERMANAGH
SLIGO
MAYO
ROSCOMMON
LONGFORD
GALWAY
OFFALY
CLARE
TIPPERARY
LIMERICK
KERRY
WATERFORD
CORK
Mullaghmore
Bundoran
Rossinver
Enniskillen
Rosses Point
Sligo
Strandhill
Manorhamilton
Belderrig
Ballycastle
Easkey
Killala
Enniscrone
Ballysadare
Blacksod
Bangor Erris
Ballina
Ballymote
Lough Arrow
Ballyconnell
Ballinamore
Dugort
Wild Nephin National Park
Kesh
Ballinafad
Carrick-on-Shannon
Achill Island
Keel
Mulranny
Foxford
Charlestown
Mohill
Newport
Castlebar
Clew Bay
Knock
Tulsk
Louisburgh
Westport
Longford
Inishturk
Ballymoe
Lanesborough
Inishbofin
Leenane
Lough Mask
Ballinrobe
Roscommon
Omey Island
Letterfrack
Cong
Dunmore
Clifden
Maam Cross
Tuam
Mount Bellew
Ballymahon
Recess
Athlone
Roundstone
Oughterard
Lough Corrib
Ballinasloe
Kilbeggan
Athenry
Galway
Carraroe
Aughrim
Tullamore
Cloghan
Spiddal
Galway Bay
Kilcolgan
Killimor
Inishmore
Ballyvaughan
New Quay
Portumna
Birr
Inishmaan
Inisheer
Carron
Gort
Aran Islands
Kilfenora
Lough Derg
Whitegate
Roscrea
Corofin
Liscannor
Inagh
Nenagh
Moneygall
Ennis
Ballina
Templemore
Urlingford
Shannon
Kilkee
Bunratty
Limerick
Thurles
Kilrush
Foynes
Kilbaha
Tarbert
Rathkeale
Adare
Cashel
Ballybunion
Fethard
Listowel
Tipperary
Cahir
Banna
Abbeyfeale
Clonmel
Charleville
Tralee
Cloghane
Castleisland
Newmarket
Buttevant
Mitchelstown
Dingle Peninsula
Castlemaine
Farranfore
Mallow
Fermoy
Dingle
Lismore
Killorglin
Killarney
Great Blasket
Rathcormack
Dungarvan
Kells
Moll's Gap
Killarney National Park
Cahersiveen
Iveragh Peninsula
Valentia Island
Kenmare
Macroom
Cork
Midleton
Youghal
Sneem
Cobh
Lauragh
Caherdaniel
Glengarriff
Dunmanway
Bandon
Adrigole
Beara Peninsula
Bantry
Kinsale
Durrus
Sheep's Head Peninsula
Ballydehob
Clonakilty
Skibbereen
Goleen
Baltimore
Mizen Head Peninsula
N15
N59
R314
R319
N5
N60
R335
N17
N61
R344
R341
N84
R336
N18
M6
R477
M18
R476
N67
N68
M7
R487
R473
N21
N24
N20
N86
N72
N70
M8
N22
N71
23
24
25
26
27
28
29

FREESKYLINE/SHUTTERSTOCK

View from Croagh Patrick (p175), Mayo

GALWAY & THE WEST OF IRELAND

EXPLORE

GALWAY & THE WEST OF IRELAND

It's little wonder the west of Ireland is top of most must-see lists – apart from the bad weather, it really has it all. There's the wild romantic beauty of County Mayo and the lonely bogs and white-sand beaches of Connemara. There's the iconic scenery of Cork and Kerry, straight out of a postcard. Between them, there's the mesmerising landscapes of The Burren in County Clare and the Aran Islands, just off the coast but a million miles away from the buzz of cosmopolitan life. But if you want that, you'll find it – in colourful Galway city and Westport.

Galway

Arty, bohemian Galway *(Gaillimh)* is one of Ireland's most engaging cities. Brightly painted pubs heave with live music, while restaurants and cafes offer front-row seats to observe buskers and street theatre. B&Bs line the major approach roads – College Rd, a 15-minute walk from the centre, has an especially high concentration. Most have on-site parking, but few central accommodation providers do, although many offer good deals at car parks. The smorgasbord of eating options ranges from a wonderful market to adventurous new eateries redefining Irish cuisine, as well as a burgeoning restaurant scene in the West End.

Westport

Bright and vibrant, even in the depths of winter, Westport is a photogenic Georgian town with tree-lined streets, riverside walkways and a great vibe. With an excellent choice of accommodation and fine restaurants and pubs renowned for their music, it's a hugely popular place, yet has never sold its soul to tourism.

Westport is Mayo's nightlife hub, and its central location makes it a convenient and enjoyable base for exploring the county. While there's an abundance of B&Bs and hotels, rooms are in short supply during summer and special events.

WHEN TO GO

Galway's festival season runs throughout the summer, so book your accommodation well in advance. Everywhere else is busier, too, including the Aran Islands and Connemara.

Easter to May and late September into October can be beautiful, with fewer visitors, although some accommodation closes earlier for winter. Winter is colder and much quieter. Many accommodations and attractions are closed.

Sligo

Pedestrian streets lined with inviting shopfronts, stone bridges spanning the River Garavogue, and *céilidhs* (traditional music and dancing sessions) spilling from pubs contrast with contemporary art and glass towers rising from the prominent corners of compact Sligo. It makes a fantastic, low-key and easily manageable base for exploring Yeats country, and the countryside outside of town is gorgeous.

You'll find some B&Bs on Pearse Rd, but there are also many central spots – some stylish – as well as large resort-style hotels catering to holidaying families.

Ennis

Clare's charming commercial hub, Ennis *(Inis)* lies on the banks of the fast-moving River Fergus, which flows east, then south into the Shannon Estuary.

Formal sights are few, but the town centre's narrow, pedestrian-friendly streets are enjoyable to wander through. There's a good hostel and several hotels in the centre, as well as a range of modest B&Bs on many of the main roads into town – some an easy walk from the centre. Handily situated 23km north of Shannon Airport, it makes an ideal base for exploring the county: you can reach any part of Clare in under two hours from here.

TRANSPORT

Motorways connect Galway with Ennis and Limerick to the south (the section between Ennis and Limerick is tolled), but you're relying on single-lane roads to get pretty much everywhere else, including Connemara, The Burren and County Mayo.

The Aran Islands are only reachable by passenger ferry – from Rossaveal in County Galway and from Doolin in County Clare – and by plane from Connemara Regional Airport.

WHERE TO STAY

On the Mullet Peninsula in northern County Mayo, **Further Space** has eco-conscious self-catering glamping pods overlooking Termoncarragh Lake. The outdoor area is sheltered from the wind, and there's a communal area for cooking.

At **Fernwood Farm** just outside Clifden, your accommodation is either in a geodesic dome set in a canopy of trees or in a house set on stilts. There's also an outdoor hot tub and sauna.

In Enniscrone, the beachside **Ocean Sands Hotel** is a great family option, whether you stay in the hotel itself or in the collection of self-catering apartments.

RESOURCES

- **Wild Atlantic Way**
  Good resource for Ireland's best-known driving route. *thewildatlanticway.com*
- **Galway Tourism**
  The place for all things Galway city and county. *galwaytourism.ie*
- **West Clare**
  Packed with information on Clare, including attractions, accommodation and places to eat. *visitclare.ie*
- **Aran Islands**
  Dedicated site to the three islands off the Galway and Clare coast. *aranislands.ie*

WHAT'S ON

- **Willie Clancy Summer School**
  The country's best traditional music festival takes place in Milltown Malbay over nine days in July.
- **Galway International Arts Festival**
  Ireland's top arts festival sees musicians, comedians and artists descend on Galway over two weeks in July.
- **Ennis Trad Festival**
  Five days of traditional music in November.
- **Mayo Dark Sky Festival**
  Celebrate the night sky over three days in early November.

23

GALWAY & THE WEST OF IRELAND

BEST OF THE WEST

DURATION: 6 DAYS

DISTANCE: 890KM / 553 MILES

GREAT FOR: FOOD & DRINK, HISTORY, OUTDOORS

BEST TIME TO GO: JULY FOR THE BEST SELECTION OF SUMMER FESTIVALS.

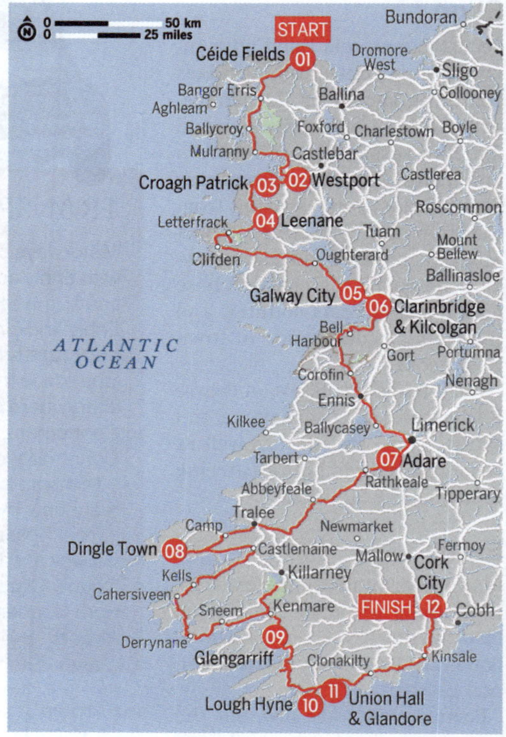

The most westerly fringe of Europe is the wild, rugged and incredibly beautiful west of Ireland, which is why Irish tourism created the Wild Atlantic Way (our Epic Trip, p22) as its signature driving route. This drive is shorter, but still takes in the best beaches in Europe, the epic landscapes of Connemara, culture-packed Galway and Clare, and the kingdom of Kerry right round to West Cork's wonderful fishing villages.

LINK YOUR TRIP

00 Sligo Surrounds
From Céide Fields continue northeast for a glimpse of Sligo's wild side.

00 Wexford & Waterford
When you hit Cork, keep going east through Ardmore to experience Ireland's sunny southeast.

01 Céide Fields

A famous wit once described archaeology as being all about 'a series of small walls'. But it's not often that said walls have experts hopping up and down with such excitement as at Céide Fields, 8km northwest of Ballycastle. During the 1930s, local man Patrick Caulfield was digging in the bog when he noticed piled-up stones buried beneath it. About 40 years later, his son Seamus, who had become an archaeologist on the basis of his father's discovery, uncovered the world's most extensive Stone Age monument, consisting of stone-walled fields, houses and megalithic tombs – as early as five millennia ago a thriving farming community had lived here. The award-winning **interpretive centre** *(heritageireland.ie)* gives a fascinating glimpse into these times. However, it's a good idea to take a guided tour of the site itself, or it may seem nothing more than, well, a series of small walls.

JACEK ROGOZ/SHUTTERSTOCK

★ BEST FOR

PHOTOGRAPHY

Take a boat tour from Dingle and visit the dolphins, whales, seals and seabirds.

Dolphin-spotting tour, Dingle (p179), Kerry

THE DRIVE: Head south to the hillside village of Mulranny – a prime vantage point for counting the 365 or so islands that grace Clew Bay. En route to the picturesque village of Newport look for signs to 15th-century Carrigahowley Castle (also called Rockfleet Castle). From there a wiggling 12km drive south leads to the atmospheric, pub-packed, heritage town of Westport.

02 Westport

Bright and vibrant even in the depths of winter, Westport (p182) is a photogenic Georgian town with tree-lined streets, riverside walks and a great vibe. Matt Malloy, the fife player from the Chieftains, opened **Matt Molloy's** *(mattmolloy.com)*, an old-school pub, years ago and the good times haven't let up.

Head to the back room around 9pm and you'll catch a *céilidh*. Or perhaps a veteran musician will simply slide into a chair and croon a few classics.

Westport House *(westporthouse.ie)* is a charming Georgian mansion with gardens and an adventure playground that make a terrific day's outing for all ages.

THE DRIVE: Just 15km southwest of town is Croagh Patrick, one of Ireland's most famous pilgrimage sites.

03 Croagh Patrick

St Patrick couldn't have picked a better spot for a pilgrimage than this conical mountain (also known as 'the Reek'). On a clear day the tough two-hour climb rewards with stunning views over Clew Bay and its sandy islets.

It was on Croagh Patrick that Ireland's patron saint fasted for 40 days and nights, and it's where he reputedly banished venomous snakes. Climbing the 764m holy mountain is an act of penance for thousands of believers on the last Sunday of July (Reek Sunday). The truly contrite take the ancient 35km pilgrim's route from Ballintubber Abbey, *Tóchar Phádraig* (Patrick's Causeway), and ascend the

GALWAY HOOKERS

Galway hookers are the iconic small sailing boats that were the basis of local seafaring during the 19th century and part of the 20th century. Small, tough and highly manoeuvrable, these wooden boats are undergoing a resurgence thanks to weekend sailors and hobbyists. The hulls are jet black, due to the pitch used for waterproofing, while the sails flying from the single mast are a distinctive rust colour. Expect to see them all along the Galway coast.

mountain barefoot. The 7km trail taken by the less repentant begins at a signed car park in the west end of the village of Murrisk.

THE DRIVE: The scenic route along Doolough Valley on the R335 to Leenane is the site of a tragic Famine walk of 1849, when in icy weather many people died as they walked from Louisburgh to Delphi in vain search of aid from a landlord. The side roads to the north and west of the valley lead to glorious beaches.

04 Leenane

The small village of Leenane (also spelt Leenaun) rests on the shore of dramatic **Killary Harbour**. Dotted with mussel rafts, the long, narrow harbour is Ireland's only fjord – maybe.

Slicing 16km inland and more than 45m deep in the centre, it certainly looks like a fjord, although some scientific studies suggest it may not actually have been glaciated. **Mt Mweelrea** (814m) towers to its north.

Leenane has both stage and screen connections. It was the location for *The Field* (1989), a movie with Richard Harris based on John B Keane's play about a tenant farmer's ill-fated plans to pass on a rented piece of land to his son.

THE DRIVE: From Leenane, an ultrascenic loop of Connemara via the N59 crosses the beauty spots of Kylemore Abbey (p192) and Connemara National Park (p201) and then on through the lively town of Clifden, where you continue east through Maam Cross into Galway city in under two hours.

05 Galway City

Galway city is a swirl of enticing old pubs that hum with trad music sessions throughout the year. More importantly, it has an overlaying vibe of fun and frolic that's addictive. Soak it up on a walk through the city's medieval centre.

Galway is often referred to as the 'most Irish' of Ireland's cities (and it's the only one where you're likely to hear Irish spoken in the streets, shops and pubs). **Tigh Neachtain** *(tighneachtain.com)*, a 19th-century pub known simply as Neachtain's (nock tans) or Naughtons and painted a bright cornflower blue, has a wraparound string of tables outside, many shaded by a large tree. It's a must-stop place where a polyglot mix of locals plop down and let the world pass them by. Nearby, the long-established and award-winning **Druid Theatre** *(druid.ie)* is famed for staging experimental works by young Irish playwrights, as well as new adaptations of classics.

Inagh Valley, Connemara, Galway
MILOSZ MASLANKA/SHUTTERSTOCK

☑ TOP TIP

THAT'S A GAS

A word of caution for visitors driving the wilds of Connemara: they're not called wilds for nothin'. There are long distances between petrol stations on those gorgeous swathes of uninhabited valley and sheep-dotted mountainside. What's more, the few stations that exist are often closed by early evening, so make sure you have enough fuel to keep you going for at least 80km. Find stations at Recess, Clifden and Kylemore.

THE DRIVE: There's plenty of time to think about lunch on the busy 20km seaside route between Galway city and County Clare. Clarinbridge and Kilcolgan offer welcome pit stops, especially if you're into oysters.

06 Clarinbridge & Kilcolgan

Some 16km south of Galway, **Clarinbridge** *(Droichead an Chláirin)* and **Kilcolgan** *(Cill Cholgáin)* are at their busiest during the **Clarenbridge Oyster Festival** *(galwaytourism.ie/event/clarenbridge-oyster-festival)*, held during the second weekend of September. However, the oysters are actually at their best from May through the summer. Oysters are celebrated year-round at **Paddy Burkes Oyster Inn** *(paddyburkesgalway.com)*, a thatched pub by the bridge in Clarinbridge that dishes up heaped servings.

> **PHOTO OPPORTUNITY**
>
> Clew Bay's many islands from the foot of Croagh Patrick.

In more scenic surroundings is another thatched inn – waterside **Moran's Oyster Cottage** *(moransoystercottage.com)*. Settle on the terrace overlooking Dunbulcaun Bay, where the oysters are reared. It's well signposted some 2km off the N18, in a cove near Kilcolgan, just south of Clarinbridge.

THE DRIVE: From the N67, it's a short jaunt to the sleepy harbour village of Kinvara. From Ballyvaughan the inspiring scenery along the R480 highlights the barren Burren and its scattered prehistoric stone structures at its best. Drive through Ennis and around the Limerick city bypass to the pretty village of Adare. It's just over two hours of driving in all.

07 Adare

Often dubbed 'Ireland's prettiest village', Adare centres on its clutch of perfectly preserved thatched cottages built by the 19th-century English landlord, the Earl of Dunraven, for workers constructing Adare Manor, now one of Ireland's fanciest hotels (and host to the 2027 Ryder Cup in golf). Today, the cottages house craft shops and some of the county's finest restaurants, with prestigious golf courses

Garinish Island (p181), Cork

FOTOGRO/SHUTTERSTOCK

nearby. Unsurprisingly, tourists are drawn to the postcard-perfect village, on the River Maigue, by the busload.

Dating back to around 1200, **Desmond Castle** *(heritageireland.ie)*, a picturesque feudal ruin, saw rough usage until it was finally wrecked for good by Oliver Cromwell's troops in 1657.

THE DRIVE: It's about two hours' drive southwest to Dingle (128km). The scenery ramps up several notches as you head from Tralee onto the peninsula – where the roads are pretty twisty – and over the famously picturesque Connor Pass.

08 Dingle Town

If you've arrived via the dramatic mountain-top Connor Pass, the fishing town of Dingle can feel like an oasis at the end of the earth...and maybe that's just what it is. Chocolate-box quaint, though grounded by a typical Kerry earthiness, its streets are crammed with brightly painted grocer-pubs and great restaurants, second-hand bookshops and, in summer, coachloads of visitors. Announced by stars in the pavement bearing the names of its celebrity customers, **Dick Mack's** *(dickmacks pub.com)* has an irrepressible sense of self. Ancient wood and ancient snugs dominate the interior, which is lit like the inside of a whiskey bottle.

There are regular boat and dolphin-spotting tours *(dingledolphin.com)* on the bay.

THE DRIVE: Dragging yourself away from Dingle, take the peninsula's lower road (R561) back, passing the windswept 5km stretch of dune-backed Inch Beach, and veer south at Castlemaine round the jewel

JOSE IGNACIO RETAMAL/SHUTTERSTOCK

Street performers, Eyre Square, Galway City

FESTIVALS OF FUN

Galway's packed calendar of festivals turns the city and surrounding communities into what feels like one nonstop party – streets overflow with revellers, and pubs and restaurants often extend their opening hours. The following are highlights:

- **Cúirt International Festival of Literature** *(cuirt.ie)* Top-name authors converge on Galway in April for one of Ireland's premier literary festivals.
- **Galway International Arts Festival** *(giaf.ie)* A two-week extravaganza of theatre, music and comedy in mid-July.
- **Galway Film Fleadh** *(galwayfilmfleadh.com)* One of Ireland's biggest film festivals, held in July.
- **Galway Race Week** *(galwayraces.com)* Horse races in Ballybrit, 7km northeast of the city, are the centrepiece each July or August of Galway's biggest, most boisterous festival of all.
- **Galway International Oyster and Seafood Festival** *(galwayoysterfest.com)* Oysters are washed down with plenty of pints in the last week in September.

of the southwest, the Ring of Kerry, through Kenmare to the magnificent Killarney National Park. The scenery becomes a lot wilder at Glengarriff on the awe-inspiring Beara Peninsula.

09 Glengarriff

Hidden deep in the Bantry Bay area, Glengarriff *(Gleann Garbh)* is an attractive village that snares plenty of passers-by. In the second half of the 19th century, Glengarriff became a popular retreat for prosperous Victorians, who sailed from England.

The tropical Italianate garden on **Garinish Island** *(garinishisland.ie)* is the top sight in Glengarriff. Subtropical plants flourish in the rich soil and warm climate. The camellias, magnolias and rhododendrons especially provide a seasonal blaze of colour. This little miracle of a place was created in the early 20th century, when the island's owner commissioned the English architect Harold Peto to design him a garden on the then-barren outcrop.

THE DRIVE: Wend your way down the N71 through Bantry and on to pretty Skibbereen, where you access the R595 and follow signs to Lough Hyne. Glengarriff to Lough Hyne is 55km.

10 Lough Hyne

This beautiful lough is one of Ireland's natural wonders, and in 1981 it became the country's first marine nature reserve. Its glacier-gouged depths were originally filled with fresh water until rising sea levels breached one end around 4000 years ago. It is now linked to the sea by a narrow tidal channel known as the Rapids, where the tide pours in and out twice a day in a rush of white water.

There are lovely walks around the lough and in the neighbouring **Knockomagh Wood Nature Reserve**. A waymarked nature trail leads up a steep hill through the forest; you're rewarded with stunning views at the top.

Atlantic Sea Kayaking *(atlanticseakayaking.com)* offers guided sea-kayak tours of the lough, including superbly atmospheric 2½-hour 'starlight paddles' after dark, where bioluminescence lights up the water in spectacular display.

THE DRIVE: Back at the N71, it's less than 10km to the dual villages of Union Hall and Glandore at Glandore Harbour.

11 Union Hall & Glandore

The pretty waterside villages of Union Hall and Glandore *(Cuan Dor)* burst into life in summer when fleets of yachts tack into the shelter of the Glandore Harbour inlet. A tangle of back roads meanders across the area; you should, too. Accessible from Glandore via a long, narrow causeway over the estuary, Union Hall was named after the 1801 Act of Union, which abolished the separate Irish parliament. There's an ATM, a post office and a general store here.

THE DRIVE: From here you can glide into Cork, 70km away, in about 1½ hours. Along the way, you'll drive through Clonakilty, where you can buy Ireland's most famous black (blood) pudding. Rather than follow the main N71 all the way, explore the picturesque R600 coastal road via Kinsale.

♥ WHY I LOVE THIS TRIP

BELINDA DIXON, WRITER

For many visitors, the best of the west is synonymous with the best of Ireland – the wild, rugged scenery is reason enough to do it, and that's before you meet the people, visit the pubs and eat the food. Six days is just about right to enjoy the experience, but you're just as likely to find a spot that you'll want to grow old in.

12 Cork City

Competing fiercely with Dublin for recognition, the south's largest city has arguably every bit as much to offer as the capital, yet on a smaller and even friendlier scale.

The River Lee flows around the centre, an island packed with grand Georgian parades, cramped 17th-century alleys and modern masterpieces, such as the opera house. Dotted around the compact centre are a host of historic buildings, cosmopolitan restaurants, local markets and cosy traditional bars. The award-winning **Glucksman Gallery** *(glucksman.org)*, in the grounds of **University College Cork** (UCC), is a startling limestone, steel and timber construction that displays the best in both national and international contemporary art and installation. It's always buzzing with people coming to attend lectures, view the artwork or procrastinate in the cafe.

River Lee, Cork City
LUCA REI/SHUTTERSTOCK

STAY AWHILE

WESTPORT

BY FIONN DAVENPORT

I'm happy pretty much anywhere along the west coast, but Westport just brings an extra big smile to my face. It's a handsome Georgian town – one of the few planned towns in Ireland – but that's only a small part of why I love it so much. There's enough here to distract you from the fact that the location is perfect – on the edge of Clew Bay and overshadowed to the south by mighty Croagh Patrick.

I love walking along the Carrowbeg River and through the estate woodland, which leads to the Georgian masterpiece that is **Westport House** *(westporthouse.ie)*, built on the remains of a castle that belonged to the pirate queen Grace O'Malley. A tour of Clew Bay is always a nice experience – **Westport Cruises** *(westportcruises.ie)* does 90-minute tours from the Quay that include seeing seal colonies and an island once owned by John Lennon.

Otherwise, it's all about eating and drinking well: my favourites include tiny **An Port Mór** *(anportmor.com)* for its Achill Island lobster and Clew Bay scallops; pizzas from **Wesport Woodfire** *(westportwoodfire.com)*; and **Savoir Fare** *(facebook.com/SavoirFareWestport)* if all I want is tasty cheese and good wines.

As good as the food scene is, the pub scene is even better. Everyone flocks to **Matt Molloy's** *(mattmolloy.com)*, which is one of the most famous pubs in Ireland, but nearby **Cobbler's** and the **Porter House** are just as good in terms of music, while **McGing's** on High St has a huge local following for its top-notch folk, bluegrass and jazz.

LINK YOUR TRIP

You can add to your Westport experiences on the **23 Best of the West** trip, which starts at the prehistoric Céide Fields in Mayo and ends in Cork city.

Left: Westport House;
Right: Matt Molloy's

FROM LEFT: GABRIELA INSURATELU/SHUTTERSTOCK, VINCENT MACNAMARA/SHUTTERSTOCK

PLACES TO STAY

As one of the most popular towns in the west, Westport has no shortage of decent acccommodation both in town and nearby. Staying just outside of town gives you more choice and views.

- **The Wyatt Hotel**
  Excellent three-star hotel overlooking the Octagon, with comfortable rooms, three restaurants and the lively Cobbler's pub on site. *wyatthotel.com*
- **The Mariner**
  Friendly, centrally located hotel with simple, clean rooms. *themariner.ie*
- **Knockranny House Hotel**
  Superb hotel just outside town with elegant rooms and sweeping views. *knockrannyhousehotel.ie*
- **Westport Woods Hotel**
  Handsome, large hotel surrounded by mature woodland. *westportwoodshotel.com*

24

GALWAY & THE WEST OF IRELAND

MUSICAL LANDSCAPES

★ BEST FOR

TUNES

Ennis, on summer nights, where local musicians showcase their skills.

Musicians, Galway City

DURATION: 5 DAYS

DISTANCE: 155KM / 96 MILES

GREAT FOR: FOOD & DRINK, HISTORY, OUTDOORS

BEST TIME TO GO: THE SUMMER MONTHS FOR OUTDOOR CÉILIDH AND MUSIC FESTIVALS.

Prepare for an embarrassment of musical riches. Join the big bawdy get-togethers of Galway's always-on music scene and Ennis' rollicking urban boozers. Then take a seat at the atmospheric small pub sessions in crossroad villages such as Kilfenora and Kilronan on the Aran Islands, where pretty much everyone joins in. Whatever way you like it, this region is undeniably one of Ireland's hottest for toe-tapping tunes.

LINK YOUR TRIP

25 Mountains & Moors
From Galway take in some of Connemara's loveliest points.

27 North Mayo & Sligo
Cruise up to Westport to join this wondrous trail around the hidden gems of north Connaught.

01 Galway City

Galway *(Gaillimh)* has a young student population and a largely creative community that give a palpable energy to the place. Walk its colourful medieval streets, packed with heritage shops, street-side cafes and pubs, all ensuring there's never a dull moment. Galway's pub selection is second to none and some swing to tunes every night of the week. **Crane Bar** *(thecranebar.com)*, an atmospheric old pub west of the River Corrib, is the best spot in Galway to catch an informal *céilidh* most nights. Or for something more contemporary, **Róisín Dubh** *(roisindubh.net)* is the place to hear emerging international and local singer-songwriters.

THE DRIVE: From Galway city centre, follow the coast road (R338) east out of town as far as the N18 and then cruise south to Ennis, where your great musical tour of Clare begins.

JON CHICA/SHUTTERSTOCK

02 Ennis

Ennis *(Inis)*, a medieval town in origin, is packed with pubs featuring trad music. **Brogan's** *(facebook.com/brogansennis)*, on the corner of Cook's Lane, sees a fine bunch of musicians rattling even the stone floors almost every night in summer, while the wood-panelled **Poet's Corner Bar** is a hideout for local musicians serious about their trad sessions. The tourist office collates weekly live music listings for the town's pubs. **Cois na hAbhna** *(coisna habhna.ie)*, a pilgrimage point for traditional music and culture, has frequent performances and a full range of classes in dance and music; it's also an archive and library of Irish traditional music, song, dance and folklore.

Traditional music aficionados might like to time a visit with **Fleadh Nua** *(fleadhnua.com)*, a lively festival held in late May.

THE DRIVE: From the N85, which runs south of The Burren, you'll arrive at the blink-and-you'll-miss-it village of Inagh. Swing right on to the smaller R460 for the run into Miltown Malbay – some 32km in all.

03 Miltown Malbay

Miltown Malbay was a resort favoured by well-to-do Victorians, though the beach itself is 2km southwest at **Spanish Point**. To the north of the Point there are beautiful walks amid the low cliffs, coves and isolated beaches. A classically friendly place in the chatty Irish way, Miltown Malbay hosts the annual **Willie Clancy Summer School**, one of Ireland's great trad music events. In town, one of a couple of genuine old-style places with occasional trad sessions is **Friel's Bar** (the sign over the door says 'Lynch's'). Another top music pub is the dapper **Hillery's**.

THE DRIVE: Hugging the coast, continue north on the N67 until you come to the small seaside resort of Lahinch (p188). Just a few streets backing a wide beach, it's renowned for surfing. From here, it's only 4km up the road to the lovely heritage town of Ennistymon.

04 Ennistymon

Ennistymon *(Inis Díomáin)* is one of those charming market towns where people go about their business barely noticing the characterful buildings lining Main St.

Behind this bustling facade there's a surprise: the roaring **Cascades**, the stepped falls of the River Inagh. After heavy rain they surge, beer-brown and foaming, and you risk getting drenched on windy days in the flying drizzle.

Not to be missed, **Eugene's** is intimate and cosy, and has a trademark collection of visiting cards covering its walls, alongside photographs of famous writers and musicians. The inspiring collection of whiskey (Irish) and whisky (Scottish) will have you smoothly debating their relative merits.

Another great trad pub is **Cooley's House**, with music most nights in summer and several evenings a week in winter.

THE DRIVE: Heading north through a patchwork of green fields and stony walls on the R481, you'll land at the tiny village of Kilfenora, some 9km

THE PIED PIPER

Half the population of Miltown Malbay seems to be part of the annual **Willie Clancy Summer School** *(scoilsamhraidhwillie clancy.com)*, a tribute to a native son and one of Ireland's greatest pipers.

The eight-day festival, now in its fourth decade, begins on the first Saturday in July, when impromptu sessions occur day and night, the pubs are packed and Guinness is consumed by the barrel – up to 10,000 enthusiasts from around the globe turn up for the event.

Specialist workshops and classes underpin the event; don't be surprised to attend a recital with 40 noted fiddlers.

later. Despite its diminutive size, the pulse of Clare's music scene beats strongly in this area.

05 Kilfenora

Underappreciated Kilfenora *(Cill Fhionnúrach)* lies on the southern fringe of The Burren. It's a small place, with a diminutive 12th-century **cathedral**, which is best known for its **high crosses**.

The town has a strong music tradition that rivals that of Doolin but without the crowds. The celebrated **Kilfenora Céilí Band** *(kilfenoraceiliband.com)* has been playing for more than a century. Its traditional music features fiddles, banjos, squeeze boxes and more and can be enjoyed most Wednesday evenings at **Linnane's Pub**. A short stroll away, **Vaughan's** *(vaughanspub.ie)* has music in the bar every night during the summer and terrific set-dancing sessions in the neighbouring barn on Sunday nights.

THE DRIVE: From Kilfenora, the R476 meanders northwest 8km to Lisdoonvarna, home of the international matchmaking festival. Posh during Victorian times, the town is a little less classy today, but friendly, good-looking and far less overrun than Doolin.

06 Lisdoonvarna

Lisdoonvarna *(Lios Dun Bhearna)*, often just called 'Lisdoon', is well known for its mineral springs. For centuries people have been visiting the local spa to swallow its waters.

Down by the river at **Roadside Tavern** *(facbook.com/TheRoadside Tavern)*, third-generation owner Peter Curtin knows every story worth telling. There are trad sessions nightly in summer and on Friday and Saturday evenings in winter. Look for a trail beside the pub that runs 400m down to two wells by the river.

A few paces from the tavern, the **Burren Smokehouse** *(burren smokehouse.ie)* is where you can learn about the ancient Irish art of oak-smoking salmon.

THE DRIVE: Just under 10 minutes' drive west, via the R478/479, you'll reach the epicentre of Clare's trad music scene, Doolin. Also known for its setting – 6km north of the Cliffs of Moher – Doolin is really three small neighbouring villages. First comes Roadford, then 1km west sits Doolin itself, then another 1km west comes pretty Fisherstreet, nearest the water.

07 Doolin

Doolin gets plenty of press as a centre of Irish traditional music, owing to a trio of pubs that have sessions throughout the year.

McGann's *(mcgannspubdoolin.com)* has all the classic touches of a full-on Irish music pub; the action often spills out onto the street.

Right on the water, **Gus O'Connor's** *(gusoconnorsdoolin.com)*, a sprawling favourite, has a rollicking atmosphere. It easily gets the most crowded and has the highest tourist quotient.

McDermott's *(MacDiarmada's; mcdermottspub.com)* is a simple and sometimes rowdy old pub popular with locals.

THE DRIVE: This 'drive' is really a sail – you'll need to leave your car at one of Doolin's many car parks to board the ferry to the Aran Islands.

08 Inishmore

The Aran Islands sing their own siren song to thousands of travellers each year, who find their desolate beauty beguiling. The largest and most accessible Aran, Inishmore *(Inis Mór)*, is home to ancient fort **Dun Aengus** *(Dún Aonghasa; heritageireland.ie)*, one of the oldest archaeological remains in Ireland, as well as some lively pubs and restaurants in the only town, **Kilronan**. Irish remains the local tongue, but most locals speak English with visitors.

Tí Joe Watty's Bar *(joewattys.ie)* is the best pub in Kilronan, with

JULIEN BEHAL/ALAMY STOCK PHOTO

Performance by the Kilfenora Céilí Band

traditional sessions most summer nights. Turf fires warm the air on the 50 weeks a year when this is needed. Informal music sessions, glowing fires and a broad terrace with harbour views make **Tí Joe Mac's** another local favourite, as is the **Bar** *(inismorbar.com)*, which has nightly live music from May to mid-October, and weekends the rest of the year.

THE DRIVE: In the summer passenger ferries run regularly between the Aran Islands. They cost €10 to €15; schedules can be a little complex – book in advance.

09 Inisheer

On Inisheer *(Inis Oírr)*, the smallest of the Aran Islands, the breathtakingly beautiful end-of-the-earth landscape adds to the island's distinctly mystical aura. Steeped in mythology, traditional rituals are very much respected here. Locals still carry out a pilgrimage with potential healing powers, known as the Turas, to the **Well of Enda**, an ever-burbling spring in the southwest.

For a week in late June the island reverberates to the thunder of traditional drums during **Craiceann Inis Oírr International Bodhrán Summerschool** *(craiceann.com)*. Bodhrán masterclasses, workshops and pub sessions are held, as well as Irish dancing.

Rory Conneely's atmospheric inn **Tigh Ruairí** (Rory's) hosts live music sessions and, here since 1897, **Tigh Ned** *(tighned.com)* is a welcoming, unpretentious place, with harbour views and lively traditional music.

PHOTO OPPORTUNITY

Set-dancing at the crossroads, in Vaughan's of Kilfenora.

STAY AWHILE

LAHINCH

BY FIONN DAVENPORT

If Lahinch sat a little closer to the equator, I suspect its main street would be lined with five-star hotels and its summer calendar anchored by a film festival. As it is, the Irish Biarritz has never needed the gloss. The big draw for me is the world-class **golf course** *(lahinchgolf.com)*, designed by Old Tom Morris and extending right from the village centre, which explains its nickname, the St Andrew's of Ireland.

For most others, though, the big draw is the **beach**, a broad crescent of sand facing into sheltered Liscannor Bay. This is one of Ireland's premier surf spots, and in summer I watch learners wobble to their feet under the patient eye of instructors: **Ben's Clinic** *(bens surfclinic.com)* and **The Green Room** *(thegreenroom.ie)* – both on the seafront – provide lessons and board rental, while families paddle in the shallows, content to let the day drift by.

One of my favourite places to eat in town is **Joe's Café**, which doesn't look like much from the outside but serves terrific fare – and all of it is sourced locally: the beef from Roughan's butchers in Ennistymon, the sausages from Loughnane's in Galway and all of their greens from Celtic Salads, a farm in The Burren. Alternatively, **Barrtrá** *(barrtra.com)* is a fabulous seafood restaurant in a whitewashed cottage overlooking fields and water.

Later, on Main St, I find a pint waiting at **O'Looney's**, the Atlantic still moving somewhere just beyond the glass. And if I want some traditional music with my pint, there's always **Kenny's** nearby.

LINK YOUR TRIP

Lahinch is on the 29 **County Clare** loop, which also includes the Aran Islands, and you can easily join the 24 **Musical Landscapes** drive too.

Left: Lahinch Golf Club;
Right: Surfing, Lahinch Beach

FROM LEFT: SHUTTERUPEIRE/SHUTTERSTOCK, MARK GUSEV/SHUTTERSTOCK

PLACES TO STAY

Lahinch is a popular holiday town, so there's no shortage of accommodation, including lots of private self-catering properties. My favourites, though, are traditional hotels.

Lahinch Coast Hotel
This handsome four-star hotel on Station Rd is a reliable favourite, with spacious, modern rooms, a good restaurant and a lively bar. The leisure centre, with its 17m pool and sauna, adds to its appeal. *lahinchcoast hotel.ie*

Atlantic Hotel
Set on the waterfront, this traditional hotel offers comfortable rooms and plenty of old-world charm, making it a welcoming and well-located base in Lahinch. *atlantichotel.ie*

25

GALWAY & THE WEST OF IRELAND

★ BEST FOR

DIVING

The turquoise water of Glassilaun Bay offers superb diving.

MOUNTAINS & MOORS

DURATION: 6 DAYS

DISTANCE: 206KM / 128 MILES

GREAT FOR: FOOD & DRINK, HISTORY, OUTDOORS

BEST TIME TO GO: WINTER, WHEN THE SEA AND LANDSCAPE ARE AT THEIR WILDEST.

Glassilaun Beach (p192), Galway

West of Galway the scenery behind the windscreen becomes increasingly wild and rugged. Crossing the Gaeltacht (Gaelic-speaking territory) beyond Spiddal, you'll take in the cottage of writer, poet and Easter Rising leader Pádraig Pearse, characterful Roundstone for exceptional food, and the impossibly blue waters of white-sand bays. A spin through Connemara's heartland to Gothic Kylemore Abbey brings you to pretty Oughterard and back on to Galway.

LINK YOUR TRIP

24 Musical Landscapes
This rip-roaring ride takes you from Galway's music bars to the best trad sessions of Clare.

26 Loughs of the West
Cruise Galway's gorgeous inland waterways on this tour of its lakes and rivers. Pick it up at Delphi, near Leenane.

01 Galway City

County Galway's namesake city is such a charmer you might not want to tear yourself away to the countryside. Arty, bohemian Galway city *(Gaillimh)* is renowned for its pleasures. Brightly painted pubs heave with live music, while cafes offer front-row seats for observing street performers, weekend hen parties run amok, lovers entwined and more.

Steeped in history, the city nonetheless has a contemporary vibe. Walking the cobblestone streets you'll find remnants of the medieval town walls between shops selling Aran sweaters, handcrafted Claddagh (crowned-heart) rings, and stacks of secondhand and new books.

THE DRIVE: The slow coastal route (R336) between Galway and Connemara takes you past

D. RIBEIRO/SHUTTERSTOCK

pretty seascapes and villages. Opposite the popular Blue Flag beach Silver Strand, 4.8km west of Galway, are the Barna Woods, a dense, deep-green natural oak forest perfect for rambling and picnicking before hitting Spiddal.

02 Spiddal

Spiddal *(An Spidéal)* is a refreshingly untouched little village, and the start of the Gaeltacht region. On your right as you approach the settlement is **Spiddal Craft Village** *(Ceardlann an Spidéil; spiddalcrafts.com)*, where you can watch woodworkers, leatherworkers, sculptors and weavers plying their crafts.

Spiddal also makes an excellent foodie pit stop – for the top-notch coffee and fresh dishes of the craft village's own **Builín Blasta** *(builinblasta.com)* cafe, or first-rate seafood at the acclaimed **O'Grady's on the Pier** *(ogradysonthepier.ie)*.

THE DRIVE: West of Spiddal, the scenery becomes more dramatic, with fields criss-crossed by low stone walls rolling to a ragged shore. Carraroe *(An Cheathrú Rua)* has fine beaches, including the Coral Strand. Exploring the small roads surrounding Greatman's Bay reveals tiny inlets often watched over by local donkeys – the perfect scenic muse for a nationalist writer such as Pádraig Pearse.

03 Patrick Pearse's Cottage

Writer, poet and teacher Pádraig Pearse (1879–1916) led the Easter Rising with James Connolly and others in 1916; after the revolt he was executed by the British.

Pearse wrote some of his short stories and plays in this small thatched cottage *(Ionad Cultúrtha an Phiarsaigh; heritageireland.ie)* in a wonderfully picturesque location. Although the interior was burned out during the War of Independence, it has been restored and contains an interesting exhibition about Pearse's life.

THE DRIVE: The scenic R340 swings south along Kilkieran Bay, an intricate system of tidal marshes, basins and bogs containing an amazing diversity of wildlife. The R342 meanders past Cashel *(An Caiseal)*, skirting Bertraghboy Bay. At Toombeola a short trip south on the R341 takes you to the picture-postcard village of Roundstone. A drive of some 28km in all.

04 Roundstone

Clustered around a boat-filled harbour, Roundstone *(Cloch na Rón)* is one of Connemara's gems.

Colourful terrace houses and inviting pubs overlook the dark recess of Bertraghboy Bay, which is home to lobster trawlers and traditional currachs (rowing boats with tarred canvas bottoms stretched over wicker frames).

Wander the short promenade for views over the water to ribbons of eroded land. Malachy Kearns' **Roundstone Musical Instruments** *(bodhran.com)* is just south of the village in the remains of an old Franciscan monastery. Kearns is Ireland's only full-time maker of traditional bodhráns (handheld goatskin drums).

Watch him work and buy a tin whistle, harp or booklet filled with Irish ballads; there's also a small free folk museum and a cafe.

THE DRIVE: The R341 shadows the coast from Roundstone to Clifden. Beaches along here have such beautiful white sand and turquoise water that, if you added 10°C to the temperature, you could be in Antigua. Don't believe us? Feast your eyes on the azure waters and brilliant white-sand beaches of Gurteen Bay and Dog's Bay ahead.

> PHOTO OPPORTUNITY
>
> Create your own historic movie still at the Quiet Man Bridge.

05 Gurteen Bay & Dog's Bay

About 2.5km west of Roundstone, look for the turn to **Gurteen Bay** (sometimes spelt Gorteen Bay). After a further 800m there is a turn for **Dog's Bay**. Together, the pair form the two sides of a dog-bone-shaped peninsula lined with idyllic beaches. Park and enjoy a day strolling the grassy heads and frolicking on the hard-packed sand.

THE DRIVE: Dust the sand off for a 47km drive. Continue north on the R341 through the village of Ballyconneely to Clifden. There pick up the N59 for a scenic cruise north. At the Letterfrack crossroads turn left, signed Connemara Loop (also signed Scuba Dive West). Continue to follow those signs along bumpy, sometimes single-track, water-view lanes until you reach Glassilaun Beach.

06 Glassilaun Beach

Although Connemara is a pearl necklace of sights, the north coast is diamond encrusted. Gorgeous beaches frame stark, raw mountain vistas and views out to the moody sea. Glassilaun Beach is arguably one of Connemara's best, offering a gorgeous, dune-backed crescent of sand. Islands dot the bay and tawny hills surge up behind.

If you're drawn to the beauty of the underwater world, **Scubadive West** *(scubadivewest.com)*, based at Glassilaun Beach, runs highly recommended courses and dives. Beginners are welcome.

THE DRIVE: Continue southeast along the final 5km stretch of road that runs along Lough Fee. In spring, when the gorse explodes in yellow bloom, the views here are, again, simply breathtaking. When you hit the N59 head right (southwest) until, suddenly, imposing Kylemore Abbey appears, backed by mountains and surrounded by water, on your right.

07 Kylemore Abbey

Magnificently situated on the shores of a lake, the crenellated 19th-century neogothic fantasy **Kylemore Abbey** *(kylemoreabbey.com)* was built for a wealthy English businessman, Mitchell Henry, who spent his honeymoon in Connemara. His wife died tragically young.

Admission also covers the abbey's tranquil **Victorian walled gardens**. There's a cafe and a teahouse on the grounds, which also offer hikes and woodland walks. Prepare for large volumes of visitors in high summer, when it's best to arrive in the early morning for uncluttered views.

THE DRIVE: The next 50km stretch, heading towards Galway via the R344 and N59, cruises through a kaleidoscopic tapestry of typical Connemara scenery. It feels like the end of the earth with

Dog's Bay Beach, Galway
MARK GUSEV/SHUTTERSTOCK

colours changing from lime green, to mustard, to purple on the mountainside – views interrupted only by drystone walls, the odd derelict cottage or an oblivious sheep crossing your path.

08 Oughterard

The writer William Makepeace Thackeray sang the praises of the small town of Oughterard *(Uachtar Árd)*, saying: 'A more beautiful village can scarcely be seen'.

Even if those charms have faded a little over the years, shadows of its former Georgian glory remain. And it is one of Ireland's principal angling centres. If you see tourists wandering around, talking with a drawl, it's probably because they are here to relive the iconic American film *The Quiet Man.*

THE DRIVE: Heading east again, stop close by for a great photo op at 16th-century Aughnanure Castle, 4km east of Oughterard, off the N59. From here it's a 27km run into Galway city for a well-deserved pint at Galway's finest, Tigh Neachtain.

SUSANNE POMMER/SHUTTERSTOCK

Quiet Man Bridge

BRIDGING THE QUIET MAN

Whenever an American cable TV station needs a ratings boost, they invariably trot out the iconic 1952 film *The Quiet Man*. Starring John Wayne and filmed in lavish colour to capture the crimson locks of his costar Maureen O'Hara, the film regularly makes the top-10 lists of ageing romantic-comedy lovers for its portrayal of rural Irish life, replete with drinking and fighting, fighting and drinking etc.

Director John Ford returned to his Irish roots and filmed the movie almost entirely on location in Connemara and the little village of Cong, just over the border in County Mayo.

One of the most photogenic spots from the film, the eponymous **Quiet Man Bridge**, is just 7km west of Oughterard off the N59. Looking much as it did in the film, the picture-perfect arched span (whose original name was Leam Bridge) is a lovely spot. Purists will note, however, that the scene based here had close-ups done on a cheesy set back in Hollywood. That's showbiz.

Hardcore fans will want to buy the superb *The Complete Guide to The Quiet Man*, by Des MacHale. It's sold in most tourist offices in the area.

Kylemore Abbey (p192), Galway

NORADOA/SHUTTERSTOCK

26

GALWAY & THE WEST OF IRELAND

★ BEST FOR

FISHING

Loughs Corrib and Mask are world-renowned for their brown trout.

LOUGHS OF THE WEST

DURATION: 4–5 DAYS

DISTANCE: 243KM / 151 MILES

GREAT FOR: HISTORY, OUTDOORS

BEST TIME TO GO: MAY FOR ULTIMATE FISHING AND THE INISHBOFIN ARTS FESTIVAL.

Lough Corrib, Galway

Following the lay of the lakes, this panoramic waterside drive takes in the very best of Loughs Corrib and Mask. Pass the picture-postcard villages of Cong and Tourmakeady before crossing the barren beauty of Connemara to dramatic mountain-backed Delphi. Cruising Connemara's filigreed northern coast, you'll discover pretty strands and ancient remains both on the mainland and on the striking island retreat of Inishbofin.

LINK YOUR TRIP

00 Shannon River Route
From the waters to the wild, continue on the west's inland waterways at Portumna.

00 North Mayo & Sligo
Continue exploring the northwest's incredible coastline, joining the route at Westport.

01 Galway City

Galway's Irish name, Gaillimh, originates from the Irish word *gaill*, meaning 'outsiders' or 'foreigners', and the term resonates throughout the city's history. Colourful and cosmopolitan – many dark-haired, olive-skinned Galwegians consider themselves descended from the Spanish Armada – this small city is best explored by strolling its medieval streets.

Bridges arc the salmon-filled River Corrib, and a long promenade leads to the seaside suburb of **Salthill**, on Galway Bay, the source of the area's famous oysters. A favourite pastime for Galwegians and visitors alike is walking along the seaside **Prom**, running from the edge of the city along Salthill. Local tradition dictates 'kicking the wall' across from the diving boards before turning around.

In and around Salthill are plenty of cosy pubs from where you can watch storms roll over the bay.

THE DRIVE: From Galway take the inspiringly named Headford Rd north onto the N84 into, well, Headford, skirting Lough Corrib, the Republic's biggest lake, which virtually cuts off western Galway from the rest of the country. At the crossroads in the centre of Headford turn left, initially following brown tourist signs for Rinnaknock Pier, then later for Greenfields.

02 Lough Corrib

Just under 7km west of Headford, Greenfields pier juts out into Lough Corrib. Over 48km long and covering some 200 sq km, it encompasses more than 360 islands, including **Inchagoill**, home to some 5th-century monastic remains, a simple graveyard and the **Lugnaedon Pillar** – a 6th-century inscribed stone.

Inchiquin Island can be accessed by a short, water-framed road from Greenfields pier. The lough is world-famous for its salmon and wild brown trout, with the highlight of the fishing calendar being mayfly season, when zillions of the small bugs hatch over a few days (usually in May) and drive the fish – and anglers – into a frenzy.

Salmon begin running around June. Upstream, signs point towards the curious **Ballycurrin Lighthouse**, built in 1772 when the lake may have seen more traffic – it's Europe's only inland lighthouse.

THE DRIVE: From Headford, take the R334 north out of town as far as Cross, where you'll join the R346, which takes you into the outstanding village of Cong, some 16km later.

03 Cong

Sitting on a sliver-thin isthmus between Lough Corrib and Lough Mask, Cong complies with romantic notions of a traditional Irish village. Time appears to have stood still ever since the evergreen American classic *The Quiet Man* (p195) was filmed here in 1951.

Though popular on the tour-bus circuit, the wooded trails between the lovely 12th-century **Augustinian abbey** *(Mainistir Chonga)* and stately **Ashford Castle** *(ashfordcastle.com)* offer genuine quietude. First built in 1228 as the seat of the de Burgo family, one-time owner Arthur Guinness (of stout fame) turned the castle into a regal hunting and fishing lodge; today it's one of Ireland's very best hotels.

A range of **cruises** *(corribcruises.com)* on Lough Corrib depart from the Ashford Castle pier.

THE DRIVE: Next comes a 2km hop. From Cong take the R345 west out of town towards Cornamona. After you see the entrance for McGrath Quarry, take the first left then look out for the lay-by signed Pigeon Hole Wood.

04 Pigeon Hole

Pick up the path leading left into the woods. You're about to discover one of some half a dozen limestone **caves** that honeycomb the Cong area. Each has a colourful legend or story to its credit.

Pigeon Hole is one of the best caves; steep, slippery, stone steps lead down towards it and subterranean water flows here in winter.

BOYCOTT BEGINNINGS

It was near the unassuming little village of Neale, near Cong, that the term 'boycott' first came into use. In 1880 the Irish Land League, in an effort to press for fair rents and improve the lot of workers, withdrew field hands from the estate of Lord Erne, who owned much of the land in the area. When Lord Erne's land agent, Captain Charles Cunningham Boycott, evicted the striking labourers, the surrounding community began a campaign to ostracise the agent. Not only did farmers refuse to work his land, people in the town refused to talk to him, provide services or sit next to him in church. The incident attracted attention from the London papers, and soon Boycott's name was synonymous with such organised, nonviolent protests. Within a few months, Boycott gave up and left Ireland.

Keep an eye out for the white trout of Cong, a mythical woman who turned into a fish to be with her drowned lover.

THE DRIVE: After heading back into Cong, it's a 15-minute drive on the R345 and R334 north to Ballinrobe.

05 Ballinrobe

The small market town of Ballinrobe *(Baile an Roba)*, on the River Robe, is a good base for exploring trout-filled Lough Mask, the largest lake in the county.

St Mary's Church has an impressive collection of stained-glass windows by Ireland's renowned 20th-century artist Harry Clarke. One depicts St Brendan 'the Navigator', with oar in hand, who reputedly sailed to America long before Columbus.

You can access Lough Mask at **Cushlough Bay**, just 5km west of town. Take the Castlebar road north and immediately on the left you'll see signs for Cushlough. Follow these along winding lanes and eventually the road will open out into a wide car park with broad lough views. Here slender boats are pulled up onto the gravel and picnic tables dot the grass; it's a delightful place to pause and take in the views.

THE DRIVE: Rejoin the N84 as it stretches north, before veering west at Partry. The landscape is made up of mostly small farm holdings, rusty bogland and tumbledown drystone walls. Follow the serene lakeside route (R300) before pit stopping to take in the lake around Tourmakeady.

06 Tourmakeady

With the Partry Mountains acting as a picturesque backdrop to its west, the small village of Tourmakeady, on the shore of Lough Mask, is part of an Irish-speaking community.

Once a flax-growing area, its name is derived from *Tuar Mhic Éadaigh*, meaning 'Keady's field', referring to the field where the flax was once laid out to dry before spinning.

Tourmakeady Woods, with a charming **waterfall** at its centre, makes a wonderful spot for a picnic. Or head another 2km along R300 and refuel at the cosy **Paddy's Thatched Bar**, overlooking a shimmering expanse of water.

THE DRIVE: Follow the swooping, curling lakeside road, pulling in at stunning Lake Nafooey, at the foot of Maumtrasna, to take in the view. Head north on the R336 through Leenane and around the harbour, passing Assleagh Falls to Delphi, a scenic 45km in all.

07 Delphi

Geographically just inside County Mayo, but administratively in County Galway, this swathe of mountainous moorland is kilometres from any significant population, allowing you to set about the serious business of relaxing.

At the southern extent of the Doolough Valley, the area was named by its most famous resident, the second marquis of Sligo, who was convinced that it resembled the land around Delphi, Greece. If you can spot the resemblance, you've a better imagination than most, but in many ways it's even more striking than its Mediterranean namesake.

At the beautiful **Delphi Resort** opt for a day's surfing, kayaking or rock climbing, followed by a stay and some pampering spa treatments.

THE DRIVE: Return to Leenane and follow the N59 southwest to Letterfrack. Go through the town's crossroads and 400m later you'll see signs pointing left to the Connemara National Park Visitor Centre.

Tourmakeady Waterfall, Mayo
REMIZOV/SHUTTERSTOCK

> **PHOTO OPPORTUNITY**
>
> Cong, with the spectacular vista of Ashford Castle and the lake as backdrop.

08 Connemara National Park

Spanning 2000 dramatic hectares of bog, mountain and heath, Connemara National Park encloses a number of the **Twelve Bens**, including Bencullagh, Benbrack and Benbaun.

The heart of the park is *Gleann Mór* (Big Glen), through which the River Polladirk flows. There's fine walking up the glen and over the surrounding mountains. There are also short, self-guided walks and, if the Bens look too daunting, you can hike up **Diamond Hill** nearby.

Various types of flora and fauna native to the area are explained, including the huge elephant hawkmoth, in the excellent **visitor centre** *(connemaranationalpark.ie)*.

THE DRIVE: Zip back east on the N59 for 9km before joining the R344 south through the Lough Inagh Valley as it skirts the brooding Twelve Bens. The N59 then sweeps west to Clifden. A few killometres north, signs point you towards Omey Island, a jagged coastal route that leads to tiny Claddaghduff *(An Cladach Dubh)*.

09 Omey Strand

Omey Island (population 20) is a low islet of rock, grass, sand and a handful of houses. Between half tide and low tide you can walk to the island (or, if you're brave, drive) across the sand at Omey Strand. Tide times are displayed on the noticeboard in the car park; the route is marked by blue road signs bearing white arrows. Don't be tempted to cross between half tide and high tide, or if there's water on the route.

THE DRIVE: Return to Claddaghduff and head north to Cleggan to park and take the 30-minute ferry to Inishbofin.

10 Inishbofin

By day sleepy Inishbofin is a haven of tranquillity. You can walk or bike its narrow, deserted lanes, green pastures and sandy beaches, with farm animals and seals for company. But with no *gardaí* (Irish Republic police) on the island to enforce closing times at the pub, by night – you guessed it – Inishbofin has wild craic.

Situated 9km offshore, Inishbofin is only just under 6km long by 4km wide, and its highest point is a mere 86m above sea level. Inishbofin's pristine waters offer superb scuba diving, sandy beaches and alluring trails that encourage exploring.

The island well and truly wakes up during the **Inishbofin Arts Festival** *(inishbofin.com)* in May, which includes accordion workshops, archaeological walks, art exhibitions and concerts.

Ferries from Cleggan to Inishbofin are run by **Inishbofin Ferry** *(inishbofinferry.ie)*.

Twelve Bens, Connemara National Park, Galway
GREG FELLMANN/SHUTTERSTOCK

27

GALWAY & THE WEST OF IRELAND

NORTH MAYO & SLIGO

★ BEST FOR

OUTDOORS

Achill Island and Easkey offer surf and blustery beach walks.

DURATION: 4–5 DAYS

DISTANCE: 266KM / 165 MILES

GREAT FOR: FOOD & DRINK, OUTDOORS, FAMILIES

BEST TIME TO GO: IN EARLY AUTUMN CROWDS HAVE ABATED AND THE SEA IS WARMEST.

Keem Bay, Achill Island, Mayo

This area has something quietly special – the rugged and remote Atlantic scenery of the west, but with fewer crowds. Grab a board and face off an invigorating roller at Achill, take a restorative seaweed bath at Enniscrone, walk in WB Yeats' footsteps round the 'Lake Isle of Innisfree' at the foot of Benbulben and enjoy the unpretentious company of lively Westport.

LINK YOUR TRIP

28 Sligo Surrounds
Continue from Sligo to explore the county's rich megalithic remains, blustery beaches and Yeats' old stomping ground.

23 Best of the West
The *crème de la crème* of Ireland's west coast; pick up this route in Westport for a scenic and cultural feast.

01 Westport

Bright and vibrant even in the depths of winter, Westport is a photogenic Georgian town with tree-lined streets, riverside walkways and a great vibe. With an excellent choice of accommodation and restaurants and pubs renowned for their music, it's an extremely popular spot, yet has never sold its soul to tourism. A couple of kilometres west on Clew Bay, the town's harbour, **Westport Quay**, is a picturesque spot for a sundowner.

Westport House, built in 1730 on the ruins of the 16th-century castle of Grace O'Malley (Gráinne Ní Mháille or Granuaile; 1530–1603; p205), is a charming Georgian mansion that retains much of its original contents and has some stunning period-styled rooms. The house is set in glorious gardens.

Children will love the Pirate Adventure Park, complete with a

MARK GUSEV/SHUTTERSTOCK

swinging pirate ship, a 'pirate's playground' and a rollercoaster-style flume ride through a water channel.

THE DRIVE: A wiggling 12km drive north of Westport is the picturesque 18th-century village of Newport. Then comes Mulranny village on a narrow isthmus overlooking the 365 islands of Clew Bay. Just before the main R319 to Achill Island take the scenic route left (signed Ocean Rd). Once on Achill, cut left to pick up Atlantic Dr, signed Wild Atlantic Way.

02 Achill Island

Ireland's largest offshore island, Achill *(An Caol)*, is connected to the mainland by a short bridge. Despite its accessibility, it has plenty of that far-flung-island feeling: soaring cliffs, rocky headlands, sheltered sandy beaches, broad expanses of blanket bog and rolling mountains.

Slievemore Deserted Village, at the foot of Slievemore Mountain, is a poignant reminder of the island's past hardships. In the mid-19th century, as the Potato Famine took hold, starvation forced the villagers to emigrate, or die.

Except in the height of the holiday season, the Blue Flag beaches at **Dooega**, **Keem**, **Dugort** and **Golden Strand** are often pretty much deserted.

THE DRIVE: The superbly scenic R319 bounces past broad inlets and high hills back towards the mainland. At the junction with the N59, turn left towards Wild Nephin National Park. You're now deep amid beautifully bleak boglands dotted with drystone walls and sheep. About 14km later follow signs for the Ballycroy Visitor Centre, and its cafe, Ginger & Wild.

03 Wild Nephin National Park

Covering one of Europe's largest expanses of blanket bog, **Wild Nephin National Park** *(nationalparks.ie/wild-nephin)* is a gorgeously scenic region, where the River Owenduff wends its way through intact bogs.

The park is home to a diverse range of flora and fauna, including peregrine falcons, corncrakes and

PHOTO OPPORTUNITY

Wild Atlantic rollers at sunset on Easkey beach.

whooper swans. A nature trail with interpretation panels leads from the visitor centre across the bog with great views to the surrounding mountains.

If you wish to explore further, the challenging, 40km Bangor Trail crosses the park and leads to some of its most spectacular viewpoints.

THE DRIVE: Ballycroy is 18km south of Bangor Erris on the N59. Continuing north from here on to the R314, you'll pass the magnificent Stone Age monument at Céide Fields before heading through Ballycastle and on to the historic town of Killala.

04 Killala

The town itself is pretty enough, but Killala is more famous for its namesake bay nearby, and for its role in the French invasion, when in 1798 more than 1000 French troops landed at Kilcummin in Killala Bay. It was hoped that their arrival would inspire the Irish peasantry to revolt against the English. The rebellion though was short-lived; the events are marked by signs at **Killala Quay** – follow signs to it from the centre of town.

Lackan Strand, just to the west, is a stunning expanse of golden sand. There's good surf here, but you'll need to bring your own equipment.

THE DRIVE: Back on the R314, it's only 12km or so down to the provincial hub of Ballina, a busy market town.

05 Ballina

Mayo's second-largest town, Ballina, is synonymous with salmon. If you're here during fishing season, you'll see droves of green-garbed waders, poles in hand, heading for the River Moy – one of the most prolific rivers in Europe for catching the scaly critters – which pumps right through the heart of town.

You'll also spot salmon jumping in the Ridge (salmon pool), with otters and grey seals in pursuit.

One of the best outdoor parties in the country, the five day **Ballina Salmon Festival** *(ballinasalmonfestival.ie)* takes place in mid-July.

THE DRIVE: Taking the N59 northeast out of town towards Enniscrone, cut back up to the coast onto the small R297, which you'll meet just over 4km from Ballina.

06 Enniscrone

Enniscrone is famous for **Kilcullen's Seaweed Baths** *(kilcullenseaweedbaths.net)*, an Edwardian bathhouse that is one of the best and most atmospheric in the country. A stunning beach known as the Hollow stretches for 5km. Surf lessons and board hire are available from Enniscrone-based **7th Wave Surf School** *(surfsligo.com)*.

THE DRIVE: Some 14km north you'll come to the little village of Easkey.

07 Easkey

Easkey seems blissfully unaware that it's one of Europe's best year-round surfing destinations. Pub conversations revolve around hurling and Gaelic football, and facilities are few. The beach is signed from the eastern edge of town. It's overlooked by a 19m-high 12th-century ruined castle tower, the remains of a formidable stronghold. The uppermost level is known as the Sailor's Bed.

THE DRIVE: From Easkey, hug the winding coast road (R297) until you see signs for Aughris Head.

THE PIRATE QUEEN

The life of Grace O'Malley (Gráinne Ní Mháille or Granuaile; 1530–1603) reads like an unlikely work of adventure fiction. Twice widowed and twice imprisoned for acts of piracy, she was a fearsome presence in the troubled landscape of 16th-century Ireland, when traditional chieftains were locked in battle with the English for control of the country.

Grace was ordered to London in 1593, whereupon Queen Elizabeth I granted her a pardon and offered her a title: she declined, saying she was already Queen of Connaught.

Westport House *(westporthouse.ie)* now resides on the ruins of Grace's 16th-century castle.

08 Aughris Head

An invigorating 5km walk traces the cliffs around remote Aughris Head, where dolphins and seals can often be seen swimming into the bay. Birdwatchers should look out for kittiwakes, fulmars, guillemots, shags, storm petrels and curlews along the way. In a stupendous setting on the lovely beach by the cliff walk, the Beach Bar is tucked inside a 17th-century thatched cottage, with cracking traditional music sessions and superb seafood.

THE DRIVE: From Aughris rejoin the N59 heading broadly east and onto the N4 towards Sligo

Easkey, Sligo

BUZZ PICTURES/ALAMY STOCK PHOTO

JACKIE ELLIS/ALAMY STIOCK PHOTO

Kilcullen's Seaweed Baths, Sligo

IRELAND'S SEAWEED BATHS

Ireland's native spa therapy is the stuff of mermaid (or merman) fantasy. Part of Irish homeopathy for centuries, steaming your pores open and then submerging yourself in a seaweed bath is said to help rheumatism and arthritis, thyroid imbalances, even hangovers. Certainly, it leaves your skin feeling baby-soft: seaweed's silky oils contain a massive concentration of iodine, a key presence in most moisturising creams.

Seaweed baths are prevalent along the west coast but two places stand out. **Kilcullen's Seaweed Baths**, set within a grand Edwardian structure in Enniscrone, is the most traditional and has buckets of character. It seems perfectly fitting to sit with your head exposed and your body ensconced in an individual cedar steam cabinet before plunging into one of the original gigantic porcelain baths filled with amber water and seaweed.

For an altogether more modern setting, try **Voya Seaweed Baths** *(voyaseaweedbaths.com)*, in Strandhill, which has a beachfront location.

If too much relaxation is barely enough, both establishments also offer the chance to indulge in various other seaweed treatments, including body wraps and massages.

until you see a sign for Dromahair (R287). Take this small, leafy road east, skirting the south of Lough Gill.

09 Lough Gill

The mirrorlike 'Lake of Brightness', Lough Gill is home to as many legends as fish. One that can be tested easily is the story that a silver bell from the abbey in Sligo was thrown into the lough and only those free from sin can hear it pealing. (We didn't hear it...)

Two magical swathes of woodland – Hazelwood and Slish Wood – have loop trails; from the latter, there are good views of Innisfree Island, subject of WB Yeats' poem *'The Lake Isle of Innisfree'*. You can take a cruise on the lake from **Parke's Castle**.

THE DRIVE: Having soaked up the atmosphere of Yeats' backyard, make your way a few kilometres north, via the R288 and R286, to the hub of Yeats country, Sligo town.

10 Sligo Town

Sligo town is in no hurry to shed its cultural traditions but it doesn't sell them out, either. Pedestrian streets lined with inviting shopfronts, stone bridges spanning the River Garavogue, and *céilidh* spilling from pubs contrast with contemporary art and glass towers rising from prominent corners of the compact town. A major draw of Sligo's **County Museum** *(sligoarts.ie)* is the Yeats room, which features photographs, letters and newspaper cuttings connected with the poet WB Yeats, as well as drawings by his brother Jack B Yeats, one of Ireland's most important modern artists.

Lough Gill, Sligo
WALSHPHOTOS/SHUTTERSTOCK

28

GALWAY & THE WEST OF IRELAND

SLIGO SURROUNDS

DURATION: 5 DAYS

DISTANCE: 155KM / 96 MILES

GREAT FOR: HISTORY, FOOD & DRINK, OUTDOORS

BEST TIME TO GO: MAY, JUNE OR SEPTEMBER FOR FEWER CROWDS AND BETTER WEATHER.

Sligo offers wild beauty, but with a sense of quietude. Lush fields, lakes and flat-topped mountains provided inspiration for William Butler Yeats – a literary legacy that resounds to this day. And among the stretches of golden sands and legendary breaks that lure the surfing cognoscenti, you'll find a bounty of prehistoric sites, luxury spa treatments, elegant Georgian towns, little fishing villages and good old-fashioned country hospitality.

LINK YOUR TRIP

33 Northwest on Adrenaline
There's plenty more surf to be found on Donegal's beach beauties. From Grange stick north on the N15.

26 Loughs of the West
From the northwest's wild coast, turn it down a little for a tour of the west's serene lakelands, from Sligo on the N17.

01 Sligo Town

For a small provincial hub, Sligo, with its galleries, museums and atmospheric old pubs, is quite the cultural magnet. Thanks largely to WB Yeats' childhood affection for, and his association with, the area, Sligo attracts visitors keen to learn more about the poet's formative environment.

In the **Yeats Memorial Building** *(yeatssociety. com)*, in a pretty setting near Hyde Bridge, you can visit the **WB Yeats Exhibition**, with a video presentation and valuable draft manuscripts; the exhibition catalogue makes a good souvenir of Sligo. The charming tearoom has outdoor tables overlooking the river.

A leading contemporary-art centre in Ireland, the **Model** *(themodel.ie)* houses an impressive collection of contemporary Irish art, including works by Jack B Yeats (WB's brother), as well as a program of experimental theatre, music and film.

JON SULLIVAN/SHUTTERSTOCK

★ BEST FOR

ANCIENT HISTORY

South Sligo is stacked with megalithic dolmens and burial grounds.

Carrowkeel Megalithic Cemetery

THE DRIVE: The N4 cuts south, then southeast towards Carrowkeel Megalithic Cemetery (don't confuse it with the other Carrowkeel, just 5km south of Sligo town). Some 20km later turn right in Castlebaldwin at McDermott's Restaurant, then head left at the fork and follow the signs. The cemetery is 2km uphill from the car park.

02 Carrowkeel Megalithic Cemetery

With a god's-eye view of the county from high in the Bricklieve Mountains, it's little wonder this hilltop site was sacred in prehistoric times. The windswept location is simultaneously eerie and uplifting, its undeveloped, spectacular setting providing a momentous atmosphere.

Dotted with around 14 passage cairns, Carrowkeel dates from the late Stone Age (3000 to 2400 BCE). Climbing up from the car park the first tomb you'll reach is Cairn G. Above its entrance is a roof-box aligned with the midsummer sunset, which illuminates the inner chamber. The only other such roof-box known in Ireland is that at Newgrange in County Meath.

Everywhere you look across the surrounding hills, you'll see evidence of early life here, including about 140 stone circles, all that remain of the foundations of a large village thought to have been inhabited by the builders of the tombs.

THE DRIVE: From the Carrowkeel turning, rejoin the country lane, turning left initially, heading south then west to Keash (sometimes spelt Kesh). At the R295 turn right for Ballymote; immediately, the Caves of Keash appear high on the ridge on your right. After Ballymote lanes lined with moss-topped walls lead you across the N4 to Riverstown and signs for the Sligo Folk Park.

03 Riverstown

The endearing **Sligo Folk Park** *(sligofolkpark.com)* revolves around a lovingly restored 19th-century cottage. Humble thatched structures complement this centrepiece, along with scattered farm tools and an exhibit that honours the old country life.

Another fine reason to come here is to attend a nonfaith monastic retreat or a course on hemp lime plastering at the green-roofed **Gyreum** *(gyreum.com)*, a pudding-shaped eco-lodge hidden by the surrounding hills.

THE DRIVE: Returning to the N4, follow the Sligo road for some 15km till you veer off onto the R292 to the seaside resort of Strandhill.

04 Strandhill

The great Atlantic rollers that sweep the shorefront of Strandhill make this long, red-gold beach unsafe for swimming. They have, however, made it a magnet for surfers. Gear hire and lessons can be arranged through the various suppliers operating out of the **National Surf Centre**. Alternatively, take a gentler, warmer dip in the **Voya Seaweed Baths**.

A few kilometres towards Sligo, you can walk – at low tide only! – to **Coney Island**. Its New York namesake was supposedly named by a man from Rosses Point. The island's wishing well is reputed to have been dug by St Patrick (who, if all these tales are to be trusted, led a very busy life). Check tide times to avoid getting stranded.

THE DRIVE: Continue along the R292 before picking up the R291 out of Sligo town to cruise the coast to Rosses Point, 8km northwest of Sligo. This road can get busy with holidaymakers in summer.

05 Rosses Point

Rosses Point has two wonderful beaches and one of Ireland's most challenging and renowned golf links, **County Sligo Golf Course** *(countysligogolfclub.ie)*, which attracts golfers from all over the world. Fringed by the Atlantic and lying in the shadow of Benbulben, this is one of Ireland's greatest and most picturesque golf links.

Offshore, the odd **Metal Man** beacon dates from 1821. **Harry's Bar** *(harrysrossespoint.com)*, on your right as you enter town, has a historic well, an aquarium and maritime bric-a-brac. The **Yeats Country Hotel**, just up the hill, serves good bar food.

THE DRIVE: Returning via the R291 you'll pick up the busy N15 as you head north to the quaint town of Drumcliff, Yeats' final resting place, at the foot of Benbulben. It's 10km in all.

> PHOTO OPPORTUNITY
>
> Drumcliff cemetery with Benbulben in the background.

06 Drumcliff

Visible right along Sligo's northern coast, **Benbulben** (525m) resembles a table covered by a pleated cloth: its limestone plateau is uncommonly flat, and its near-vertical sides are scored by earthen ribs.

Benbulben's beauty was not lost on WB Yeats. Before the poet died in Menton, France, in 1939, he had requested that, should he die there, 'after a year or so' he be dug up and brought to Sligo. Someone was buried here, but there is an ongoing debate as to whether it was actually Yeats. Still, **Yeats' grave** is next to the doorway of the Protestant church in Drumcliff, and his youthful bride Georgie Hyde-Lee is buried alongside.

Historic **Lissadell House** *(lissadellhouse.com)*, west of Drumcliff off the N15 just past **Yeats Tavern**, is open for guided tours from June to August.

THE DRIVE: The light on Benbulben, looming in the distance inland, often changes the mountain from dark blue to purple or a mossy shade of green. Continue on the N15 less than 9km into the small village of Grange.

07 Grange

From the village of Grange, signs point towards **Streedagh Strand**, a grand crescent of sand that saw some 1100 sailors perish when three ships from the Spanish Armada were wrecked nearby.

Views extend from the beach to the cliffs at **Sliabh Liag** (Slieve League) in Donegal. Locals regularly swim here, even in winter.

Don't leave Grange without stopping into **Langs pub** *(langs.ie)* for a bite or to water the horses in the well-preserved front bar, with bottles of Guinness among the old washing powder and cereal boxes. It's one of the county's finest old grocery-draper-bars.

THE DRIVE: Keep heading north on the N15 until you reach the sleepy crossroads of Cliffony. In the centre of the village take a left, following signs for the R279 to Mullaghmore.

08 Mullaghmore

The sweeping arc of dark golden sand and the safe shallow waters make the pretty fishing village of Mullaghmore a popular family destination. Take time to drive the scenic road looping around Mullaghmore Head, where wide shafts of rock slice into the Atlantic surf.

Benbulben

DAMIENJKENNEDYPHOTOGRAPHY/SHUTTERSTOCK

En route you'll pass **Classiebawn Castle** – closed to the public – a neogothic turreted pile built for Lord Palmerston in 1856 and later home to the ill-fated Lord Mountbatten, who was killed here in 1979 when the Irish Republican Army (IRA) rigged his boat with explosives.

Mullaghmore Head is becoming known as one of Ireland's premier **big wave surf spots**, with swells of up to 30m allowing for Hawaiian-style adventure. Mullaghmore's clear waters, rocky outcrops and coves are also ideal for diving.

THE DRIVE: Once back on the N15 it's a straight run for some 27km back to Sligo, where you can enjoy a creamy pint in a snug at one of the region's finest traditional pubs, Thomas Connolly on Holborn St.

Classiebawn Castle

MNSTUDIO/SHUTTERSTOCK

MICHAEL QUIRKE: WOODCARVER OF WINE STREET

The inconspicuous studio of Michael Quirke, woodcarver, raconteur and local character, is filled with the scents of locally felled timbers and offcuts of beech stumps. A converted butcher shop on Wine St in Sligo town, it retains some of the implements of the butcher's trade, including an electric bone saw.

Quirke, himself formerly a butcher, began to use his tools for cutting and carving wood in 1968. He divided his time between his twin callings for 20 years, after which he gave up meat, so to speak.

Quirke's art is inspired by Irish mythology, a subject about which he is passionate and knowledgeable, and as he carves he readily chats with the customers and the curious who enter his shop and end up staying for hours. He draws unforced connections between Ireland's shifting myths, music, history, flora, fauna and contemporary events, as well as comparisons in the wider world, such as Australian First Nations and Native North American lore.

As he talks and carves, Quirke frequently pulls out a county map, pointing to places that spring from the conversation, leading you on your own magical, mystical tour of the county.

29

GALWAY & THE WEST OF IRELAND

COUNTY CLARE

★ BEST FOR

RAMBLING

Take blustery cliff walks, or cross The Burren on foot.

DURATION: 8-9 DAYS

DISTANCE: 299KM / 185 MILES

GREAT FOR: FOOD & DRINK, OUTDOORS, HIKING

BEST TIME TO GO: SPRING FOR THE AWAKENING OF NATURE IN THE BURREN.

Walking route, The Burren

From friendly market towns Ennis and Ennistymon down the cliff-fringed coast of Clare to its southernmost tip, the raggedly beautiful Loop Head, you'll encounter sandy strands and quiet coves just begging for company. In the summer you can island-hop between the Aran Islands, discovering historic relics and a taste of a simpler life, before returning to the mainland's homely resorts of Kilrush and Kilkee.

LINK YOUR TRIP

23 Best of the West
Having sampled the delicious Clare coast, take a wild southerly bite of Kerry and West Cork from Limerick down.

25 Mountains & Moors
If you like The Burren, you'll love Connemara. Join this trip at Ballyvaughan and wander west at Galway.

01 Ennis

Ennis *(Inis)* is the busy commercial centre of Clare. It lies on the banks of the smallish River Fergus, which runs east, then south into the Shannon Estuary. It's the place to stay if you want a bit of urban flair; a little short on sights, Ennis' strengths are its food, lodging and traditional entertainment.

The town's medieval origins are indicated by its irregular, narrow streets. Its most important historical site is **Ennis Friary** *(heritageireland.ie)*, founded in the 13th-century by the O'Briens, kings of Thomond, who also built a castle here.

THE DRIVE: A jaunt north, initially on the R476 towards Corofin, opens up the wondrous karst limestone of The Burren's heartland. Make sure you stop and take in primroses and other flora dotted in the crevices in spring. Skirting The Burren National Park, you'll turn left onto

TOLOBALAGUER.COMS/SHUTTERSTOCK

the N67 to get to Ballyvaughan, some 55km in all.

02 Ballyvaughan

Something of a hub for the otherwise dispersed charms of The Burren, Ballyvaughan *(Baile Uí Bheacháin)* sits between the hard land of the hills and a quiet leafy corner of Galway Bay. Just west of the village's junction is the **quay**, built in 1829 at a time when boats traded with the Aran Islands and Galway, exporting grain and bacon and bringing in turf – a scarce commodity in the windswept rocks of The Burren.

THE DRIVE: From Ballyvaughan the R477 clings to the coast, a leisurely 40-minute, shore-side ride down to Doolin, offering sweeping views over to the Aran Islands on your right. At Doolin, park and catch one of the ferries that run (between mid-March and October) to Inishmore, the first of three splendid castaway isles.

03 Inishmore

Most visitors who venture out to the islands don't make it beyond 14km long Inishmore *(Inis Mór)* and its main attraction, **Dun Aengus**, the stunning stone fort perched perilously on the island's towering cliffs.

The arid landscape west of Kilronan *(Cill Rónáin)*, Inishmore's main settlement, is dominated by stone walls, boulders, scattered buildings and the odd patch of deep-green grass and potato plants. It gets pretty crowded in summer but on foot or bike (for hire at the pier), you can happily set your own pace.

There's an EU Blue Flag white-sand beach (awarded for cleanliness) at **Kilmurvey**, peacefully situated west of bustling Kilronan. A **craft village**, where you'll find local women hand-knitting traditional Aran sweaters, sits nearby.

THE DRIVE: Prebook your seasonal interisland boat ticket (€10 to €15) with one of the ferry companies and check their sailing schedules for the latest crossing times.

04 Inishmaan

The least-visited of the islands, with the smallest population, Inishmaan *(Inis Meáin)* is a rocky respite. Early Christian monks seeking solitude were drawn to Inishmaan, as was the author JM Synge, who spent five summers here between 1898 and 1902. The island they knew largely survives today: stoic cows and placid sheep, impressive old forts and warm-hearted locals, who may tell you, with a glint in their eye, that they had a hard night on the whiskey the previous evening.

Inishmaan's scenery is breathtaking, with a jagged coastline of startling cliffs, empty beaches, and fields where the main crop seems to be stone. **Teach Synge**, a thatched cottage on the road just before you head up to the fort, is where JM Synge spent his summers.

05 Inisheer

Inisheer *(Inis Oírr)*, the smallest of the Aran Islands with a population of only around 200, has a palpable sense of enchantment, enhanced by the island's deep-rooted mythology, devotion to traditional culture and ethereal landscapes.

MARK GUSEV/SHUTTERSTOCK

Ferry from Doolin to the Aran Islands

GETTING TO & FROM THE ARAN ISLANDS

Flights and ferries serve the Aran Islands. Seasonal boats shuttle regularly from Doolin to the islands; ferries also run year-round from Rossaveal in County Galway.

From mid-March to October, **Doolin 2 Aran Ferries** and the **Doolin Ferry Co** *(doolinferry.com)* link the Arans with the mainland – they also run interisland services.

It takes around half an hour to cover the 8km from Doolin to Inisheer; a boat from the mainland to Inishmore takes at least 1¼ hours, while ferries from Doolin to Inishmaan take up to an hour. Expect to pay €45 to €55 return. Interisland boats cost €23 to €25. Each firm has an office at Doolin Pier or you can book online.

The ferry firms also offer various combo trips and Cliffs of Moher boat tours, which are best done late in the afternoon when the light is from the west.

Year-round, ferries also run to the Aran Islands from Rossaveal, 37km west of Galway. **Aran Island Ferries** *(aranislandferries.com)* has two to three crossings daily; a shuttle bus is available from Galway city.

Aer Arann Islands *(aerarannislands.ie)* has flights to each of the islands up to six times a day; the journey takes about 10 minutes and can be done as a day trip. Flights go from **Connemara Regional Airport** *(Aerfort Réigiúnach Chonamara)*; a shuttle bus links it with Galway city, 30km to the east.

Wandering the lanes with their ivy-covered stone walls and making discoveries here and there is the best way to experience the island.

At **O'Brien's Castle** *(Caisleán Uí Bhriain)*, a 100m climb to the island's highest point yields dramatic views over clover-covered fields to the beach and harbour.

Much more modern is an iconic island sight – the freighter, Plassy, that was thrown up on the rocks in 1960 in a storm. An aerial shot of the wreck was used in the opening sequence of the seminal TV series *Father Ted*.

THE DRIVE: Back on the mainland, it's back behind the wheel. From Doolin, it's a scenic 10-minute cruise on the coastal R478 to the famed, unmistakable Cliffs of Moher.

06 Cliffs of Moher

Star of a million tourist brochures the Cliffs of Moher *(Aillte an Mothair, or Ailltreacha Mothair)* are one of Ireland's most visited sights. But, as at many at-times overcrowded attractions, you have to get beyond the coach parties to experience what's drawn visitors in the first place - entirely vertical cliffs that rise to a height of 214m, with edges falling away abruptly into the constantly churning sea. A series of heads, the dark limestone seems to march in a rigid formation that amazes, no matter how many times you look.

Luckily crowds thin the further you get from the coach park. And if you're willing to walk for 10 minutes south past the end of the 'Moher Wall', there's a trail along the cliffs to **Hag's Head** – few venture this

Cliffs of Moher

PATRYK KOSMIDER/SHUTTERSTOCK

PHOTO OPPORTUNITY

A sunset shot over the Atlantic from Dun Aengus, Inishmore.

far. A vast **visitor centre** *(cliffsofmoher.ie)* is set back into the side of a hill, Hobbit house style.

For uncommon views of the cliffs and wildlife you might consider a **cruise**. The boat operators in Doolin offer popular tours of the cliffs.

THE DRIVE: A 10km drive through an ever-flattening landscape takes you to the small seaside resort of Lahinch (p188). From there the N67 darts 4km due east to the authentic rural market town of Ennistymon.

07 Ennistymon

Ennistymon (*Inis Díomáin*; sometimes spelt Ennistimon) is a genuinely charming market town. Here a postcard-perfect main street is lined with brightly coloured shopfronts and traditional pubs that host fantastic trad sessions throughout the year. From the roaring **Cascades**, the stepped falls of the River Inagh, there are picturesque walks downstream.

Each Saturday morning the stalls of a **farmers market** fill Market Sq.

THE DRIVE: Next comes a 74km picturesque trip down the coastal N67 and then the R487. The landscape between the old-fashioned resort of Kilkee and Loop Head in the south has subtle undulations that suddenly end in dramatic cliffs falling off into the Atlantic. It's a windswept place with timeless striations of old stone walls.

08 Loop Head

Discriminating travellers come here for coastal views that are in many ways more dramatic than the Cliffs of Moher. On a clear day, Loop Head *(Ceann Léime)*, Clare's southernmost point, has magnificent views south to the Dingle Peninsula crowned by Mt Brandon (952m), and north to the Aran Islands and Galway Bay. There are bracing walks in the area including **heritage trails** around Kilkee and a 15km clifftop circuit. A working **lighthouse** (complete with fresnel lens) is the punctuation on the far southwestern point.

THE DRIVE: A scenic 40km drive north on the R487 and east on the N67 brings you to the bustling local resort of Kilrush.

09 Kilrush

Kilrush *(Cill Rois)* is a small, atmospheric town that overlooks the Shannon Estuary and the hills of Kerry to the south. From the town's big marina, you can head out on cruises run by **Dolphin Discovery** *(discoverdolphins.ie)* to see the pods of bottlenose dolphins that live in the estuary, an important calving region for the mammals.

The remarkable 'lost' **Vandeleur Walled Garden** *(vandeleurwalledgarden.ie)* was the private domain of the wealthy Vandeleur family – merchants and landowners. The gardens are just east of the centre and have been redesigned and planted with colourful tropical and rare plants.

THE DRIVE: After all that sea air and seafood you'll be ready for a straight 40-minute jaunt (on the N68) inland back to Ennis.

Ennistymon

PATRYK KOSMIDER/SHUTTERSTOCK

0 50 km
0 25 miles
SCOTLAND
Campbeltown
North Channel
Rathlin Island
Ballintoy
Ballycastle
35
Bushmills
Armoy
Cushendun
Waterfoot
A44
30
Glenarm
Portrush
Downhill
Coleraine
Ballymoney
Limavady
Kilrea
Broughshane
Larne
Ballymena
Kells
Ballynure
ANTRIM
Antrim
M2
Newtownabbey
Bangor
Newtownards
BELFAST
M1
Lisburn
34
Comber
Hillsborough
DOWN
Downpatrick
Malin Head
Ballyliffin
32
Moville
Buncrana
Lough Foyle
Muff
A2
Burt
Derry
N13
Tory Island
Dunfanaghy
Carrigart
Milford
Gortahork
Gweedore
N56
31
Letterkenny
Arranmore Island
Leabgarrow
Dungloe
Fintown
Narin
Glenties
Maghera
Ardara
Glencolumbcille
DONEGAL
Carrick
Killybegs
Sliabh Liag Sea Cliffs
N15
Stranorlar
Donegal
Rossnowlagh
Donegal Bay
Ballyshannon
Bundoran
Grange
LEITRIM
FERMANAGH
Claudy
Strabane
DERRY
Dungiven
Maghera
Castledawson
Sperrin Mountains
Toome
Newtownstewart
Creggan
Cookstown
Lough Neagh
Omagh
TYRONE
Dromore
A5
Dungannon
Ballygawley
Portadown
Lurgan
Tandragee
Banbridge
Armagh
Fivemiletown
Enniskillen
A1
Rathfriland
Castlewellan
ARMAGH
Lisnaskea
Upper Lough Erne
Monaghan
Newtownhamilton
Newry
Clones
MONAGHAN
Castleblayney
Kilkeel
Belturbet
Cootehill
Carlingford
Carrickmacross
Dundalk
Erris Head
Portacloy
Belderrig
33
Ballycastle
Kilglass
Dromore West
Sligo
N16
Manorhamilton
Belmullet
MAYO
Killala
Enniscrone
Ballysadare
SLIGO
Bangor Erris
Crossmolina
Ballina
Tubbercurry
Ballymote
Lough Allen
Ballinamore
Killeshandra
Cavan
Achill Island
Ballycroy
Lough Conn
Foxford
Gurteen
Boyle
Carrick-on-Shannon
Charlestown
Swinford
Ballaghaderreen
CAVAN
Kingscourt
Ardee
Dunleer
Irish Sea
Mulranny
Castlebar
Kiltimagh
ROSCOMMON
Virginia
Louisburgh
Westport
Ballyhaunis
Tulsk
Longford
Kells
LOUTH
Drogheda
Castlepollard
Navan
Leenane
Lough Mask
Ballinrobe
Ballymoe
Balbriggan
Letterfrack
Dunmore
Roscommon
Lough
LONGFORD
MEATH
Mullingar

NICOLAS D'HOEDT/LONELY PLANET

Narin's Blue Flag beach (p230), Donegal

BELFAST & THE NORTH OF IRELAND

EXPLORE

BELFAST & THE NORTH OF IRELAND

Ireland's north is made for road trips. Routes swoop from hard, stark hills to soft, sandy shores, and cliff-hanging roads snake into wild lands peppered with loughs, glens and bogs. There are epic sights like the Giant's Causeway and the cliffs at Slieve League, but in between you'll find stately homes, romantic castles and countless beaches where you can find solitude as well as a host of activities, from surfing to horseback riding.

Within easy reach are the north's main cities of Derry and Belfast – hives of cosmopolitan activity that provide fascinating insights into a now receded troubled past.

Belfast

A former industrial powerhouse with a troubled past, Belfast has pulled off a remarkable transformation into a hip city with a vibrant nightlife. In the south of the city, the Lisburn Rd has lots of high-end boutiques and homewares stores, while the compact city centre is full of high-street names, as well as a number of independent shops selling top-quality local arts and crafts, and plenty of specialist food and drink.

And speaking of food, from fine dining to market grazing, it's easy to eat well in Belfast. Many of Belfast's midrange restaurants punch well above their price bracket, with menus of expertly prepared dishes served in contemporary dining spaces. The city's top restaurants include two Michelin-star establishments, both located in the city centre. Most fine-dining restaurants offer tasting menus, usually with optional wine pairings; be sure to book several weeks in advance for weekend tables.

In terms of accommodation, the range of places to stay in Belfast widens every year, from backpacker hostels to boutique havens. Most budget and midrange accommodation is south of the centre, in the leafy university district around

WHEN TO GO

June is the best time to spot puffins nesting at the Rathlin West Light Seabird Centre. July's warm weather makes this the best month for hiking in the Mournes and Sperrins, and October sees the Belfast International Arts Festival bring three weeks of theatre, music, dance and talks to the city.

Botanic Ave, University Rd and Malone Rd, around a 20-minute walk from City Hall. Business and luxury boutique hotels proliferate in the city centre. Most of these don't have dedicated car parks, but they do have deals with local providers.

Derry (Londonderry)

Northern Ireland's second-largest city continues to flourish as an artistic and cultural hub. It's had a substantial makeover in the last decade, particularly visible on the redeveloped waterfront and in the Guildhall area, where planners have taken full advantage of the city's splendid riverside setting. Derry is also gaining a reputation as a foodie city, with several excellent restaurants specialising in fresh local produce having opened in recent years.

All of the usual supermarkets are represented in the city, and you'll have no trouble getting every kind of provision you'll need for your driving trips. Derry also has a good range of sleeping options, most of them within walking distance of the main sights in the city centre. It's best to book accommodation in advance during festivals and events, as places are likely to fill up.

TRANSPORT

The easiest way to get around Northern Ireland is by car; roads are good and traffic is rarely a problem (although avoid routes in and around Belfast at rush hour).

Buses serve urban areas and connect the province's main towns and cities, with less frequent services to most (but not all) rural villages. Some towns are linked to Belfast by train.

WHERE TO STAY

Four luxury lodges set in a forest near Coleraine make up the **Burrenmore Nest**, including two set on stilts at canopy level.

In Belfast's Queen's Quarter, **Regency House** is a luxury boutique hotel in an elegant Georgian terrace; everything is seriously classy, including the Drawing Room restaurant.

An Cúlú is the Irish for 'retreat', and this stunning home near Donegal town is the perfect spot to disappear to if you're a family or big group – plus there's a beach nearby.

Stay in one of **Finn Lough's** stylish bubble domes, spread throughout a forest in Fermanagh.

RESOURCES

- **Go Visit Donegal**
  Visitor information and tips for Donegal. *govisitdonegal.com*
- **Discover Northern Ireland**
  Official tourist site for Northern Ireland. *discovernorthernireland.com*
- **Visit Belfast**
  Information on stays, attractions, transport, festivals, events and itineraries. *visitbelfast.com*
- **Visit Belfast**
  Local website highlighting news and events, with tourist information. *thebelfasttimes.com*
- **The Big List Entertainment**
  Listings for Belfast and beyond. *thebiglist.co.uk*

WHAT'S ON

- **Féile an Phobail**
  Ireland's largest community festival takes place in West Belfast over 10 days in August.
- **Cathedral Quarter Arts Festival**
  Ten days of drama, music, poetry, street theatre and art exhibitions in and around Belfast's Cathedral Quarter in early May.
- **Irish National Surfing Championships**
  Bundoran hosts the best surfers in the country, usually in autumn (September to November).

30

BELFAST & THE NORTH OF IRELAND

THE NORTH IN A NUTSHELL

DURATION: 10 DAYS

DISTANCE: 470KM / 292 MILES

GREAT FOR: HISTORY, OUTDOORS

BEST TIME TO GO: MARCH TO JUNE AND SEPTEMBER MEAN GOOD WEATHER BUT FEWER CROWDS.

★ BEST FOR

SCENERY

Stops 16 to 20 head into the heart of wild, wind-whipped Donegal.

Malin Head (p229), Donegal

On this road-trip-to-remember you'll drive routes that cling to cliffs, cross borders and head high onto mountain passes. You'll witness Ireland's turbulent past and its inspiring path to peace. And you'll also explore rich faith, folk and music traditions, ride a horse across a sandy beach, cross a swaying rope bridge and spend a night on a castaway island. Not bad for a 10-day drive.

LINK YOUR TRIP

34 From Bangor to Derry
Encounter seaside fun, a grand stately home and the king's official residence. Begin 20km east of Belfast at Bangor.

04 Tip to Toe
Take in the cream of Irish music and poetry. Start where this trip stops: Glencolumbcille.

01 Belfast

In bustling, big-city Belfast the past is palpably present – walk the city's former sectarian battlegrounds for a profound way to start exploring the North's story. Next, cross the River Lagan and head to the Titanic Quarter. Dominated by the towering yellow Harland and Wolff (H&W) cranes, it's where RMS *Titanic* was built. **Titanic Belfast** *(titanicbelfast.com)* is a stunning multisensory experience: see bustling shipyards, join crowds at Titanic's launch, feel temperatures drop as it strikes that iceberg, and look through a glass floor at watery footage of the vessel wreckage.

Slightly to the west, don't miss the **Thompson Graving Dock** *(titanicdistillers.com/pages/dry-dock-tour)*, where you descend into the immense dry dock where the liner was fitted out.

THE DRIVE: As you drive the M3/M2 north, the now-familiar H&W cranes recede. Take the A26 through Ballymena; soon the Antrim *(Aontroim)* Mountains loom large to the right. Skirt them, following the A26 then the A44 into Ballycastle, 96km from Belfast.

02 Ballycastle

Head beyond the sandy beach to the harbour at the appealing resort of Ballycastle (p232). From here, daily **ferries** *(rathlin-ferry.com)* depart for **Rathlin Island**, where you'll see sea stacks and thousands of guillemots, kittiwakes, razorbills and puffins.

THE DRIVE: Pick up the B15 towards Ballintoy, which meanders up to a gorse-dotted coastal plateau where hills part to reveal bursts of the sea. As the road plunges downwards, take the right turn to the Carrick-a-Rede Rope Bridge (10km).

03 Carrick-a-Rede Rope Bridge

The **Carrick-a-Rede Rope Bridge** *(nationaltrust.org.uk/carrick-a-rede)* loops across a surging sea to a tiny island 20m offshore. This walkway of planks and wire rope sways some 30m above the waves, testing your nerve and head for heights.

The bridge was originally put up each year by salmon fishers to help them set their nets, and signs along the 1km clifftop hike to the bridge detail the fascinating process. Declining stocks have put an end to fishing, however. If you want to cross the bridge, it's best to book a ticket online in advance as numbers are limited.

THE DRIVE: The B15 then the A2 snake west along clifftops and past views of White Park Bay's sandy expanse. Swing right onto the B146, passing Dunseverick Castle's fairytale tumblings, en route to the Giant's Causeway (11km).

04 Giant's Causeway

Stretching elegantly out from a rugged shore, the **Giant's Causeway** *(nationaltrust.org.uk)* is one of the world's true geological wonders. Clambering around this jetty of fused geometric rock chunks, it's hard to believe it's not human-made.

Legend says Irish giant Finn McCool built the causeway to cross the sea to fight Scottish giant Benandonner.

More prosaically, scientists tell us the 60-million-year-old rocks were formed when a flow of molten basaltic lava cooled and hardened from the top and bottom inwards. It contracted and the hexagonal cracks spread as the rock solidified.

Entry to the causeway site is free, but to use the National Trust car park you'll need to buy a ticket that includes the **Giant's Causeway Visitor Experience**.

THE DRIVE: Continue west, through Bushmills, with its famous distillery, picking up the A2 Causeway Coastal Route, signed to Portrush. You'll pass wind-pruned trees, crumbling Dunluce Castle and Portrush's long sandy beaches before arriving at Portstewart (16km).

05 Portstewart

Time for some unique parking. Head through resort-town Portstewart, following signs for the Strand (beach). Ever-sandier roads descend to an immense shoreline that doubles as a **car park** *(nationaltrust.org.uk/portstewart-strand)*. It's a decidedly weird experience to drive and park *(£8.50)* on an apparently endless expanse of hard-packed sand. It's also at your own risk, which doesn't deter the locals (but do stick to central, compacted areas).

Nearby, a 1km **walking trail** meanders up a sand ladder, through huge dunes and past marram grass and occasional orchids.

THE DRIVE: Take the A2 west, through Coleraine towards Downhill. About 1km after the Mussenden Temple's dome appears, take Bishop's Rd left up steep hills with spectacular Lough Foyle views. Descend, go through Limavady and onto the B68 (signed Dungiven). Soon a brown country park sign points to Roe Valley (42km).

> ☑ TOP TIP
>
> ### THE BORDER
>
> Driving 20 minutes north out of Derry will see you entering another country: the Republic of Ireland. On road signs, be aware speed limits will suddenly change from mph to km/h, while wording switches from English to Irish and English. Stock up on euros in Derry or visit the first post-border ATM.

06 Roe Valley

This beguiling **country park** is packed with rich reminders of a key Irish industry: linen production. The damp valley was ideal for growing the flax that made the cloth; the fast-flowing water powered the machinery.

The **Green Lane Museum**, near the car park, features sowing fiddles, flax breakers and spinning wheels. Look out for nearby watchtowers, built to guard linen spread out to bleach in the fields, and **Scutch Mills**, where the flax was pounded.

THE DRIVE: Head back into Limavady to take the A2 west to Derry (28km). Green fields give way to suburbs then city streets.

07 Derry

Northern Ireland's second city offers another powerful insight into the North's troubled past and the remarkable steps towards peace. It's best experienced on foot.

Partway round, drop into the **Tower Museum** *(towermuseumcollections.com)*. Its imaginative 'Story of Derry' exhibit leads you through the city's history, from the 6th-century monastery of St Colmcille (Columba) to the 1969 Battle of the Bogside. Some time in 2027, the museum is set to close and its exhibits will move to the new **DNA Museum** *(dnamuseum.com)*.

THE DRIVE: The A2 heads north towards Moville. Soon speed-limit signs switch from mph to km/h: welcome to the Republic of Ireland. Shortly after Muff take the small left turn, signed Iskaheen, up the hill. Park beside Iskaheen church (11km).

08 Iskaheen

It's completely off the tourist trail, but Iskaheen church's tiny **graveyard** offers evidence of two of Ireland's most significant historical themes: the poverty that led to mass migration and the consequences of sectarian violence. One gravestone among many is to the McKinney family, recording a string of children dying young: at 13 years, 11 months, nine months and six weeks. It also bears the name of 34-year-old James Gerard McKinney, one of 13 unarmed civilians shot dead when British troops opened fire on demonstrators on Bloody Sunday, 30 January 1972.

Carrick-a-Rede Rope Bridge (p225), Antrim

WIRESTOCK CREATORS/SHUTTERSTOCK

CAUSEWAY COAST WALKS

The official **Causeway Coast Way** *(walkni.com)* stretches for 53km from **Ballycastle** to **Portstewart**, but individual chunks can be walked whenever you feel like stretching your legs. Day hikes include the supremely scenic 16.5km section between **Carrick-a-Rede** and the **Giant's Causeway** – one of the finest coastal walks in Ireland. Shorter options also abound, including a 2km ramble around **Portrush**, a 1.5km stroll on sandy **White Park Bay** and a 300m scramble around ruined **Dunluce Castle**.

THE DRIVE: Rejoin the R238 north, turning onto the R240 to Carndonagh, climbing steeply into rounded summits. After quaint Ballyliffin and Clonmany, pick up the Inis Eoghain Scenic Route signs towards Mamore's Gap, and park at the Glenevin Waterfall car park.

09 Glenevin Waterfall

Welcome to Butler's Bridge – from here a 1km trail winds beside a stream through a wooded glen to Glenevin Waterfall, which cascades 10m down the rock face. It's an utterly picturesque, gentle, waymarked route – the perfect leg stretch.

THE DRIVE: The Inis Eoghain snakes south up to Mamore's Gap, a high-altitude, white-knuckle mountain pass that climbs 260m on single-lane, twisting roads, past shrines to the saints. After a supremely steep descent (and glorious views) go south through Buncrana, and onto Fahan (37km), parking beside the village church.

10 Fahan

St Colmcille founded a monastery in Fahan in the 6th century. Its creeper-clad ruins sit beside the church.

Among them, hunt out the beautifully carved **St Mura Cross**. Each face of this 7th-century stone slab is decorated with a cross in intricate Celtic weave. The barely discernible Greek inscription is the only one known in Ireland from this early Christian period and is thought to be part of a prayer dating from 633.

THE DRIVE: Take the N13 to Letterkenny, before picking up the R245 to Rathmelton (aka Ramelton) , a 10km sweep north through the River Swilly valley. Turn off for the village, heading downhill to park beside the water in front of you (50km).

11 Rathmelton (Ramelton)

In this picture-perfect town, rows of Georgian houses and rough-walled stone warehouses curve along the River Lennon. Strolling right takes you to a string of three-storey, three-bay Victorian warehouses; walking back and left up Church Rd leads to the ruined **Tullyaughnish Church** with its Romanesque carvings in the eastern wall.

Glenevin Waterfall, Donegal

BONN BONN FOTO/SHUTTERSTOCK

Walking left beside the river leads past Victorian shops to the three-arched, late-18th-century Rathmelton Bridge.

THE DRIVE: Cross the town bridge, turning right (north) for Rathmullan. The hills of the Inishowen Peninsula rise ahead and Lough Swilly swings into view – soon you're driving right beside the shore. At Rathmullan (11km), make for the harbour car park.

12 Rathmullan

Refined, tranquil Rathmullan was the setting for an event that shaped modern Ireland. In 1607 a band of nobles boarded a ship here, leaving with the intention of raising an army to fight the occupying English. But they never returned. Known as the Flight of the Earls, it marked the end of the Irish (Catholic) chieftains' power. Their estates were confiscated, paving the way for the Plantation of Ulster with British (Protestant) settlers. Beside the sandy beach, look for the striking modern sculpture, depicting the earls' departure, waving to their distressed people as they left.

THE DRIVE: Head straight on from the harbour, picking up Fanad/Atlantic Dr, a roller-coaster road that surges up Lough Swilly's shore, round huge Knockalla, past the exquisite beach at Ballymastocker Bay and around Fanad Head. It then hugs the (ironically) narrow Broad Water en route to Carrigart (74km), with its village-centre horse-riding centre.

13 Carrigart

Most visitors scoot straight through laid-back Carrigart, heading for the swimming beach at Downings. But they miss a real treat: a horse ride on a vast beach. The **Carrigart Riding Centre** *(instagram.com/carrigartstables)* is just across the main street from sandy, hill-ringed Mulroy Bay, meaning you can head straight onto the beach for an hour-long ride amid the shallows and the dunes. There are hourly trips, and it's best to book.

THE DRIVE: Head south for Creeslough. An inlet with a creamy, single-towered castle soon pops into view. The turn-off comes on the plain, where brown signs point through narrow lanes and past farms to Doe Castle (12km) itself.

> **PHOTO OPPORTUNITY**
>
> Crossing the Carrick-a-Rede Rope Bridge as it wobbles above the waves.

14 Doe Castle

The best way to appreciate the charm of early-16th-century Doe Castle *(heritageireland.ie)* is to wander the peaceful grounds, admiring its slender tower and crenellated battlements. The castle was the stronghold of the Scottish MacSweeney family until it fell into English hands in the 17th century. It's a deeply picturesque spot: a low, water-fringed promontory with a moat hewn out of the rock.

THE DRIVE: Near Creeslough, the bulk of Muckish Mountain rears up before the N56 to Dunfanaghy undulates past homesteads, loughs and sandy bays. Once in Dunfanaghy, with its gently kooky vibe, welcoming pubs and great places to sleep, look out for the signpost pointing right to Horn Head (25km).

15 Horn Head

This headland provides one of Donegal's best clifftop drives: along sheer, heather-topped quartzite cliffs with views of an island-dotted sea. A circular road bears left to the coastguard station – park to take the 20-minute walk due north to the signal tower.

Hop back in the car, continuing east – around 1km later a viewpoint sits atop cliffs 180m high. There's another superb vantage point 1km further round – on a fine day you'll see Ireland's most northerly point, **Malin Head**.

THE DRIVE: The N56 continues west. Settlements thin out, the road climbs and the pointed peak of Mt Errigal fills more and more of your windscreen before the road swings away. At tiny Crolly follow the R259 towards the airport then turn right, picking up signs for Leo's Tavern (35km).

16 Meenaleck

You never know who'll drop by for one of the legendary sing-alongs at **Leo's Tavern** *(leostavern.com)* in Meenaleck. It's owned by Bartley Brennan, brother of Enya and her siblings Máire, Ciaran and Pól (aka the group Clannad). The pub glitters with gold, silver and platinum discs and is packed with musical mementos – there's live music nightly in summer.

THE DRIVE: Continue west on the R259 as it bobbles and twists beside scattered communities and an at-first-boggy then sandy shore. Head on to the pocket-sized port of Burtonport, following ferry signs right, to embark for Arranmore Island (25km).

♥ WHY I LOVE THIS TRIP

ISABEL ALBISTON, WRITER

Starting in Belfast, a city whose turbulent history seems finally to come second to its flourishing future, this trip gives a sense of the north's past and present while showcasing a stunning natural landscape so old – the striking hexagonal rocks of the Giant's Causeway date back 60 million years – it makes the region's troubles seem like a blip on the timeline.

17 Arranmore Island

Arranmore *(Árainn Mhór)* offers a true taste of Ireland. Framed by dramatic cliff faces, vast sea caves and clear sandy beaches, this 9km by-5km island sits 5km offshore. Here you'll discover a prehistoric triangular fort and an offshore bird sanctuary fluttering with corncrakes, snipes and seabirds.

Irish is the main language spoken, pubs put on turf fires and traditional-music sessions run late into the night. **The Arranmore Ferry** *(arranmoreferry.com)* takes 20 minutes and runs up to eight times a day.

THE DRIVE: The R259 bounces down to Dungloe, where you take the N56 south into a rock-strewn landscape that's backed by the Blue Stack Mountains. After a stretch of rally-circuit-esque road, the sweep of Gweebarra Bay emerges. Take the sharp right towards peaceful Narin (R261), following signs to the beach *(trá)*, 45km from Arranmore Island.

DETOUR

Fintown Railway

Start: 17 Arranmore island

You've been driving for days now – time to let the train take the strain. The charming **Fintown Railway** *(antraen.com)* runs along a rebuilt 5km section of the former County Donegal Railway track beside picturesque Lough Finn. It's been lovingly restored to its original condition and a return trip in the red-and-white, 1940s diesel railcar takes around 40 minutes. To get to the railway, head east on the R252, off the N56 south of Dungloe. Then settle back to enjoy the ride.

18 Narin

You've now entered the beautiful Loughrea Peninsula, which glistens with tiny lakes cupped by undulating hills. Narin has a spectacular 4km-long, wishbone-shaped Blue Flag beach, the sandy tip of which points towards Inishkeel Island. You can walk to the island at low tide along a 500m sandy causeway. Your reward? An intimate island studded with early Christian remains: St Connell, a cousin of St Colmcille, founded a monastery here in the 6th century.

THE DRIVE: Continue south on the R261 through tweed-producing Ardara. Shortly after leaving town, take the second turning (the first turning after the John Malloy factory outlet), marked by a hand-painted sign to 'Maghera', following a road wedged between craggy hills and an increasingly sandy shore. In time the Assarancagh Waterfall (14km) comes into view.

19 Assarancagh Waterfall

Stepping out of the car reveals just what an enchanting spot this is. As the waterfall streams down the sheer hillside, walk along the road (really a lane) towards the sea. This 1.5km route leads past time-warp farms – sheep bleat and the tang of peat smoke scents the air.

At tiny **Maghera** head through the car park, down a track, over a boardwalk and onto a truly stunning expanse of pure-white sand. This exquisite place belies a bloody past. Local legend has it that some 100 villagers hid from Cromwell's forces in nearby caves – all except one were discovered and massacred.

THE DRIVE: Drive west through Maghera on a dramatic route that makes straight for the gap in the towering hills. At the fork, turn right, heading deeper into the remote headland, making for Glencolumbcille (20km).

20 Glencolumbcille

The welcome in the scattered, pub-dotted, bayside village of Glencolumbcille *(Gleann Cholm Cille)* is warm. This remote settlement also offers a glimpse of a disappearing way of life. **Glencolmcille Folk Village** *(glenfolkvillage.com)* took traditional life of the 1960s and froze it in time. Its thatched cottages recreate daily life with genuine period fittings, while the craft shop sells wines made from such things as seaweed, as well as marmalade and whiskey truffles – a few treats at your journey's end.

North West 200

WILL BROADHEAD/ALAMY STOCK PHOTO

NORTH WEST 200 ROAD RACE

Driving this delightful coast can have its challenges, so imagine doing it at high speed. Each May the world's best motorcyclists do just that, going as fast as 300km/h in the **North West 200** *(northwest200.org)*, which is run on a road circuit taking in Portrush, Portstewart and Coleraine. This classic race is Ireland's biggest outdoor sporting event and one of the last to take place on closed public roads anywhere in Europe. It attracts up to 150,000 spectators; if you're not one of them, it's best to avoid the area on the race weekend.

STAY AWHILE

BALLYCASTLE

BY ISABEL ALBISTON

With a thriving trad music scene, breathtaking coastal views, a sandy beach that's generally safe for swimming and fantastic food, Ballycastle is my favourite place to stay on the north coast. The main street is lined with independent local businesses; I always make a stop at **Ursa Minor** *(ursaminor-bakehouse.com)*, where some of Ireland's best sourdough loaves are baked. And when it comes to historic pubs with lively trad sessions, you're spoilt for choice. Dating from 1761, the **Boyd Arms** feels like a living museum (the Guinness is great here, too), but it's not even the town's oldest family-run pub; that distinction is held by **House of McDonnell**, established in 1744. While you're in town, be sure to try the fish and chips from **Morton's** by the harbour.

Another reason I love Ballycastle is the spectacular views of the Fairhead cliffs and Rathlin Island. **Kintra Boat Tours** *(kintraboattours.co.uk)* runs trips from the harbour, including a two-hour spin to see the seals, lighthouses and seabirds of Rathlin Island from the water, passing sea stacks where puffins can be seen nesting in the spring and summer months. Alternatively, take a boat trip along the coast as far as the Carrick-a-Rede Rope Bridge, with views of Kinbane Castle along the way. You might even spot dolphins and basking sharks. Ballycastle is also the starting point of the **Causeway Coast Way**, a scenic 50km hiking trail. After your walk, soothe your aching muscles in a seaweed bath at **Sea Haven Therapy** *(seahaventherapy.com)*.

LINK YOUR TRIP

Ballycastle is midway on the drive 34 **From Bangor to Derry**, or continue west into Donegal on 30 **The North in a Nutshell**.

FROM LEFT: JOAQUIN OSORIO CASTILLO/SHUTTERSTOCK, JORGE TUTOR/ALAMY ATOCK PHOTO

Left: Guinness, House of McDonnell; Right: Morton's

PLACES TO STAY

Ballycastle's accommodation options range from traditional B&Bs to a luxury hotel.

- **An Caisleán**
  A traditional, family-run B&B located a short walk from the beach and the town centre. The guest lounge is great for post-road-trip card games. *corratavey.ie*

- **Marine Hotel**
  An excellent choice for families, with spacious rooms, some of which have sea views. Activities include yoga, sea swimming and bike hire. *marinehotelballycastle.com*

- **Salthouse Hotel**
  Perched on a hilltop on the outskirts of town, this modern, carbon-neutral and sumptuously decorated luxury hotel has outstanding views of the coastline, two restaurants and a spa. Catch performances by local musicians in the bar. *thesalthousehotel.com*

31

BELFAST & THE NORTH OF IRELAND

DELIGHTS OF DONEGAL

★ BEST

TWO DAYS

From tweed town via mountain to classic Irish island: stops 6 to 8 deliver the essence of Donegal.

Dunlewey Lough (p236)

DURATION: 7 DAYS

DISTANCE: 427KM / 265 MILES

GREAT FOR: HISTORY, OUTDOORS

BEST TIME TO GO: EASTER TO OCTOBER – SIGHTS AND ACTIVITIES ARE OPEN; WEATHER MIGHT BE BETTER.

This trip prompts diverse sensations: looming Mt Errigal is overwhelming; a swim at Downings beach feels liberating; and driving the high mountain passes is heart-in-the-mouth stuff. Relax on boat trips around Donegal Bay to 600m-high sea cliffs and an island, then encounter international art, Ireland's traditional industries and piles of hand-cut peat beside the road. On this trip you gain a true insight into delightful Donegal.

LINK YOUR TRIP

28 Sligo Surrounds
A five-day meander through culture-packed Sligo. Head for Sligo town, 50km south of this trip's start.

32 Inishowen Peninsula
An exhilarating foray onto a remote headland. Start in Derry, 20km east of this trip's finish.

01 Rossnowlagh

There's more to the happy-go-lucky resort of Rossnowlagh than its superb 3km sandy beach. Deep in a forest (signed off the R231 south of town), a **Franciscan Friary** *(rossnowlaghfriary.ie)* offers tranquil gardens and the Way of the Cross walk, which meanders up a hillside smothered with rhododendrons and with spectacular views.

THE DRIVE: The R231 heads north through a gently rolling landscape, joining the N15 for a smooth run into Donegal town (19km). Head for the waterfront, parking near the pier.

02 Donegal Town

With its handsome castle, waterside location and Blue Stack Mountains backdrop, Donegal town is a delightful stop. Drink in the beauty of Donegal Bay on the

NICOLAS D'HOEDT/LONELY PLANET

Donegal Bay Waterbus *(donegalbaywaterbus.com)*, a 1¼-hour boat tour that will see you gazing at historic sites, seal-inhabited coves, an island manor and a ruined castle.

THE DRIVE: Take the N56 west. The Blue Stack Mountains retreat in your wing mirror, an open coast road unfurls and soon the wafer-thin St John's peninsula comes into view. Turn off left, heading out to its tip for 32km.

03 St John's Point

This improbably thin finger of land pokes into the sea, culminating at St John's Point. Driving the 11km lane to the tip feels like driving into the ocean. The point itself has a small sandy beach, rich bird and plant life, total tranquillity and (inevitably) remarkable, wrap-around views.

THE DRIVE: Continue west on the N56 then take the R263 through fish-scented Killybegs. After its harbour full of trawlers, signs appear for Sliabh Liag, the towering mountains that loom ever closer ahead. After Carrick comes tiny Teelin *(Tieleann)*, 34km from St John's Point.

04 Sliabh Liag

From the road so far, Sliabh Liag (Slieve League) has looked like an impressive mountain range, but these sheer 600m-high sea cliffs are utterly awe-inspiring when seen from the water at their base. Boats leave from Teelin; book with **Sliabh Liag Boat Trips** *(sliabhleagueboattrips.com)*.

THE DRIVE: Back at Carrick, edge west on the R263 before turning left on the minor route signed Malin Beg *(Málainn Bhig)*. It cuts behind the massive peaks of Sliabh Liag, threading through an increasingly remote landscape, dotted with isolated farms and scored while cutting strips of hand-cut turf (peat). It's 12km to Malin Beg.

05 Malin Beg

Malin Beg is one of Donegal's wildest spots, which is quite something in a county crammed with them.

An undulating sea-monster-like headland snakes in the waves. Sligo's coast appears distant to the south, and a creamy lighthouse sits just offshore. The bay below is bitten out of low cliffs; descend 60 steps to firm, red-tinged sand, a spot sheltered from Malin Beg's howling winds.

THE DRIVE: Go north through Glencolumbcille *(Gleann Cholm Cille)*, picking up signs for Glengesh Pass. A steep climb past bogs and wandering sheep leads to a plunging road, winding into the valley below. Go north onto the N56 to reach Ardara (34km).

06 Ardara

Heritage-town Ardara is the heart of Donegal's traditional tweed industry; the **Heritage Centre** charts its transformation from cottage industry to global product.

Turn right out of the centre and stroll up the hill to the **Eddie**

Doherty *(handwoventweed.com)* shop to see a vast loom, piles of rugs and rolls of cloth. Staff will happily explain more.

THE DRIVE: The N56 sweeps north towards Dungloe (signed Glenties). After Dungloe, Mt Errigal's pyramidal peak rears from a lough-studded landscape. Turn onto the R251, climbing steadily towards it and Dunlewey (70km).

07 Dunlewey

Isolated, exposed loughside Dunlewey *(Dún Lúiche)* offers a true taste of mountain life. The scenery overwhelms everything here; human habitation seems very small.

Experience the landscape's full impact on a boat trip run by the **Dunlewey Centre** *(Ionad Cois Locha; dunleweycentre.com)*, as a storyteller expounds on ghoulish folklore.

THE DRIVE: Rejoin the N56, heading briefly west before taking the R258 around Bloody Foreland *(Cnóc Fola)*, a spectacular shore so named because sunsets turn its rocks crimson. Turn towards the tiny harbour (Magheraroarty, 32km) that eventually swings into view. From here the 45-minute crossing to Tory Island on the ferry can be wild.

08 Tory Island

Some 11km offshore, craggy Tory Island *(Oileán Thóraí)* is a fiercely independent community with its own Irish dialect, tradition of electing a 'king' and style of 'naive' art, plus early Christian remains and 100 seabird species.

THE DRIVE: The N56 undulates north past loughs in a sheep-grazed landscape where the ever-present bulk of Muckish Mountain looms to the right. Continue east through Dunfanaghy; 5km later turn left into Ards Forest Park (42km).

09 Ards Forest Park

From the main car park, pick up the trail that meanders east through ash and oak towards a **Capuchin Friary** *(ardsfriary.ie)*. Follow the path further down still and you'll stumble upon the exquisite **Isabella's Cove** then **Lucky Shell Bay**. Allow two hours return.

THE DRIVE: Rejoin the N56 east, before taking the R245, an increasingly windy road backed by the rugged hills of the Fanad Peninsula, to Carrigart *(Carraig Airt)*. Head through amiable Carrigart to Downings, 24km from Ards Forest Park.

> ☑ TOP TIP
>
> ### GLENVEAGH NATIONAL PARK
>
> **Glebe House and Gallery** sits beside the stunning **Glenveagh National Park** *(Páirc Náisiúnta Ghleann Bheatha; glenveaghnationalpark.ie)*, home to Glenveagh Castle. This 16,500-sq-km wilderness features forests, mountains, shimmering lakes and green-gold bogs, and makes for magnificent walking. The **visitor centre** provides free maps.

10 Downings

The beach at Downings (or Downies) is simply superb: rolling green hills meet an immense curl of bright-white sand. It's also, unlike many local beaches, safe to swim here; the Atlantic makes for a chilly, but memorable, dip.

THE DRIVE: Return to the N56, turning towards Letterkenny, with the Derryveagh Mountains gathering ahead. Turn onto the R255 (signed Glenveagh National Park), climbing towards those peaks. Turn right onto the R251, and park at the Glenveagh National Park visitor centre (25km).

11 Glenveagh Castle

Modelled on Scotland's Balmoral Castle, **Glenveagh Castle** *(nationalparks.ie)* is a characterful building with a dark history. Learn all about it on a self-guided tour, taking in the flamboyantly decorated rooms of the round tower and the tartan-and-antler-encrusted Music Room.

THE DRIVE: Return to the R251 which swings south and descends, revealing a glittering Lough Gartan. At the water's edge, follow Glebe Gallery signs right (11km).

12 Glebe Gallery

This is a true treat: the top-notch artwork at **Glebe Gallery** *(heritageireland.ie)* belonged to English painter Derrick Hill. Works include pieces by Tory Island's 'naive' artists, plus Picasso, Landseer, Hokusai, Jack B Yeats and Kokoschka.

THE DRIVE: The R251 winds south through woodland,

NICOLAS D'HOEDT/LONELY PLANET

Glenveagh Castle, Glenveagh National Park

hugging the lough shore. Turn onto the R250 towards Letterkenny; soon you'll see Newmills Corn and Flax Mills signed on your right (11km).

13 Newmills Corn and Flax Mills

A whirring, creaking, gushing delight, this restored, three-storey, water-powered **corn mill** *(heritage ireland.ie)* is full of in-motion grinding stones, drive shafts, cogs and gears.

THE DRIVE: After Letterkenny join the N13 east towards Derry. The River Swilly uncurls to your left. Take the R238/239 turn, then the left towards Inch Island (signed 'Inch Island Wildfowl Reserve'). Once over the causeway the (signed) road to Inch Pier (53km) snakes along tranquil, tree-lined lanes.

14 Inch Island

At Inch's tiny pier, park on the right (don't block the fishers' track to the left). Few tourists make it to this compact crescent of sand. It's a place to rest, skim stones and watch waves.

PHOTO OPPORTUNITY

Snap red deer in Glenveagh National Park.

THE DRIVE: Return to the R238, which sweeps north past a 5km sandy beach to Buncrana. By now Lough Swilly is stretching far ahead. Head for Buncrana's shoreline (20km).

15 Buncrana

Bustling Buncrana provides a fitting trip finale, courtesy of stunning sunsets; locals will tell you the ones over Lough Swilly are the best around. A path leads beside the water to pint-sized, 1718 **Buncrana Castle** – it and neighbouring **O'Doherty's Keep** provide ideal sun-going-down vantage points.

32

BELFAST & THE NORTH OF IRELAND

INISHOWEN PENINSULA

DURATION: 3 DAYS

DISTANCE: 165KM / 103 MILES

GREAT FOR: FOOD & DRINK, HISTORY, OUTDOORS

BEST TIME TO GO: EASTER TO OCTOBER SHOULD HAVE BETTER WEATHER, AND MORE THINGS ARE OPEN.

★ BEST

DRIVE

The white-knuckle ascent up mountainous Mamore's Gap.

Mamore's Gap (p241), Donegal

This trip isn't about skimming Ireland's surface through big-name sights. Instead it's a route to the heart of the country's compelling narratives: faith, poverty, mass migration, territorial disputes, the Troubles. With unsigned, cliff-side roads that look more like farm tracks, you'll probably get a little lost. But locals are helpful if you do – and asking for directions is a great conversation starter.

LINK YOUR TRIP

30 The North in a Nutshell
The cream of the north in one glorious route; pick it up from this trip's end at Buncrana.

34 From Bangor to Derry
Belfast and the sight-packed Antrim *(Aontroim)* coast. It stops where this trip starts: Derry.

01 Derry

Kick-start your Inishowen trip by exploring the historic city of Derry. From the city walls, take in views of the Bogside district, the predominantly Catholic residential area where Derry's most notorious and tragic event took place. On 30 January 1972, 13 civilians were shot dead by the British Army during a Civil Rights march, on a day that became known as Bloody Sunday. The **Museum of Free Derry** *(museumoffreederry.org)* chronicles the history of the Bogside, the Northern Ireland Civil Rights Association and the events of Bloody Sunday. Most moving are the funeral cards of those killed on Bloody Sunday and the jackets worn that day by Michael McDaid and Jim Wray, with holes from the bullets that killed them.

THE DRIVE: Take the A2 north towards Moville. Derry's retail parks quickly give way to fields and mountain views, and the

LUKASSEK/SHUTTERSTOCK

silvery Lough Foyle emerges to your right. Soon road signs switch from mph to km/h: welcome to the Republic of Ireland. Shortly after Muff, turn left to Iskaheen (11km), head up the hill and park beside the village church.

02 Iskaheen

Head across the road, through the creaking gate and into the old graveyard. There you'll see evidence of spectres that have long stalked Ireland: poverty, high death rates and the Troubles. Among many gravestones recording multiple deaths, hunt out the broad memorial to the McKinney family. Its losses include a 24-year-old woman, a nine-month-old boy and three girls, aged 13 years, 11 months and six weeks. It also commemorates 34-year-old James Gerard McKinney, one of 13 unarmed demonstrators shot dead by British troops in Derry on 30 January 1972 – Bloody Sunday.

THE DRIVE: Head back to the R238 drinking in the panorama of Lough Foyle as you go. Next comes a 15-minute, scenic shoreside cruise north to Moville. Just before town, take the left turn, signed Cooley Cross, which appears next to a small lay-by on the right, 20km from Iskaheen.

03 Cooley Cross

The 3m-high cross you've parked beside has an unusual ringed head – through it negotiating parties are said to have shaken hands to seal agreements. The atmospheric tumbling of ruins beyond features the remnants of an early monastery founded by St Patrick. At the foot of the enclosure, set against some great lough views, sits the tiny, hut-like **Skull House**. This roofed, gabled structure is a tomb-shrine associated with St Finian, an abbot of the early monastery.

THE DRIVE: Rejoin the R238, heading left for the 10-minute drive along the shore to Greencastle. Opposite, Magilligan Point's sandy beaches curl into view. Soon after entering Greencastle (5km) take the right to the Maritime Museum.

04 Greencastle

Packed with boats and top seafood restaurants, the thriving port of Greencastle also has a fine **Maritime Museum** *(inishowen maritime.com)*. It explores the history of the surrounding seas, with fascinating exhibits from the sunken wrecks of Lough Foyle, exhibitions exploring the demise of the Spanish Armada and examples of Drontheim fishing boats, once produced en masse in Greencastle and widely used along Ireland's north-coast and beyond.

THE DRIVE: Continue north. Just after the Fisheries College take the right, following signs to Inishowen Head. Houses thin out and the road narrows before the black-and-white Inishowen lighthouse edges into your windscreen. Park just beyond, beside Stroove Beach (5km).

05 Inishowen Head

From Stroove Beach's curling sands, join the footpath that winds north, initially on the road then onto a track, up towards Inishowen Head itself. This stiff 2.5km climb reveals spectacular views over

Lough Foyle to the ribbon of sand framing **Magilligan Point**. On clear days you can spot Scotland's islands to the northeast. Edge high enough and you'll see the jagged rocks and golden sands of Kinnagoe Bay – where *La Trinidad Valencera* of the Spanish Armada came to grief.

THE DRIVE: Motor north, initially along your walk route, before curving left. Opposite the Maritime Museum turning, head up an unsigned, steep, narrow, roller-coaster road (it even has grass in the middle) to Culdaff. This is a difficult to navigate route with very steep hills; an alternative is to backtrack to Moville via the R241 coastal road and take the R238 to Culdaff. At Culdaff, take the R238 towards Gleneely. Turn right 1km along, opposite the modern church. Clonca Church appears 1km later.

06 Clonca Church

The towering gable ends and huge windows of the roofless shell of 17th-century Clonca Church frame views of the Donegal mountains. Inside sits the intricately carved tombstone of Scott Magnus MacOrristin – spot the carved writing sloping down the side, and the sword and hurling-stick motifs.

Outside, a tall cross stands in a field; clamber down to see the depiction of the loaves-and-fishes miracle on its weathered face, amid ornate swirls and zigzags.

THE DRIVE: The R238/R243 leads from Culdaff to quaint Malin village. Next make for Malin Head (25km from Clonca Church), a spectacular drive through Trawbreaga Bay's lowlands, past massive dunes at Five Fingers Strand and the hulk of Knockamany. You emerge onto a rugged coast dotted with whitewashed cottages. Take the right, signed Banba's Crown.

07 Malin Head

Open your car door at Malin Head and step into a weather-battered landscape of tumbling cliffs and sparse vegetation – welcome to Ireland's most northerly point.

The clifftop tower beside you was built in 1805 by the British admiralty and later used as a Lloyds signal station. WWII lookout posts are dotted around.

Dunree Head, Donegal

AGAGLOWALA/SHUTTERSTOCK

PHOTO OPPORTUNITY

The gorgeous sandy-bay views from Inishowen Head.

To the west a path leads to **Hell's Hole**, a chasm where the incoming waters crash against rock formations. Just to the east of the head sits **Ballyhillin Beach**, known for its semi-precious stones.

THE DRIVE: From Malin village take the R238 through Carndonagh to Clonmany then follow signs to **Mamore's Gap**, heading straight for the by-now-large-looming mountains. At the crossroads the Inis Eoghain Scenic Route goes up what looks like a farm track. Wayside shrines and another first-and-second-gear ascent follow, before a brake-burning descent. At the plain, head right to Dunree Head (50km).

08 Fort Dunree

Dunree Head overlooks Lough Swilly, a highly strategic stretch of water that's been navigated by Norsemen, Normans, Ireland's fleeing aristocracy and part of Britain's WWI naval fleet.

The 19th-century Fort Dunree *(fortdunree.com)* commands the water. Along with some menacing artillery, films explore the fort's past, while an underground bunker conjures up daily life. The scenery and the birdlife are stunning.

THE DRIVE: Head south to Buncrana, past the mountains of Bulbin and Aghaweel, rising up to your left. The waters of Lough Swilly sweep off to the right, backed by the ranges of the Fanad Peninsula. At the appealing town of Buncrana (19km) head for the shore, initially signed Swilly Ferry, and park opposite the leisure centre.

PICTORIAL PRESS LTD/ALAMY STOCK PHOTO

John Newton

AMAZING GRACE

John Newton, the composer of 'Amazing Grace', was inspired to write his legendary song after his ship, the *Greyhound*, took refuge in the calm waters of Lough Swilly during a severe storm in 1748. He and his crew were welcomed in Buncrana after their near-death experience and his spiritual journey from slave trader to antislavery campaigner had its beginnings here.

He went on to become a prolific hymn writer and later mentored William Wilberforce in his fight against slavery.

For more on the story, visit *amazinggrace.ie*.

09 Buncrana

From the car park a path leads across the grass and along the coast, with Lough Swilly and the Fanad Peninsula's hills in front of you.

Make for **Buncrana Castle**, built in 1718. Wolfe Tone was imprisoned here following the unsuccessful French invasion in 1798. Beside the castle you'll find **O'Doherty's Keep**, a 15th-century tower built by the local O'Doherty chiefs, but burned by the English and rebuilt for their own use.

From here, the waymarked Shore Path continues north for 4km to **Straghill Strand**, a remote beach with beautiful views across the lough.

33

BELFAST & THE NORTH OF IRELAND

★ BEST FOR

OUTDOORS

Stops 3 to 8 for surfing, clambering around cliffs and soaking in seaweed baths.

NORTHWEST ON ADRENALINE

DURATION: 4 DAYS

DISTANCE: 365KM / 227 MILES

GREAT FOR: HISTORY, OUTDOORS

BEST TIME TO GO: EASTER TO OCTOBER MEANS BETTER WEATHER AND OPENING HOURS.

Céide Fields, Mayo

If you're after an Irish adventure, this trip delivers in spades. Along with adrenaline-fuelled surfing and hiking, you'll take in Donegal's highest mountain, Ireland's highest sea cliffs and the world's largest Neolithic monument. Other heritage crowds in, too: an abbey, a castle and a seafaring past. And then there's the drive itself, from sand-dusted seaside lanes to exhilarating mountain roads – it's a roller-coaster ride.

LINK YOUR TRIP

04 Tip to Toe
Wind south to Wexford, past the pick of Ireland's historic sites. Join it at stop 4: Sligo town.

31 Delights of Donegal
Head further north for exquisite beaches and a sandy horseback ride. Pick it up where this trip stops: towering Mt Errigal.

01 Erris Head

Where better to start a road trip than at the end of the road – literally. The parking area for Erris Head *(Ceann Iorrais)* appears where the rough lane peters out. From there waymarks (posts with purple arrows) direct you on a two-hour, 5km loop walk around this wind-buffeted headland.

The path leads over footbridges and earth banks, across fields and along sheep tracks. The views from the high cliffs are spectacular, taking in islands, sea stacks and rock arches.

Belmullet Tourist Office *(visit erris.ie)* has free guides; to get to the trailhead from Belmullet, initially follow signs to An Baile Glas, then pick up signs for Ceann Iorrais.

THE DRIVE: Motor southeast across the narrow neck of land that fuses Belmullet to the rest of County Mayo. Soon, turn

NICOLAS D'HOEDT/LONELY PLANET

left onto the R314, towards Ballycastle. After it climbs a lush ravine and attaches itself to the coast, a wood and glass pyramid suddenly pops up on the right. It's your next stop: Céide Fields (45km).

02 Céide Fields

Céide Fields *(heritageireland.ie)* is considered the world's most extensive Neolithic monument. Half a million tonnes of rock make up the field boundaries, houses and megalithic tombs that have been found so far.

Today it's a barren, wind-blasted spot, but five millennia ago a thriving farming community lived here, growing wheat and barley and grazing sheep and cattle. Although important, this story is hard to tell engagingly (to the uninitiated the site could resemble tumbles of stone) but a sleek, award-winning visitor centre cleverly recreates life in early farming communities. Better still, take a guided tour.

THE DRIVE: The R314 heads east, revealing a vast sea stack at Downpatrick Head. Gradually, exposed hills give way to rolling fields. After one-street Ballycastle comes congested Ballina, where you take the N59 north (signed 'Sligo'). Soon the R297 peels off to Enniscrone, 56km from Céide Fields. Drive up the main street, passing several signs to the beach, before turning left at the sign for Cliff Rd.

03 Enniscrone

Right beside Enniscrone's stunning 5km beach sits **Kilcullen's Seaweed Baths** *(kilcullenseaweedbaths.net)*. Step into this Edwardian spa and soon you'll be steaming away in a cedar cabinet then submerging yourself in a gigantic porcelain bath filled with orangey water and bits of seaweed.

It's used to treat arthritis and rheumatism, but the baths' high iodine content means this traditional natural therapy also acts as an intense moisturiser. It's also a great way to recover from, and prepare for, this trip's adventures.

THE DRIVE: You could head south back to the N59, but it's more fun to stay on the R297 as it bobbles and twists beside flat coastal fields. Eventually it rejoins the N59 to sweep east to Ballysadare. There take the N4 to Sligo (56km); Sligo Abbey is signed from the ring road.

04 Sligo Town

Sligo town is an inviting stop: stone bridges frame the river; pedestrian streets are lined with attractive shops; and pub music sessions overflow onto the footpath.

In the centre is **Sligo Abbey** *(heritageireland.ie)*, a Dominican friary founded around 1252. The abbey survived the worst ravages of the Tudor era and it has the only sculpted altar to survive the Reformation.

The doorways reach only a few feet high at the abbey's rear – the ground around it was swollen by mass graves from years of famine and war.

THE DRIVE: Heading north out of Sligo town on the N15 sees the mountains of Benbulben and Truskmore looming ever

NICOLAS D'HOEDT/LONELY PLANET

☑ TOP TIP

GAELTACHT

This part of Ireland is the **Donegal Gaeltacht**, one of many areas where Irish culture and language are championed. Initially you'll notice it mostly in road signs, as here they tend to be in Irish only (elsewhere it's Irish and English). We use English transliterations with Irish names included in brackets.

Mt Errigal, Donegal

larger. At Ballyshannon take the R231 to Rossnowlagh. When sand starts edging onto the road, you know you're near the resort's Blue Flag beach. Make for Fin McCool Surf School , a total trip of 53km.

05 Rossnowlagh

Rossnowlagh's spectacular 3km-long beach is a wide, sandy stretch beloved by families, walkers and surfers throughout the year. The gentle rollers are great for learning to ride the waves, or to hone your skills. **Fin McCool Surf School** *(finmccoolsurfschool.com)* offers tuition and gear hire; the waters of Donegal Bay offer an exhilarating ride.

THE DRIVE: From Rossnowlagh's sand-dusted road, the R231 winds north through rolling fields before rejoining the N15. This sweeps on towards Donegal town, with the Blue Stack Mountains now appearing behind. On the roundabout on its fringes, pick up the signs for Donegal (20km).

06 Donegal Town

Mountain-backed, pretty Donegal town was for centuries the stamping grounds of the chiefs who ruled northwest Ireland from the 15th to 17th centuries: the O'Donnells.

They built **Donegal Castle** *(heritageireland.ie)* in 1474 and it served as the seat of their formidable power until 1607, when the English ousted Ireland's chieftains.

Rory O'Donnell torched his own castle before leaving for France in the infamous Flight of the Earls. Their departure paved the way for the Plantation of Ulster by thousands of Scots and English Protestants, creating divisions still felt today.

The castle was rebuilt in 1623 and it's a wonderfully atmospheric place to visit, with rooms furnished with French tapestries and Persian rugs.

> **PHOTO OPPORTUNITY**
>
> The 600m-high sea cliffs at Sliabh Liag are a photographer's dream.

THE DRIVE: As the N56 heads west the Blue Stacks range to your right and more mountains shade the horizon ahead. Take the R263, tracing the shore before cutting inland to a peak-lined landscape threaded with rough stone walls. Gradually the brooding Sliabh Liag (Slieve League) mountains come to dominate the view. At Carrick turn left, signed Sliabh Liag, and nudge round the mountain edge to the lower car park (46km).

07 Sliabh Liag

The Cliffs of Moher get more publicity, but the spectacular polychrome sea cliffs at Sliabh Liag (Slieve League, *slieveleague.com*) are higher – some of the highest in Europe, plunging 600m to the sea.

From the lower car park, a path skirts up around the near-vertical rock face to the aptly named **One Man's Pass** – look out for two rocks nicknamed the 'school desk and chair'.

Sunset can be stunning, with waves crashing dramatically far below and the ocean reflecting the day's last rays. It's a strenuous hike to the summit, and rain and mist can appear unexpectedly, making conditions slippery. You can drive further up to the second car park, but be sure to close the gate behind you.

THE DRIVE: Take the L1125 northwards, passing through Carrick and Meenaneary, then turn right onto the L1505 Meenadiff Rd. The abandoned village of An Port lies at the far western end of a single-lane road (22km).

08 An Port

On the edge of the Atlantic Ocean sits the abandoned village of An Port, where a small pier looks out to towering sea stacks. Near the car park are the remains of a cluster of deserted stone houses. As you walk between the cottages, imagine the life of the fisherfolk and their families who once lived in this wild place. While local stories say the village was abandoned during the Famine and in its aftermath, the real story is that An Port's decline was slower and more gradual.

THE DRIVE: Pick up the (signed) Glengesh Pass road, a long climb into a wild landscape that crests to reveal sweeping valley views. A dizzying, hairpin descent lurches to the N56 and towards **Mt Errigal**, the massive pointed peak that edges ever nearer. The R251 climbs through Dunlewey village; when Errigal is directly on your left, turn into the small, walled parking area (77km).

09 Mt Errigal

Towering Mt Errigal (752m) seemingly dares you to attempt the tough but beautiful climb to its pyramid-shaped peak. Watch the weather: it's a dangerous trek on misty or wet days, when visibility is minimal.

The easiest path to the summit covers 5km and takes around three hours (two up, one back); the **Dunlewey Centre** *(Ionad Cois Locha; dunleweycentre.com)* can direct you to the starting point. Even if you don't climb, drink in this remarkably exposed, remote landscape of peaks, loughs and bogs.

34

BELFAST & THE NORTH OF IRELAND

FROM BANGOR TO DERRY

DURATION: 4 DAYS

DISTANCE: 165KM / 103 MILES

GREAT FOR: HISTORY, OUTDOORS

BEST TIME TO GO: MARCH TO OCTOBER BRINGS BETTER WEATHER; AVOID AUGUST TO DODGE HOLIDAY CROWDS.

★ BEST

TWO DAYS

Stops 8 to 11 take in the Causeway, castles, ruins and golden sands.

Mussenden Temple (p248), Derry

This drive delivers a true taste of Ireland's gloriously diverse North: the must-see stops of the Giant's Causeway and Carrick-a-Rede; castles and historic homes at Mount Stewart, Hillsborough, Dunluce and Downhill; and superb scenery, from Slemish to sea-sprayed cliffs and immense sand dunes. While in Belfast and Derry, you'll experience two vibrant cities progressing beyond a painful past.

LINK YOUR TRIP

30 The North in a Nutshell
Head west to wild Donegal for sandy shores, live-music sessions and a castaway island. Pick it up at this trip's end in Derry.

32 Inishowen Peninsula
Drive north onto a remote headland with exquisite scenery, shipwrecks and white-knuckle drives. Start in Derry.

01 Bangor

Start your journey through the North's scenic and historic highlights at a stop with a pop-culture twist. Pedal round the ornamental lake at Bangor's kitsch-rich **Pickie Funpark** *(pickiefunpark.com)* in one of its famous swan-shaped boats then play a round of crazy golf.

THE DRIVE: From Bangor's pastel-painted seafront terraces, pick up the A21 south to Newtownards. From there the A20 runs south towards Mount Stewart (initially signed Portaferry). Soon the vast, island-dotted Strangford Lough emerges to your right; the road clings to its winding shore to Mount Stewart House (16km).

02 Mount Stewart

Magnificent,18th-century **Mount Stewart** *(nationaltrust.org.uk)* is one of Northern Ireland's grandest stately homes. Lavish plasterwork combines with antiques and artworks that

THOMAS BRESENHUBER/SHUTTERSTOCK

include a painting of the racehorse Hambletonian by George Stubbs. Garden highlights include griffin and mermaid statues on the Dodo Terrace, and the **Temple of the Winds**, a mock Gothic ruin with great views of the Strangford Lough.

THE DRIVE: Head north, back along the A20 beside scenic Strangford Lough into Newtownards. There, take the A21 southwest through Comber. Soon the B178 to Hillsborough (40km) cuts off to the right, across a lush landscape of fields, woods and farms.

03 Hillsborough

Set in elegant Hillsborough, the rambling, late-Georgian **Hillsborough Castle** *(hrp.org.uk)* is the king's official residence in Northern Ireland. Book ahead for guided tours taking in opulent state drawing and dining rooms and the Lady Grey Room, where former UK prime minister Tony Blair and former US president George W Bush had talks on Iraq.

Garden delights include yew- and lime-tree walks, an icehouse and a lake.

THE DRIVE: Head north on the A1 then join the M1 for Belfast. Exit onto the A55/Outer Ring, then follow signs for Queens University, Botanic Gardens or your destination, Ulster Museum (16km).

04 Belfast

Bustling Belfast has big-city appeal. As well as walking through its former sectarian strongholds, drop by the **Ulster Museum** *(nmni.com)*, one of Belfast's biggest draws. Highlights of its beautifully designed displays are the Armada Room; Takabuti, a 2500-year-old Egyptian mummy; the Bann Disc and the Snapshot of an Ancient Sea Floor.

THE DRIVE: From Belfast, pass the Grand Opera House and then take the M2 north, then the A26 to Ballymena and then the A42 to Broughshane. There, turn right onto the B94, following the hard-to-see sign to Slemish. Follow another sign, which points left almost immediately, before the mountain itself emerges, an immense, hump-topped plateau of rock (67km).

05 Slemish

Craggy Slemish (438m) is where Ireland's patron saint St Patrick is said to have tended goats. On St Patrick's Day, thousands make a pilgrimage to its summit. It's a steep but pleasant 30-minute climb that's rewarded with fine views.

THE DRIVE: Head back to Broughshane then peel off right onto Knockan Rd towards Clogh. Next take the A43 north towards Waterfoot.

In time the road suddenly rises, settlements thin out and you're in the glens: sweeping ridges of steep-sided hills. After a steep valley descent, emerge onto the coast to go north to Cushendall (32km), parking beside its beach.

06 Cushendall

From Cushendall's beach, walk 1km north, scrambling up the coast path to the picturesque ruins of **Layde Old Church**. Here views stretch as far as the Scottish coast. Founded by the Franciscans, Layde was used as a parish church from the early 14th century. Today the picturesque ruins have grand memorials to the MacDonnells (earls of Antrim from 1620) in the graveyard, and an ancient, weathered ring-cross by the gate.

THE DRIVE: The A2 heads north, through pretty Cushendun, before climbing steeply to open heathland. At the holiday resort of Ballycastle, pick up the B15, which winds beside fields and windswept cliffs to the Carrick-a-Rede Rope Bridge (34km).

07 Carrick-a-Rede Rope Bridge

A wobbling bridge is an unusual spot to stretch your legs, but it's unforgettable nonetheless. The **Carrick-a-Rede Rope Bridge** is a 20m-long, 1m-wide contraption of wire and planks that stretches 30m above rock-strewn water. It sways and bounces beneath your feet before you emerge onto a tiny island dotted with reminders of its past as a salmon fishery. Book your ticket online in advance to cross the bridge.

THE DRIVE: Rejoin the B15 then the A2 before turning right onto the scenic B146, which clings to the coast, passing ruined Dunseverick Castle en route to the Giant's Causeway (11km).

08 Giant's Causeway

The Giant's Causeway is this coast's must-see sight: a remarkable, ragged ribbon of regular, closely packed, hexagonal stone columns that dips gently beneath the waves. The spectacular rock formation is Northern Ireland's only UNESCO World Heritage site and is one of Ireland's most impressive and atmospheric landscape features.

To park on-site you'll need to buy a ticket to the **Giant's Causeway Visitor Experience**.

> **PHOTO OPPORTUNITY**
>
> The spectacular Giant's Causeway, your must-have north-coast snap.

THE DRIVE: Head through Bushmills, with its historic distillery and great sleeping options, onto the A2 to Portrush. Soon sea views flood in, then Dunluce Castle's ragged ruins (8km) spring suddenly into view. Be aware: the castle turn-off comes immediately afterwards, down a sloping track on the right.

09 Dunluce Castle

The atmospheric remains of Dunluce Castle cling to a dramatic basalt crag. Built between the 15th and 17th centuries, it was once the coast's finest castle and the seat of the powerful MacDonnell family.

A narrow bridge leads from the mainland courtyard across a dizzying gap to the main fortress, where you can roam the shells of buildings and listen to the sea pounding on the cliffs.

THE DRIVE: Taking the A2 towards Portrush, you're soon sandwiched between creamy cliffs and a huge golden beach far below. At Portrush (6km), sand dunes dotted with golf courses take over; head for the central East (Curran) Strand car park.

10 Portrush

You can't leave the Antrim *(Aontroim)* coast without some head-clearance time beside the sea. The East Strand car park borders the 3km Curran Strand, a dune-backed golden ribbon of sand that makes for a glorious walk. Or make for nearby **Troggs Surf Shop** *(troggs.com)*, which runs lessons (bookings advised) and hires out bodyboards/surfboards *(per day £10/20)* and wetsuits *(per day £10)*.

THE DRIVE: The A2 heads west, passing through seaside Portstewart and shop-packed Coleraine. Next the cupola of Downhill Demesne's Mussenden Temple eases into view. Skip the Bishop's Gate entrance and take the Lion's Gate (24km).

11 Downhill Demesne

In 1774 the eccentric Bishop of Derry built himself a palatial, clifftop home: **Downhill Demesne** *(nationaltrust.org.uk)*. It burnt down in 1851, was rebuilt in 1876 and finally abandoned after WWII.

Today it features follies (ornamental buildings), mausoleums and a giant, ruined house. Trails lead past a dovecote onto a grassy headland and the elegant **Mussenden Temple**. From inside, the cliff-edge views are extraordinary,

Giant's Causeway, Antrim
ENRIQUE ARNAIZ LAFUENTE/SHUTTERSTOCK

☑ TOP TIP

GIANT'S CAUSEWAY

The causeway is stunning but it can get swamped by visitors. If you can, visit midweek or out of season to experience it at its most evocative. Sunset in spring and autumn is the best time for photographs.

reaching from Portrush round to the shores of Lough Foyle.

THE DRIVE: The A2 continues west, through the fertile lowlands that frame Lough Foyle, and onto the city of Derry (41km).

12 Derry

Northern Ireland's second city surprises some with its riverside setting and impressive, 17th-century walls. The best way to explore them, and the city's inspiring progress beyond sectarian violence, is by walking the city walls.

Make sure you drop into **St Columb's Cathedral** *(stcolumbscathedral.org)*. This stately church was completed in 1633, making it Derry's oldest building. In the porch look for the hollow mortar shell fired into the churchyard during the Great Siege of 1688. Inside the shell were the terms of a surrender that never came.

DERRY OR LONDONDERRY?

Derry-Londonderry is a city with two names. Nationalists always use Derry, and the 'London' part of the name is often crossed through on road signs. Some staunch Unionists insist on Londonderry, which is still the city's (and county's) official name. All the same, most people, regardless of political persuasion, call it Derry in everyday speech. Traditionally, road signs in Northern Ireland point to Londonderry and those in the Republic point to Derry (or Doíre in Irish). Attempts by the council to change the city's official name to Derry were foiled by a 2007 High Court ruling that the city's legal name could only be changed by legislation or royal prerogative. Many local businesses, as well as buses and trains, use the clunky Derry-Londonderry.

St Columb's Cathedral, Derry
ALEX_MASTRO/SHUTTERSTOCK

35

BELFAST & THE NORTH OF IRELAND

THE ANTRIM COAST

★ BEST FOR

SOLITUDE

Stops 4 and 5 see you well away from the crowds.

East Lighthouse (p254), Rathlin Island

DURATION: 3 DAYS

DISTANCE: 110KM / 68 MILES

GREAT FOR: HISTORY, OUTDOORS

BEST TIME TO GO: AVOIDING AUGUST MEANS LESS-CROWDED SIGHTS; EASTER TO JULY AND SEPTEMBER SHOULD MEAN BRIGHTER DAYS.

Many visitors belt around the Antrim *(Aontroim)* coast, cramming the big-name sights into a day. But this trip can be taken slowly, allowing time to marvel at less-obvious sights and discover a side to Antrim that many people miss. This mystical landscape's extraordinary rock formations, ruined castles and wooded glens have made the region an atmospheric backdrop for the TV series *Game of Thrones*, with numerous filming locations here.

LINK YOUR TRIP

30 The North in a Nutshell
Head west to Donegal's wild, beach-fringed coast. Begin where this trip ends: Bushmills.

34 From Bangor to Derry
Take in seaside fun, history-rich Belfast and two stately homes. Start 60km southeast of Ballymena, at Bangor.

01 Ballymena

Start exploring the Antrim *(Aontroim)* coast with the potted history offered by the **Mid-Antrim Museum** at the **Braid** *(thebraid.com)*. Audiovisual displays evoke a rich history stretching from the county's prehistoric inhabitants to the present. Prepare for stories of Irish chiefs, the mass settlement of Scottish and English Protestants (called Plantation) and the historic events behind the island's political banners – both Unionist/Loyalist (mostly Protestants who want to preserve the union with Britain) and Nationalist/Republican (mostly Catholics who want the North to be part of the Irish Republic).

The *Modern Times* film montage is another highlight, encompassing the *Titanic*, WWI, the Depression, civil rights, footballer George Best and former US president Bill Clinton.

THE DRIVE: As the A43 heads north towards Waterfoot, the

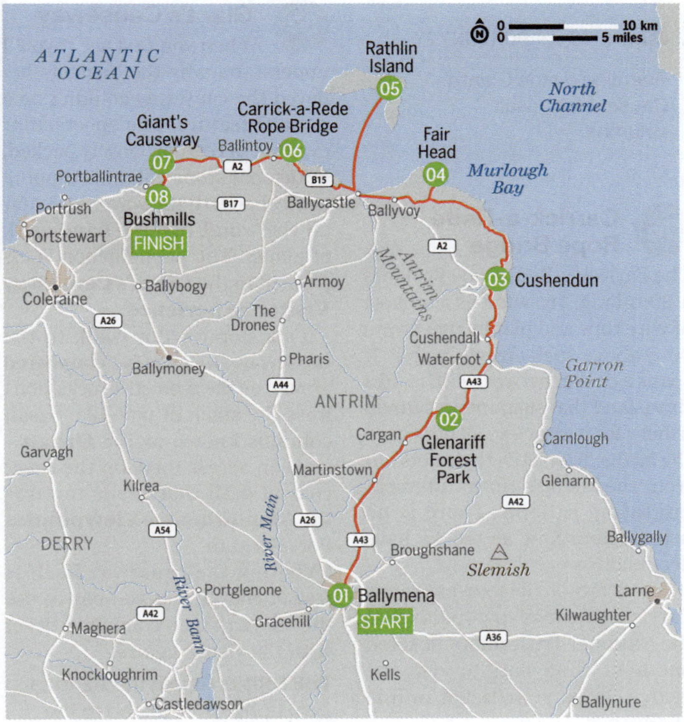

MIKE-HUBERT.COM/SHUTTERSTOCK

Antrim *(Aontroim)* Mountains rise closer. Suddenly there's a landscape shift: houses peter away, the road climbs and trees thin out, revealing rock ridges and plunging valleys. Turn right into Glenariff Forest Park (23km), onto a track that winds between dense conifers. The trees clear abruptly, exposing plummeting hills.

02 Glenariff Forest Park

The pick of the trails at Glenariff Forest Park is the **Waterfalls Walk**. From the car park (surely one of the North's most scenic; *parking £5*) this 3km, waymarked, circular trail runs beside the Glenariff River and past the Ess-na-Larach and Ess-na-Crub waterfalls, along paths cut into the sheer gorge sides, up stairways and along boardwalks set on stilts on the water.

The forest is a mix of native species (look out for oak, elm and hazel) and introduced trees, notably pine and Douglas fir. You've a fair chance of spotting red squirrels, hen harriers and Irish hares darting among the trees.

The teahouse beside the car park offers the chance to refuel and see more stunning gorge views.

THE DRIVE: Continue on the A43, descending steeply through hairpin bends into a wide, U-shaped glacial valley with suddenly revealed sea views. Follow the A2 north along the shore, through the busy little town of Cushendall to Cushendun (17km).

03 Cushendun

Follow the shoreline to the right, past the fisher's cottage on the south side of pretty Cushendun, until you reach a series of caves sculpted from porous rock; *Game of Thrones* fans will recognise this as a filming location for the Stormlands.

Head back along the seafront and over the bridge, this time going straight on to the village itself. Its central cluster of Cornish-style cottages was built between 1912 and 1925 and designed by Clough Williams-Ellis, the architect of Portmeirion in north Wales. They were commissioned by Lord Cushendun and his Cornish wife, Maud. Her grave in the village churchyard bears the inscription, 'To a Cornish woman who loved the Glens and their people'.

THE DRIVE: Pick up the (signed) Torr Head Scenic Route, a heart-in-the-mouth route of winding first-gear gradients that clings to increasingly stark cliffs. Ignore the Torr Head turn-off and instead peel off right to Murlough Bay (signed), reaching a car park 300m after the turning (16km).

04 Fair Head

By now the 180m-high basalt cliffs of Fair Head rear to your left. Walk towards them, following a 1km moderate clifftop path (waymarked by yellow circles) to the top. Once there, look out for rock climbers (this is one of the region's best climbing sites) and the spectacular gully bridged by a fallen rock, called Grey Man's Path. A stunning panorama sweeps from **Rathlin Island** in the west to Scotland's Mull of Kintyre in the east. Keep an eye out for whales and dolphins swimming offshore.

THE DRIVE: Heading west on the A2, the landscape becomes steadily less rugged. Soon golf courses replace sheep-grazed hills and sandy beaches replace that precipitous shore. At the cheery resort of Ballycastle (20km), park in the ferry-terminal car park.

05 Rathlin Island

Time to leave the car behind and stay overnight on Rathlin Island *(rathlin360.com)*, a 6.5km-by-4km windswept slab of rock, 6km offshore.

From mid-April to August it's home to hundreds of seals and thousands of nesting seabirds. The Royal Society for the Protection of Birds' **Rathlin West Light Seabird Centre** *(rspb.org.uk/rathlin island)* provides extraordinary views of sea stacks thick with guillemots, kittiwakes, razorbills and puffins.

Scottish hero Robert the Bruce hid here in 1306 after being defeated by the English. Inspired by a spider's determined web-spinning, he subsequently triumphed at Bannockburn.

His cave is beneath the **East Lighthouse**.

From July to August, 10 ferries a day (less often off season) make the 25- to 45-minute crossing. Book in advance.

THE DRIVE: From the Rathlin Island ferry terminal the B15 climbs north towards Ballintoy. As Rathlin Island recedes behind you, a coastal plateau of rugged heathland unfurls. The plateau runs along then steeply down to the Carrick-a-Rede Rope Bridge turn (19km) on the right.

PHOTO OPPORTUNITY

Standing on the Giant's Causeway's basalt columns.

06 Carrick-a-Rede Rope Bridge

The Carrick-a-Rede Rope Bridge is a 20m-long, 1m-wide assemblage of wire rope and planks that sways 30m above rock-strewn water. It spans a chasm between cliffs and a tiny island that sustained a salmon fishery for centuries – fishers used the bridge to stretch their nets out from the island's tip to intercept migrating salmon. There is no fishing here now as stocks have declined.

Now firmly on the tour-bus route, Carrick-a-Rede is so popular that the National Trust offers ticketed one-hour time slots to visit the bridge. Book your ticket online in advance.

It's a heart-in-the-mouth walk across the bridge. From the island you can see last night's stop, Rathlin Island, and the site of your walk on the sheer cliffs of Fair Head.

THE DRIVE: Heading west, the B15 then the A2 deliver more bursts of rugged coastal driving – the golden beach unfurling below is White Park Bay. Turn onto the B146, getting even closer to the shore. This road glides past ruined Dunseverick Castle en route to the coast's big draw: the Giant's Causeway (11km).

07 Giant's Causeway

When you first see it you'll understand why the ancients believed the causeway couldn't be a natural feature. The spectacular expanse of regular, closely packed, hexagonal stone columns dipping gently beneath the waves looks for all the world like the handiwork of giants. The phenomenon is explained in the **Giant's Causeway Visitor Experience**.

It's a sloping 1km walk to the causeway. Once you've clambered around on the geometric rocks, don't miss the stack of pipe-like basalt columns known as the **Organ** – you can access them on the lower coastal path that heads towards the **Amphitheatre Viewpoint** at Port Reostan.

Visiting the causeway itself is free of charge, but you pay to use the car park on a combined ticket with the visitor centre.

THE DRIVE: Rejoin the A2 for a 3km uphill drive inland to the small town of Bushmills. Signs point towards the world-famous distillery on its western edge.

08 Bushmills

What better way to finish a trip full of the flavour of the Antrim *(Aontroim)* coast than with a true taste of Ireland – Bushmills Irish Whiskey? **Old Bushmills Distillery** *(bushmills.eu/about-the-distillery)* is the world's oldest legal distillery. During ageing, the alcohol content drops from around 60% to 40%. The spirit lost through evaporation is known as 'the angels' share'. Tours include a sample of a 12-year-old Single Malt Distillery Reserve, only available on-site.

Old Bushmills Distillery
DAVID K PHOTOGRAPHY/SHUTTERSTOCK

TOOLKIT

eft: Doo Lough (p34), Mayo
ABUSCAA/SHUTTERSTOCK

ARRIVING

Most people arriving in Ireland come via Dublin Airport; if you're arriving by boat, there's a port in the city as well as a ferry terminal in Dun Laoghaire. Ferries from Wales and France arrive in Rosslare, County Wexford, while all ferry arrivals into Northern Ireland are at either Belfast City Port or at Larne, 37km north of the city.

CAR RENTAL AT AIRPORTS

All the main car-rental agencies are represented at all of Ireland's airports.

The car-rental desks can be found in the arrivals concourses of all airports, including both Dublin terminals.

It is strongly advised that you book in advance rather than just show up, as rates are cheaper; as well as this, demand is high during the summer months and holiday periods.

Picking up a prebooked car is easy: all you need is your booking reference, ID and driving licence. Note that motorbikes and mopeds are not available for rent.

Those aged under 21 are not allowed to hire a car, and for the majority of rental companies, you have to be at least 25 and have had a valid driving licence for a minimum of one year.

Many rental agencies will not rent to people over 70 or 75.

AIRPORT TO CITY CENTRE

	DUBLIN	BELFAST	SHANNON
TRAIN	No train	17mins £2	No train
COACH	35mins €8	10mins £2.20	30mins €2.60
TAXI	25mins €35	14mins £18	30mins €40

ENTERING IRELAND

Dublin is the primary point of entry for most visitors to Ireland, but you can also fly into Cork, Shannon or Belfast. Dublin also has two ferry ports and is the country's rail hub.

BREXIT

Despite the UK (and Northern Ireland) leaving the EU after Brexit, there are no border controls between the Republic and Northern Ireland.

PRECLEARANCE

For travel to the US, Dublin and Shannon airports operate preclearance facilities, which means you pass through US immigration before boarding your aircraft.

VISAS

Visas for both the Republic and Northern Ireland are not not required by citizens of the EU, Australia, New Zealand, the US and Canada. Citizens of Australia, Canada, New Zealand and the US can visit for up to three months.

GETTING AROUND

BEST WAYS TO GET AROUND

The most convenient way to explore Ireland's every nook and cranny is by car. Car rental is available in all major towns and at all airports, but book in advance, especially during the summer when demand sometimes outstrips supply.

DRIVING INFO

Drive on the left

30

Speed limits are in kilometres per hour in the Republic and miles per hour in Northern Ireland.

.05

Blood alcohol limit is 50mg/100mL

PUBLIC TRANSPORT

The extensive network of public and private buses is the most cost-effective way to get around. There's services to and from most inhabited areas.

The Irish Rail *(Iarnród Éireann)* network links Dublin to all major urban centres, including Belfast.

MAKING SENSE OF LOCAL NETWORKS

The Transport for Ireland (TFI) public transport network includes national bus and train services, as well as Luas trams and the DART in Dublin.

For Northern Ireland, Ulsterbus runs bus services to all towns and cities. Translink operates the north's five train lines.

SPEED LIMITS

Republic speed limits are 120km/h on motorways, 100km/h on national roads, 80km/h on regional roads, and 50km/h in towns. Northern Ireland speed limits are 70mph (112km/h) on motorways, 60mph (96km/h) on main roads and 30mph (48km/h) in built-up areas.

THE GRATEFUL FINGER

In Ireland, narrow roads mean you often have to pull over to let an oncoming driver pass. The general rule is that the obstruction is on your side of the road, you have to give way to oncoming traffic. The standard 'thank you' is a barely perceptible lift of the index finger, which rises a few centimetres from the steering wheel, and the usual acknowledgement is to lift your own finger in return.

CAR RENTAL COSTS

Car rental From **€60/day**

Petrol/Diesel **Approx €1.74/litre**

EV charging **35–40c/kWh**

Dublin–Cork train **€25–€45**

ACCOMMODATION

HOW MUCH FOR A NIGHT IN A...

glamping pod
€120–180

B&B
€80–200

five-star castle hotel
€500–1500

LOOKING FOR A BED

The relocation of a number of multinational companies to Dublin is one factor that has contributed to the city's housing crisis. Rents have soared, and housing is scarce. In 2025, the Department of Housing reported that there were more than 10,925 homeless people living in the city.

In some popular tourist areas of the country, such as the Dingle Peninsula in County Kerry, a shortage of affordable housing is partly because of properties being bought up as holiday homes and landlords choosing to rent properties on short-stay accommodation platforms such as Airbnb.

B&BS

Their status may be seriously challenged by a glut of midrange hotels, but the bed-and-breakfast remains the bedrock of Irish accommodation, offering the closest thing to homestays you'll find in the country.

A good B&B host will pick you up at the station, make you feel at home and kickstart your day with the ubiquitous 'Full Irish' fry-up.

CASTLE HOTELS

From elegant manor houses to bona fide Norman fortifications, Ireland's castle hotels are a mix of four-star decadence and five-star opulence.

The best of them offer unparalleled amenities and services, from Michelin-star cuisine and world-class golf to private butler service and even helicopter transfers – all delivered in a relaxed ambience that is quintessentially Irish.

CAMPING

Camping and caravan parks aren't as common in Ireland as they are elsewhere in Europe. Some hostels have camping space for tents and also offer house facilities, which makes them better value than main camping grounds. Most caravan parks are open only from Easter (March/April) to the end of September or October.

SUSTAINABLE OPTIONS

Sustainability is an overused buzzword in tourism, but many hotels in Ireland recognise the value of being greener. The number of eco-friendly options has grown dramatically, from cabins in pristine forests to coastal yurts with stunning sea views. Many traditional hotels have taken positive steps towards carbon neutrality by reducing landfill waste and water usage, and cutting back on electricity and gas.

CANAL BARGES

For something a little different, you should consider staying on the water. Canal barges are an unhurried and pleasurable way to see the countryside (plus you can go from Dublin right out to the Shannon by canal), while a cabin cruiser is a popular way of exploring Ireland's rivers, notably the Shannon Erne Waterway, which encompasses the Shannon River and Lough Erne.

CARS

CAR RENTAL

The main car-rental firms and some local operators are well-represented in Ireland's major towns and cities. Car rental is easy and straightforward. Advance hire rates start at around €50 a day for a small car (unlimited mileage). Shop around and use price comparison sites as well as company sites (which often have great deals not available on booking sites).

Car-sharing services, where you can rent a car by the hour, are increasingly popular. GoCar (pictured) is Ireland's largest provider, and bookings are made through its app, which has a GPS map telling you where you can pick up and drop off the vehicle; it uses your phone as the key.

HOW MUCH TO HIRE A CAR?

Mercedes EQB
€130 per day

Toyota C-HR Hybrid
€190 per day

Tesla Model 3
€500 per day

INSURANCE

Theft protection and third-party liability insurance are included in the basic car-rental rate.

The excess is usually around €1500, but you can reduce it to zero with a Collision Damage Waiver.

All rental agreements also include unlimited mileage and 24-hour breakdown cover.

EVS

Car-rental companies are also ramping up their EV fleets, especially in the luxury categories, and in 2026, there were around 3100 charging stations around the island, with 2500 in the Republic.

The majority will currently charge at 22kW, taking around four hours to fully charge a typical car, while 'fast charging' points use 43kW to charge most batteries to 80% in around 30 minutes. The most cost-effective way to pay for charging is to get a charge-point access card from the ESB (the Electricity Supply Board), which administers most points. Pay-as-you-go charges range from €0.59/kWh (Standard), to €0.66/kWh (Fast), to €0.682/kWh (High Power).

FRANK333/SHUTTERSTOCK

RESPONSIBLE TRAVEL

CLIMATE CHANGE & TRAVEL

Lonely Planet urges all travellers to engage with their travel carbon footprint, which will mainly come from air travel. While there often isn't an alternative, travellers can look to minimise the number of flights they take and use cleaner ground transport, such as trains.

One proposed solution – purchasing carbon offsets – unfortunately does not cancel out the impact of individual flights. While most destinations will depend on air travel for the foreseeable future, for now, pursuing ground-based travel where possible is the best course of action.

The **UN carbon footprint calculator** shows how flying impacts a household's emissions

The **ICAO's Carbon Emissions Calculator** allows visitors to analyse the CO_2 generated by point-to-point journeys

Sustainable Travel Ireland
sustainabletravelireland.ie
Lists all of Ireland's sustainable businesses.

Bord Bia: Irish Food Board
bordbia.ie
Has a whole section on sustainable enterprises.

Green Travel
greentravel.ie
Helps you travel and consume sustainably.

SUPPORT LOCAL

An added bonus to visiting The Burren in County Clare is that many local businesses – from surf schools to hotels – are part of **Burren Ecotourism** *(burren.ie)*, a network dedicated to enhancing local and sustainable tourism.

CHOOSE SUSTAINABLE VENUES

If you're in rural County Leitrim and pass by the village of Rossinver, stop by the fabulous cafe at the **Organic Centre** *(theorganiccentre.ie)*, where everything is made using produce grown in their own garden.

GET BACK TO NATURE

Why not sleep in a tree tent under the stars or in a shelter that you've just built? At **Finnebrogue Woods** *(finnebroguewoods.com)* in Downpatrick, County Down. Let yourself reconnect with nature.

SAFE TRAVEL

HEALTH INSURANCE

EU citizens equipped with a European Health Insurance Card (EHIC) will be covered for most medical care – but not for non-emergencies or emergency repatriation.

While other countries, such as Australia, also have reciprocal agreements with Ireland and Britain, many do not.

In Northern Ireland, everyone receives free emergency treatment at accident and emergency (A&E) departments of state-run hospitals, irrespective of nationality.

VALUABLES

Don't leave any luggage or valuables visible in your car when you park, especially if you're parking on the street. If you must leave your things in the car, keep as much as you can in the boot (trunk) or under the seats, and try to use a covered car park where your car won't attract unwanted attention.

ATM SKIMMING

ATM skimming, where your card information is stolen, is an issue. Before inserting your card, check for hidden cameras or an unusually bulky slot. Many ATMs now have drop-down shields that allow you to insert your PIN safely. ATMs attached to banks are commonplace, and convenience stores also have ATMs that are perfectly fine to use if you take the appropriate precautions.

CAR BREAKDOWN

Most car-rental companies offer breakdown cover as part of their extra insurance policies. In the event of a breakdown, place your warning triangle 45m behind the car (but not if you're on a motorway); call the Motorway Emergency Assistance number (0818-715-100) if you're on a motorway; call the dedicated emergency number if you're in a rental car.

DRUGS

Illegal drugs are widely available, especially in nightclubs. Small quantities of cannabis usually attract a fine or a warning, but harder drugs are treated more seriously. Public drunkenness is technically illegal – but only an issue if you cause trouble. Should you find yourself under arrest, you have the right to remain silent and to contact either a lawyer or your embassy.

IN CASE OF EMERGENCY

999

Call 999 for police, fire or ambulance.

NUTS & BOLTS

GOOD TO KNOW

Time zone
UTC (UTC+1 in summer)

Country code
+353 (Republic); +44 (Northern Ireland)

Population
5 million (Republic); 1.8 million (Northern Ireland)

CURRENCY: EURO (€); POUND (£)

OPENING HOURS

- **Pubs:** Standard hours are 10.30am to 11.30pm Monday to Thursday, with later hours at weekends (usually until 12.30am).
- **Restaurants:** Lunch service starts around 10am. Dinner is rarely served past 9.30pm.
- **Shops:** In the cities, most are open all week, with late opening on Thursdays. In smaller towns, shops close on Sundays.

COVERAGE

Wi-fi and 4G/5G networks prevail; in some rural areas, 3G is as strong as the signal gets. Most accommodation has free wi-fi (although some still charge a fee), as do many cafes and restaurants.

WEIGHTS & MEASURES

In the Republic, all but liquid measures for alcohol are metric, so it's metres and kilometres on the roads.

In Northern Ireland, imperial measurements prevail; all is measured in yards and miles.

ELECTRICITY

230V AC/50HZ

BEST WAYS TO PAY

Everywhere takes cash, and most outlets also use cashless payments. You can tap up to €50 with a card; larger amounts require that you put your card in the machine and insert your PIN. Contactless – with your phone – is accepted everywhere that takes cards.

TIPPING ETIQUETTE

In hotels, only tip porters who carry luggage *(€2 per bag)*; in pubs, tipping isn't expected unless table service is provided *(€2 to €3 per round of drinks)*. Tip 10% to 15% for decent service in restaurants, and up to 18% to 20% in more expensive places. Tip 10% to 15% or round up to the nearest euro for taxis.

EURO & STERLING

While the euro is the currency in the Republic of Ireland, you'll need a stash of sterling for cash purchases in the North. Some places (around the border, usually) will advertise exchange services, but the rates are not very good – you're better off using a bank.

HOW MUCH FOR A...

pint of beer
€6–10

Guinness Storehouse ticket
€22–30

Heritage Card
€40 (gives access to 45 attractions)

latte
€3.80

INDEX

Drives 000
Map pages **p000**

C

H

I

J

K

L

THE WRITERS

This is the 5th edition of Lonely Planet's Best Road Trips Ireland guidebook, updated with new material by Fionn Davenport and Isabel Albiston.

Writers on previous editions whose work also appears in this book are included below.

Fionn Davenport

Fionn has been writing travel guides since the pre-internet age. He doesn't miss not having a smartphone, but it makes it much harder to get happily lost. *@fionndavenport*

Isabel Albiston

After twenty years living in and writing about different parts of the world, Isabel now lives in Belfast, not far from where she grew up. *@isabel_albiston*

Contributing writers

Belinda Dixon, Catherine Le Nevez, Neil Wilson

Send us your feedback

We love to hear from travellers – your comments keep us on our toes and help make our books better. Our well-travelled team reads every word on what you loved or loathed about this book. Although we cannot reply individually to your submissions, we always guarantee that your feedback goes straight to the appropriate writers, in time for the next edition.

BEHIND THE SCENES

This book was produced by the following:

Destination Editor
James Smart

Coordinating Editor
Bridget Blair

Production Editor
Ailbhe MacMahon

Image Researcher
Nicolas D'Hoedt

Cartographer
Vojtech Bartos

Assisting Editor
Kevin Ebbutt

Cover Researcher
Sam Ubinas

Thanks to
Will Allen, Marc Blackwell, Melanie Dankel, Alison Killilea, Vicky Smith, Saralinda Turner

Product Development
Sofie Andersen, Melinda Anderson, Marc Backwell, Alison Killilea, Darren O'Connell, James Smart, Saralinda Turner, Robin Yule

Acknowledgments

Digital Model Elevation Data
Contains public sector information licensed under the Open Government Licence v3.0 website nationalarchives.gov.uk/doc/open-government-licence/version/3/

Cover photographs
Front: Glanmore Lake, Kerry (p123); Helen Hoston/Shutterstock
Back: Ross Castle, Kerry (p132); Ronin83/Shutterstock

Visit **lonelyplanet.com/contact** to submit your updates and suggestions or to ask for help. Our award-winning website also features inspirational travel stories and news.

Note: We may edit, reproduce and incorporate your comments in Lonely Planet products such as guidebooks, websites and digital products, so let us know if you are happy to have your name acknowledged. For a copy of our privacy policy visit **lonelyplanet.com/legal**

lonely planet

Published by Lonely Planet Global Limited
CRN 554153
Digital Depot, Roe Lane off Thomas Street, Dublin
D08 TCV4, Ireland (EU authorised representative)
5th edition – Sep 2026
ISBN 9781838698072

10 9 8 7 6 5 4 3 2 1
Printed in Malaysia